Gerard Mai

The poetry of Gerard Manley Hopkins was among the most innovative writing of the Victorian period. Hopkins was an experimental and idiosyncratic writer whose work remains important for any student of Victorian literature.

Taking the form of a sourcebook, this guide to Hopkins's poetry offers:

- extensive introductory comment on the contexts, critical history and interpretations of his work, from composition to the present
- annotated extracts from key contextual documents, reviews and critical works
- unabridged texts of twenty-nine of Hopkins's most important poems, with detailed annotations
- cross-references between documents and sections of the guide, in order to suggest links between texts, contexts and criticism
- suggestions for further reading.

Part of the *Routledge Guides to Literature* series, this volume is essential reading for all those beginning detailed study of Hopkins's work and seeking not only a guide to the poems, but also a way through the wealth of contextual and critical material that surrounds them.

Alice Jenkins is a lecturer in the department of English at the University of Glasgow.

Routledge Guides to Literature*

Editorial Advisory Board: Richard Bradford (University of Ulster at Coleraine), Jan Jedrzejewski (University of Ulster at Coleraine), Duncan Wu (St Catherine's College, University of Oxford)

Routledge Guides to Literature offer clear introductions to the most widely studied authors and literary texts. Each book engages with texts, contexts and criticism, highlighting the range of critical views and contextual factors that need to be taken into consideration in advanced studies of literary works. The series encourages informed but independent readings of texts by ranging as widely as possible across the contextual and critical issues relevant to the works examined and highlighting areas of debate as well as those of critical consensus. Alongside general guides to texts and authors, the series includes 'sourcebooks', which allow access to reprinted contextual and critical materials as well as annotated extracts of primary text.

Available in this series

Geoffrey Chaucer by Gillian Rudd
Ben Jonson by James Loxley
William Shakespeare's The Merchant of Venice: A Sourcebook edited by S. P. Cerasano
William Shakespeare's King Lear: A Sourcebook edited by Grace Ioppolo
William Shakespeare's Othello: A Sourcebook edited by Andrew Hadfield
John Milton by Richard Bradford
John Milton's Paradise Lost: A Sourcebook edited by Margaret Kean
Alexander Pope by Paul Baines
Mary Wollstonecraft's A Vindication of the Rights of Woman: A Sourcebook edited by Adriana Craciun
Jane Austen by Robert P. Irvine
Jane Austen's Emma: A Sourcebook edited by Paula Byrne
Jane Austen's Pride and Prejudice: A Sourcebook edited by Robert Morrison
Mary Shelley's Frankenstein: A Sourcebook edited by Timothy Morton
The Poems of John Keats: A Sourcebook edited by John Strachan
Charles Dickens's David Copperfield: A Sourcebook edited by Richard J. Dunn
Charles Dickens's Bleak House: A Sourcebook edited by Janice M. Allan
Herman Melville's Moby-Dick: A Sourcebook edited by Michael J. Davey
Harriet Beecher Stowe's Uncle Tom's Cabin: A Sourcebook edited by Debra J. Rosenthal
Walt Whitman's Song of Myself: A Sourcebook and Critical Edition edited by Ezra Greenspan
Robert Browning by Stefan Hawlin
Henrik Ibsen's Hedda Gabler: A Sourcebook edited by Christopher Innes
Thomas Hardy by Geoffrey Harvey
Charlotte Perkins Gilman's The Yellow Wallpaper: A Sourcebook and Critical Edition edited by Catherine J. Golden
Kate Chopin's The Awakening: A Sourcebook edited by Janet Beer and Elizabeth Nolan

D. H. Lawrence by Fiona Becket
The Poems of W. B. Yeats: A Sourcebook edited by Michael O'Neill
E. M. Forster's A Passage to India: A Sourcebook edited by Peter Childs
Samuel Beckett by David Pattie
Thomas Hardy's Tess of the D'Urbervilles: A Sourcebook edited by Scott McEathron
Charles Dickens's Oliver Twist: A Sourcebook edited by Juliet John

* Some books in this series were originally published in the Routledge Literary Sourcebooks series, edited by Duncan Wu, or the Complete Critical Guide to English Literature series, edited by Richard Bradford and Jan Jedrzejewski.

The Poems of
Gerard Manley Hopkins
A Sourcebook

Edited by Alice Jenkins

Routledge
Taylor & Francis Group

LONDON AND NEW YORK

First published 2006
by Routledge
2 Park Square, Milton Park, Abingdon, Oxon OX14 4RN

Simultaneously published in the USA and Canada
by Routledge
711 Third Avenue, New York, NY 10017

Routledge is an imprint of the Taylor & Francis Group

Selection and editorial matter © 2006 Alice Jenkins

Typeset in Sabon and Gill Sans by RefineCatch Limited, Bungay, Suffolk

British Library Cataloguing in Publication Data
A catalogue record for this book is available from the British Library

Library of Congress Cataloging in Publication Data
The poems of Gerard Manley Hopkins : a sourcebook / edited by Alice Jenkins.
    p. cm. — (Routledge guides to literature)
    Includes bibliographical references and index.
Hopkins, Gerard Manley, 1844–1889—Criticism and interpretation—Handbooks,
manuals, etc. I. Jenkins, Alice, 1970– II. Series.

PR4803.H44Z775   2006
821'.8—dc22

2005017601

ISBN10: 0–415–25523–6   ISBN13: 9–78–0–415–25523–3 (hbk)
ISBN10: 0–415–25524–4   ISBN13: 9–78–0–415–25524–0 (pbk)

For CCM,

From a very <u>late</u> Santa Claus!

Jill xx

2020

For Catherine, Norman and Susan

Contents

4: Further Reading

Acknowledgements

I am very grateful to Duncan Wu and to Liz Thompson at Routledge for their help and support throughout the planning and writing of this book.

Marion Purllant started me reading this poetry twenty years ago; I owe my enthusiasm for Hopkins to her.

Generous colleagues at Glasgow University, particularly Alexander Broadie, Susan Castillo, Norman Gray, Vicky Gunn, Vassiliki Kolocotroni, Donald Mackenzie, Sister Brigid McNally, Rob Maslen, Costas Panayotakis, Nick Selby, Susan Stuart and Nicky Trott have provided a great deal of help and advice.

As always I am deeply grateful to my parents for their support and encouragement.

Alfred Hickling encouraged me to start this book; Juliet John and Catherine Steel were extraordinarily generous in supporting the finishing of it.

I would like to thank the following for permission to reprint copyright material:

'Wreck of the Deutschland', 'Spelt from Sibyl's Leaves', 'As Kingfisher Catch Fire', 'Hurrahing in Harvest', 'God's Grandeur', 'Henry Purcell', 'The Leaden Echo and the Golden Echo', 'To Seem the Stranger', 'I Wake and Feel', 'Carrion Comfort', 'My Own Heart Let Me Have More Pity On', 'Where Art Thou Friend' from *Gerard Manley Hopkins* by Catherine Phillips, 1986. Reproduced by permission of Oxford University Press.

Excerpts from *Selected Letters*, Gerard Manley Hopkins, edited by Catherine Phillips, 1991. Reproduced by permission of Oxford University Press.

Excerpts from *The Notebooks and Papers of Gerard Manley Hopkins*, Gerard Manley Hopkins, edited by Humphrey House, 1959. Reproduced by permission of Oxford University Press.

Excerpts from *The Sermons and Devotional Writings*, Gerard Manley Hopkins, edited by Christopher Devlin, 1959. Reproduced by permission of Oxford University Press.

Excerpts of the Editor's preface and notes by Robert Bridges from *The Poems of Gerard Manley Hopkins*, 1st edn, Gerard Manley Hopkins, 1918. Reproduced by permission of Oxford University Press.

Excerpts from *The Printed Voice of Victorian Poetry*, Eric Griffiths, 1989. Reproduced by permission of Oxford University Press.

Excerpts from *Gerard Manley Hopkins: A Study of Poetic Idiosyncrasy in Relation to Poetic Translation*, 2nd edn, W. H. Gardner, 1958. Reproduced by permission of Oxford University Press.

By William Empson, from *Seven Types of Ambiguity*, copyright © All Rights Reserved. Reprinted by permission of New Directions Publishing Corp.

From *Seven Types of Ambiguity*, William Empson, published by Chatto & Windus. Reprinted by permission of The Random House Group Ltd.

Excerpts from *New Bearing in English Poetry*, F. R. Leavis, 1932, reprinted by kind permission of Robin Leavis.

Excerpts from *Gerard Manley Hopkins and the Victorian Temper*, Alison G. Sulloway, 1972, Routledge. Reprinted by permission of the publisher.

Excerpts from *The Madwoman in the Attic: The Woman Writer and the Nineteenth-Century Literary Imagination* by Sandra M. Gilbert and Susan Gubar, 1979, Yale University Press. Reprinted by permission of the publisher.

From 'Gerard Manley Hopkins and "Women and Men" as Partners in the Mystery of Redemption' by Alison G. Sulloway, from *Texas Studies in Literature and Language*, 31: 1, pp. 44–5. Copyright © 1989 by the University of Texas Press. All rights reserved.

Excerpts from *The Language of Gerard Manley Hopkins* by James Milroy, 1977, Andre Deutsch. Reprinted by kind permission of the author.

Exerpts from 'Hopkins the Purist (?): Some Comments on the Sources and Applications of Hopkins's Principles of Poetic Diction', James Milroy in John S. North and Michael D. Moore (eds), *Vital Candle: Victorian and Modern Bearings in Gerard Manley Hopkins*, 1984, University of Waterloo Press. Reprinted by kind permission of John North and James Milroy.

Excerpts from *Victorian Poetry: Poetry, Poetics and Politics*, Isobel Armstrong, 1993, Routledge. Reprinted by permission of the publisher.

Reprinted by permission of the publisher from *The Disappearance of God: Five Nineteenth-Century Writers*, J. Hillis Miller, pp. 288–93, 295, 352–5, 359, Cambridge, Mass.: Harvard University Press, Copyright © 1963 by the President and Fellows of Harvard College, renewed © 1991 by Jospeh Hillis Miller.

Excerpts from 'The Wreck in Deutschland' by Helen Vendler in Anthony Mortimer (ed.) *The Authentic Cadence*, 1992, Fribourg University Press. Reprinted by kind permission of Helen Vendler.

Excerpts from 'Violence, Creativity and the Feminine: Poetics and Gender Politics in Swinburne and Hopkins', Thaïs E. Morgan in Anthony H. Harrison and Beverly Taylor (eds) *Gender and Discourse in Victorian Literature and Art*. Copyright © 1992 by Northern Illinois University Press. Used by permission of the publisher.

Annotations, Footnotes and Abbreviations

Annotation is a key feature of this series. Both the original notes from reprinted texts and new annotations by the Editor appear at the bottom of the relevant page. The reprinted notes are prefaced by the author's name in square brackets, e.g. '[Robinson's note]'.

L I	*The Letters of Gerard Manley Hopkins to Robert Bridges*, ed. Claude Colleer Abbott (London: Oxford University Press, 1935). NB: the index to these letters is not in this volume but in L II (see below).
L II	*The Correspondence of Gerard Manley Hopkins and Richard Watson Dixon*, ed. Claude Colleer Abbott (London: Oxford University Press, 1935). NB: the index at the back of this volume is to both L I and L II: a reference to L I is given as 'i' and to L II as 'ii'.
L III	*Further Letters of Gerard Manley Hopkins, Including His Correspondence with Coventry Patmore*, ed. Claude Colleer Abbott, 2nd rev. edn (London: Oxford University Press, 1956).
S	*The Sermons and Devotional Writings of Gerard Manley Hopkins*, ed. Christopher Devlin (London: Oxford University Press, 1959)
J	*The Journals and Papers of Gerard Manley Hopkins*, ed. Humphry House, completed by Graham Storey (London: Oxford University Press, 1959).
AV	Authorised Version of the Bible, sometimes known as the King James Bible. Translated in 1611 at the behest of King James I, and designed specifically for English Protestants, this is the Bible Hopkins used while a member of the Church of England.
DR	Douai-Reims (now more commonly called the Douay) Bible. Completed in 1610, this was the official Roman Catholic Bible in English in the nineteenth century. Hopkins once commented that the Douay 'is of course an inferior version' but he nonetheless insisted on checking Biblical quotations in it rather than any other translation (L III, pp. 41, 42).
Phillips	*Gerard Manley Hopkins*, ed. Catherine Phillips, Oxford Authors, (Oxford: Oxford University Press, 1986; repr. Oxford World's Classics, 2002).

White   Norman White, *Hopkins: A Literary Biography* (Oxford:
               Clarendon Press, 1992; paperback edn 1995).

Introduction

'One of two kinds of clearness one shd. have – either the meaning to be felt without effort as fast as one reads or else, if dark at first reading, when once made out *to explode*.' (L I, p. 90)[1]

Reading Gerard Manley Hopkins is an exhilarating and often bewildering business. Compared with other Victorian poets such as Alfred Tennyson, Robert Browning or Matthew Arnold, Hopkins produced a fairly small corpus of poetry, and if we exclude translations, fragments and juvenilia we are left with a body of verse that centres round one ode and three dozen or so sonnets. But within this small volume is an extraordinary density of linguistic and prosodic experiment, and a complexity of thought, imagination and reference that would be dazzling even if it were not expressed in such innovative language. Hopkins makes heavy demands on the reader: even among the trusted circle of readers who saw his poetry during his lifetime, most expressed some degree of perplexity or even resistance to his uncompromising technique. But equally there is a unique excitement and satisfaction to be gained from reading his poetry when meaning, sound and technique come together explosively.

Hopkins chose a life that isolated him both from worldly social interaction and from public literary activity. By converting to Roman Catholicism as an undergraduate, he set himself outside the conventional middle-class society into which he had been born and by deciding to become a Jesuit priest, he put the major career and personal decisions of his life into the hands of his superiors in the Society of Jesus. Duties as a theology student, then a curate and parish priest and later a professor of classics in the new Roman Catholic university in Dublin meant that Hopkins had little opportunity, even if he had had the inclination, to participate in literary circles. His own scrupulousness and anxiety contributed to this isolation, with the result that very few of his poems, and none of the great ones, were read by more than a handful of family and acquaintances until his friend and literary executor Robert Bridges began to publish them, five years after Hopkins's death. Nonetheless, though his own work was so little known, for much of his life Hopkins was an enthusiastic reader and often astute critic of contemporary poetry. He was not disconnected from the literary or political

---

1 For this and all other abbreviations see list on **pp. xv–xvi**.

history of his own times; his letters show him commenting passionately on turbulent Anglo-Irish relations during the Home Rule agitation of the 1870s and 1880s and on the miserable conditions of the poor in industrial England, as well as giving opinions on new works by Algernon Swinburne, George Eliot and Thomas Hardy.

But on many topics with which Victorian literature was greatly concerned, Hopkins's poems have almost nothing to say. It is no good looking to Hopkins for explorations of human relationships, for example. Human figures in the poems are almost always represented as alone, like the speaker himself in 'To Seem the Stranger', the eponymous 'Henry Purcell', or the tall nun in stanza 24 of 'The Wreck of the Deutschland'. In the 'Terrible Sonnets', written around 1885 at the nadir of Hopkins's spiritual, physical and mental health, isolation leads to such disintegration of the self that the speaker can find himself hanging in peril from the 'mountains' of his own mind. At other times this isolation is transformed into joy by the presence in the poem of a reminder of God's work in the world: the windhover, the beauty of human faces and bodies in 'The Leaden Echo and the Golden Echo', or the clouds that yield the Saviour in 'Hurrahing in Harvest'.

Hopkins's poetry registers an extraordinary intensity of experience. One result of the poems' concentration on individuals distanced from the social world is that Hopkins is able to explore emotional responses to nature, to God and introspection in close-up, fuelled by the detailed observations that his interests in art and philology and his religious training in examination of his own conscience taught him to make of all kinds of phenomena. Much influenced by the Victorian critic John Ruskin's insistence on seeing the natural world accurately and freshly, Hopkins's writing about nature connects him with Victorian anxieties about industrialization and yearnings for a rural world. Equally, the intensity of Hopkins's dramatized expressions of faith and of despair is important for an understanding of Victorian religious experience.

This Sourcebook aims to introduce Hopkins's best-known poems through the contexts of his own and his contemporaries' writing about them, and modern critical interpretations. The first section of the book provides some of Hopkins's prose writing about poetry and some documents intended to illuminate the impact that a conversion to Roman Catholicism had on young men in the nineteenth century. It is difficult for many modern readers to appreciate the controversy surrounding such a decision: perhaps even more than coming out as gay today, Victorian conversions were often momentous upheavals in the lives of the individual and his or her family and circle of friends, and without an insight into this aspect of Hopkins's life much of the poetry – for instance, Part the First of 'The Wreck of the Deutschland' – would be needlessly obscure.

The next section gives extracts from criticism of Hopkins, beginning with comments from three of the people who read the poems during Hopkins's lifetime, poets themselves as well as his friends. Then come some of the early reactions of important critics to the publication of the poems in the 1918 and 1930 editions. I have grouped the extracts from more recent criticism into clusters, four centring on major critical themes and debates and four on readings of particular poems or groups of poems. In the 'Key Poems' section are twenty-nine of Hopkins's poems, including of course 'The Wreck of the Deutschland' and what I have estimated to be the most often taught of the sonnets and other poems. The poems are annotated with brief explanations of difficult references and locutions and with occasional explications by Hopkins or comments from critics. At the beginning of the book is a chronology designed to help readers compare the date of particular poems with events in Hopkins's life and with selected landmarks in Victorian poetry and literature.

1

Contexts

Contextual Overview

Hopkins's career as a poet was almost entirely obscure within his own lifetime. He himself lacked the direct engagement in a public literary culture that influenced the writings and the careers of his contemporaries Tennyson, the Brownings, Matthew Arnold and even Christina Rossetti. Partly in consequence, his poetry was almost wholly unaffected by concerns of marketability, literary fashion or reviews. It is enormously distinctive: though it has some resemblance to the work of contemporary poets such as Algernon Swinburne and Walt Whitman, Hopkins's poetry cannot be mistaken for that of any other Victorian poet. Those of his contemporaries to whom he showed his poems often responded with bafflement; later readers have frequently been puzzled about how to locate his poetry in literary history. To place him in the context of other Victorian writers is in some ways to pre-empt a critical judgement about his work. To many early twentieth-century readers of Hopkins, for instance, it seemed clear that the context within which his work could best be analysed was that of modernist, not Victorian, poetry. But for the past couple of decades critics have emphasized the importance of historicizing Hopkins, of relocating him among the Victorian writers whom he read, and in the religious, political and social contexts in which (and, to some extent, alongside which) he lived.

Gerard Hopkins was born in 1844 to a middle-class couple in London, the eldest of their nine children. His father worked in marine insurance (critics have sometimes drawn attention to the fact that the economic importance of shipwrecks to the family may have played a part in Gerard Manley Hopkins's choice of subject when he decided to return to writing poetry in 1875). As was typical among their class, the family were members of the Church of England. This was the Established Church which had split from the Roman Catholic Church during the Reformation in the sixteenth century and which still played an official and active part in many aspects of British life, including education, parliamentary politics and welfare provision as well as strictly religious functions.

Hopkins was an academically successful schoolboy and won an 'Exhibition' (a kind of scholarship) to study at Oxford University, where he went in April 1863. He was an undergraduate at Balliol College, where intellectual prowess was highly regarded. Here Hopkins was taught by the formidable Benjamin Jowett, Regius Professor of Greek and controversial theologian who opposed the growing

High Church movement within the University. Other tutors included Walter Pater, the inadvertent founding father of the Aestheticist movement, by which later writers including Oscar Wilde and Ernest Dowson were much influenced.[1] Hopkins was happy in his studies and his new friendships. At this time he met Robert Bridges, the man who was to become the reader and later the editor of his poems, and through him Digby Dolben, a boy of seventeen for whom Hopkins felt a very close and powerful attachment and attraction. Both these new friends were poets: Hopkins too had been writing poetry since he was a schoolboy, and having won prizes, had reason to consider himself a budding poet, though he also had a share of his family's talent for the visual arts.

Oxford in the mid- and late nineteenth century was in some ways a place conducive to homosocial relationships; the student body was entirely male, fellows were still forbidden from marrying and, as in much Victorian middle-class society, it was socially acceptable for male friends to be demonstrative of their affection.[2] Most critics now agree that Hopkins's adult sexuality was largely directed towards male rather than female objects of desire; the early friendship with Dolben was of a pattern with later emotional attractions to men.[3] Critics and biographers have disagreed over the extent and nature of Hopkins's attachment to Dolben, though all agree that no overt sexual contact took place. Dolben and Hopkins had many interests and perhaps even habits of mind in common. As well as being a poet, Dolben was greatly inclined towards religious mysticism; he baited his Protestant father and schoolteachers by joining a quasi-monastic order and by revelling in the Victorian High Church leanings towards medieval religious aesthetics and practices. He seems to have had a considerable influence on Hopkins, who had already been affected by the High Church movement in Oxford. When Dolben drowned in 1867, still in his teens, Hopkins wrote 'there can very seldom have happened the loss of so much beauty (in body and mind and life) and of the promise of still more as there has been in his case', but added 'he had gone on in a way wh. was wholly and unhappily irrational'.[4]

---

1   Pater's *The Renaissance: Studies in Art and Poetry* (1873) states the fundamental creed of Aestheticism: 'the service of philosophy, of speculative culture, towards the human spirit, is to rouse, to startle it to a life of constant and eager observation. Every moment some form grows perfect in hand or face; some tone on the hills or the sea is choicer than the rest; some mood of passion or insight or intellectual excitement is irresistibly real and attractive to us, – for that moment only. Not the fruit of experience, but experience itself, is the end [i.e. purpose]. A counted number of pulses only is given to us of a variegated, dramatic life. [. . .] How shall we pass most swiftly from point to point, and be present always at the focus where the greatest number of vital forces unite in their purest energy? To burn always with this hard, gem-like flame, to maintain this ecstasy, is success in life. [. . .] For art comes to you proposing frankly to give nothing but the highest quality to your moments as they pass, and simply for those moments' sake.' (Walter Pater, *The Renaissance*, ed. Adam Phillips (Oxford: Oxford University Press, 1986), pp. 152–3.
2   See Denis Donoghue, 'The Oxford of Pater, Hopkins, and Wilde', in C. George Sandulescu, ed., *Rediscovering Oscar Wilde* (Gerrards Cross: Smythe, 1994).
3   For more on the effect of Hopkins's sexuality on some of his poems, see Modern Criticism pp. 64–9.
4   L I, pp. 16–17. Bridges edited a selection of Dolben's poems in 1911; in 1981 Martin Cohen published a wider selection together with Dolben's letters. Neither of these books is easy to get hold of now, but Val Cunningham's excellent anthology *The Victorians: An Anthology of Poetry and Poetics* (Oxford: Blackwell, 2000) reprints five Dolben poems.

Irrationality was something Hopkins himself was accused of at the time of his conversion to Roman Catholicism late in his undergraduate career.[5] Conversion was very much in the air at Oxford during the 1860s, as it had been since the beginning of the 'Oxford Movement' in the 1830s. It is important for an understanding of Hopkins's position as a convert to recognize the broad distinctions between the basic varieties of Christian faith in the Victorian period. Nineteenth-century Christianity covered a wide spectrum of kinds of belief and practice, from the ultra-Protestant Nonconformist (or 'dissenting') sects such as Methodists at one end, to the Roman Catholic Church at the other. In the middle was the Church of England, which was split into several rival sub-groups, never officially defined but nonetheless recognizable by their nearness to one or the other end of the spectrum. Thus, the 'High Church', 'Tractarian' and 'Anglo-Catholic' parts of the Church of England approached nearer to Roman Catholicism in many of their doctrines and practices than mainstream or 'Broad Church' Anglicans liked. High Church believers adopted practices such as auricular confession (private, individual confession of sins to a clergyman who gave absolution, or forgiveness on behalf of God) from the Roman Catholic Church, hence the term 'ritualism' often applied to Tractarianism and other High Church movements. Hopkins, for example, began to make confession to Canon Henry Parry Liddon, a controversial High Church don at the University, in 1865, while he was still a member of the Church of England.

Tractarianism, a High Church movement led by John Henry Newman, Edward Pusey and John Keble – all Oxford academics, hence the alternative name 'the Oxford Movement' – had been highly influential in parts of English society in the 1830s and early 1840s. The poet Christina Rossetti and the novelist Charlotte M. Yonge were among the many middle-class writers to be profoundly affected by the religious beliefs of the movement.[6] But in 1840 Newman published *Tract 90*, which sought to undermine the fundamental distinction between Protestant and Roman Catholic doctrine centring on the 'Real Presence' or otherwise of Christ in the bread and wine used at Holy Communion. Newman argued that none of the basic teachings of the Church of England was incompatible with those of the Roman Catholic Church. A great scandal was created by this attack on the basis of the Church of England's definition of itself and its beliefs. In 1845 Newman converted to Roman Catholicism (he became a Cardinal in the Church in 1879) and precipitated the end of Tractarianism. When Hopkins and his generation were students at Oxford, the heyday of the movement was already twenty years in the past, but its influence continued to lead to conversions: several of Hopkins's friends converted at around the same time as he did.

---

5   Hopkins's father wrote to him: 'You say years would not be sufficient to go into the question by Study – therefore you will not study at all, but decide without any deliberation. Is not that almost absurd?' (L III, p. 97).
6   Aspects of Rossetti's Tractarian beliefs are visible in her religious poetry, including 'The Lowest Place', where she asks God: 'Give me the lowest place: or if for me / That lowest place too high, make one more low / Where I may sit and see / My God and love Thee so' (publ. 1866). Charlotte M. Yonge was one of the best-selling novelists of the nineteenth century; her domestic tragedy, *The Heir of Redclyffe* (1854), is wholly infused by Tractarian yearning for a fantasized medieval chivalrous spirituality.

Why were conversions so controversial in Victorian Britain? A very brief out-line of the history of the Roman Catholic Church in England will help to answer the question. The early history of the relationship between the newly formed Church of England and the Roman Catholic Church is one of persecutions: under Henry VIII, Mary Tudor and Elizabeth I bloody attempts were made to use state power to enforce conformity to one or other Church. Despite the Catholic sym-pathies of later monarchs, particularly Charles I and James II, the Church of England remained the established (i.e. state) church. The 'Glorious Revolution' of 1688, when William and Mary of Orange were brought over from Holland to replace James II, reinforced the Protestant succession of the monarchy and hence the central place of the Church of England in the political, social and cultural life of the nation. Laws restricting the freedom of Roman Catholics to worship as they chose and to participate in many economic and state functions, from serving as members of parliament to simply buying land, remained in place until a wave of new legislation in the late eighteenth and early nineteenth centuries created a more equal religious and political situation for Roman Catholics.

The Act of Union of 1801, when Ireland was unified with Great Britain (England, Wales and Scotland), added a largely Roman Catholic Irish populace to that of the other countries in the Union, and so contributed considerably to the impetus towards the improvement of the position of Roman Catholics in Britain. At the same time, however, popular anti-Catholic prejudice remained strong and bitter in British politics. The Gordon Riots of 1780 were followed by half a century of further protests, both violent and parliamentary, against the repeal of repressive anti-Catholic legislation.[7] The Catholic Emancipation Act of 1829 lifted the restriction on Catholics sitting as members of parliament and made Roman Catholic schools possible. By the time of Hopkins's conversion in 1865 almost all the legal restrictions on Roman Catholics in Britain had been lifted. Coming to Balliol College as he did a generation after the great upheaval of the Oxford Movement, he missed the worst of the university's anti-Catholic stance. Although Oxford and Cambridge had to this point insisted that students and fellows be members of the Church of England, just a few months before Hopkins's conversion his college passed a resolution admitting Catholic students.

Although the legal position of Roman Catholics in Britain was much easier by the 1860s than it had been for at least two centuries, there remained nonetheless a widespread suspicion of Roman Catholic doctrine and particularly of the priests, nuns and the institutions of the Church. This suspicion was revived by anxieties about the influence of the Oxford Movement and its apparent goal of minimizing the distance separating the Church of England from the Church of Rome. One manifestation of the growing confidence of the High Church faction was the founding of a number of religious communities, modelled on Roman Catholic religious orders, for both men and women. Digby Dolben was a member of one of these communities; Christina Rossetti's sister Maria joined another; Newman

---

7   The Gordon Riots were a popular protest against the Relief Act passed two years earlier, which repealed some particularly harsh anti-Roman Catholic legislation. Linda Colley's book *Britons: Forging the Nation, 1707–1837* (New Haven, Conn.: Yale University Press, 1992) shows strikingly the important role that anti-Catholicism played in British nation-building during the late eighteenth and early nineteenth centuries.

founded one shortly before his conversion; and Hopkins's sister Milicent became a member of another. For many members of the Church of England, the development of these quasi-Roman Catholic religious orders was a sign of the growing influence of the Catholic Church and would lead to the weakening of the Protestant Church which had, some argued, guaranteed religious and political toleration and political and social stability in Britain for several centuries. In 1850 the diocesan hierarchy was restored in Britain: the Roman Catholic Church was able to establish bishops and parish priests throughout England. When John Henry Newman, seven years after his own conversion, announced that 'something very strange is passing over this land [. . .] it is the coming in of a Second Spring; it is a restoration in the moral world', his sense that a revivification of Roman Catholicism was taking place in Britain was shared by many of his co-religionists and was a source of alarm to the more militantly Protestant parts of the Church of England.[8] The national debate about the place of Roman Catholics, particularly Roman Catholic priests and nuns, in English life made its way into contemporary literature: novels such as Elizabeth Harris's broadly pro-Catholic *From Oxford to Rome* (1847) and *Rest in the Church* (1848), and William Sewell's anti-Catholic *Hawkstone* (1845), explored, often in heated or polemical terms, questions of conversion, fidelity and the changes apparent in British religious life. In the light of this debate, Hopkins's conversion can be seen as being far from unique among the middle-class young men of his day but nonetheless as representing part of a sustained challenge from the Roman Catholic Church to the elite social and intellectual structures of the period. Conversion set Hopkins outside many of the conventions of middle-class Victorian life: it profoundly affected his social, familial and political relationships, and a number of critics have argued that it affected his relationship with the English language.[9]

Less than two years after he was received into the Roman Catholic Church by Newman, Hopkins decided to make a further commitment to his religious beliefs by becoming a priest. He chose the Society of Jesus, or Jesuits, an elite order which had a reputation for valuing intellectual rigour and which had had a particularly chequered history in Britain. Even within the Roman Catholic Church the influence of the Jesuits had sometimes been considered too great: in 1773 Pope Clement XIV suppressed the society but it survived in weakened form until it was restored by Pope Pius VII forty years later. Founded in 1539 by a Spanish priest, Ignatius Loyola, the Jesuits were particularly active as missionaries in the New World and the Far East and probably appealed to Hopkins's hope that England would be re-converted to Roman Catholicism. Life as a Jesuit involved extensive training: all incomers, whether converts or not, spent three years studying philosophy and several more studying theology, interspersed with retreats during which they worked through the Spiritual Exercises of St Ignatius, a thorough and extremely demanding system of meditation and confession. Once ordained as a priest, the Jesuit was sent to work in whatever parish or other institution the

8   J. H. Newman, 'The Second Spring', preached 13 July 1852, in *Sermons Preached on Various Occasions* (London: Longmans, Green, 1857), pp. 195–7.
9   For a particularly vivid instance of this argument, see Eric Griffiths, *The Printed Voice of Victorian Poetry* (Oxford: Clarendon Press, 1989), esp. pp. 323–4.

society considered him suited to; his superiors found it difficult to place Hopkins satisfactorily since he seems to have been unhappy and less than effective in a number of posts. In 1884, seven years after his ordination, having tried parish work and school teaching, he was sent to Ireland to be the Professor of Greek at the Roman Catholic University in Dublin, and remained there until he died in 1889, frequently ill, depressed and overworked.

When Hopkins made the decision to become a priest he wrote to his friend Alexander Baillie: 'I want to write still and as a priest I very likely can do that too, not so freely as I shd. have liked, e.g. nothing or little in the verse way, but no doubt what wd. best serve the cause of my religion.'[10] But before entering the Jesuit Novitiate, he burned copies of the poems he had written up to that point (the juvenile poems of his that survive were preserved in copies given to other people) and 'resolved to write no more, as not belonging to my profession, unless it were by the wish of my superiors', as he later wrote to his friend Richard Watson Dixon, a poet and Church of England clergyman.[11] Hopkins's temperament combined with the fervent religious climate of his times to make him a notably scrupulous, ardent and zealous follower of his faith and of the Society of Jesus's rules and practices. Even as an undergraduate he had taken a very hard line with himself in matters of discipline, apparently welcoming the opportunity to impose punishments on himself for minor offences, though in maturity his health, both mental and physical, would not permit him to follow through all the demands he and his chosen order placed on him. His resolution not to write poetry unless he was asked to do so as part of his work as a priest held through his twenties, until in 1875 a superior suggested that he write a poem commemorating the death of five nuns in a shipwreck.[12]

The resulting poem, 'The Wreck of the Deutschland' (see Key Poems, pp. 113–28), is one of the masterpieces of Victorian poetry: intensely emotional, structurally complex, innovative with both words and rhythm, it explores the nature of suffering. The poem puts its acknowledgement of the fear and pain that come with physical or mental anguish into conflict with a theology that welcomes suffering as a sign of God's presence in the world and his care for the individual. Despite some initial hopes that it would be published, it did not reach an audience beyond Hopkins's family and friends in his lifetime – a sign of what was to come. A few later attempts were made by Hopkins and various friends to publish his poetry but they came to nothing, frustrated partly by concern that the public would find the poems too difficult to understand, and partly by Hopkins's own prohibitions and interventions. A very small fraction of his poetry was published in his lifetime – one example is 'The Silver Jubilee', written for the twenty-fifth anniversary of the appointment of the Bishop of Shrewsbury – and none of these is among the poems in this Sourcebook, since none is widely critically considered to be among Hopkins's major poems.[13]

---

10 L III, p. 231. He added: 'But if I am a priest it will cause my mother, or she says it will, great grief and this preys on my mind very much and makes the near prospect quite black' (pp. 231–2).

11 L II, p. 14.

12 In the seven years between his entering the novitiate and beginning 'The Wreck of the Deutschland', Hopkins wrote several presentation pieces and some Latin translations, but most of these are very difficult to date conclusively and are certainly not major works.

13 For 'The Silver Jubilee' see Phillips, p. 119.

After 'The Wreck', Hopkins felt he was no longer bound by his resolution not to write poetry, and he continued for the rest of his life to compose poems, most of them fuelled by strong emotion. Some express bursts of intense joy – especially the poems written during his time as a theological student at St Beuno's in Wales, such as 'Hurrahing in Harvest' (see Key Poems, **p. 136**) and 'The Windhover' (**p. 133**). Others, particularly the 'Terrible Sonnets' (see Key Poems, **pp. 146–52**) dating from a prolonged period of loneliness, physical illness and severe depression while drudging as a Professor of Greek in Dublin, were written in despair over his sense of his failures as a priest and a poet.[14] None of them had more than a tiny audience composed of friends and family members to whom Hopkins sent handwritten copies.

Robert Bridges, who survived his friend by forty years, published the first edition of Hopkins's *Poems* in 1918, though he had included some in slightly earlier anthologies. Coming out at the end of the First World War, it took some time for the 750 copies to sell, but a second edition followed in 1930, and within a few years Hopkins was being recognized by critics as a major poet and was having a significant influence on Modernist poetry. The introduction to the Critical History section of this sourcebook (**pp. 41–6**) explores the post-1918 history of Hopkins's writing further.

How should we understand Hopkins's place in the literary context of his day, since he published almost no poetry and had no part in the public sphere of Victorian culture? First, we should not underestimate his engagement with literary culture as a reader, though as a writer his impact was almost negligible until the twentieth century. Though his access to contemporary literature was often through reviews in journals rather than via the works themselves, Hopkins's correspondence shows him to have been an enthusiastic reader and a confident, sometimes incisive critic. He read poems by Bridges and Dixon with immensely detailed attention and reported his criticisms of them, sometimes in less than flattering terms. Clearly his correspondence with these two poets, and with Coventry Patmore, acted in a sense as his substitute for the public literary sphere. His attention to other poets, though less detailed, was often energetic and sensitive. His essay-like letter to his friend A. W. M. Baillie on Tennyson's poetry (see Contemporary Documents, **pp. 23–6**) shows his critical imagination at work in characteristic ways, classifying poetry by degree of individuality and prizing uniqueness, inspiration and 'freshness'. His famous comment to Dixon that Robert Browning has 'a way of talking (and making his people talk) with the air and spirit of a man bouncing up from table with his mouth full of bread and cheese and saying that he meant to stand no blasted nonsense' mixes critical acuity with Hopkinsian humour.[15] Other critical judgements mix attention to the work with dislike of the writer or the writer's views, and sometimes with anxiety about comparison with his own work. His attention often went to other poets' metrics, as in his discussion of Walt Whitman: 'this savagery of his art, this rhythm in its last ruggedness and decomposition into common prose, comes near

---

14 For a good account of this period, see Norman White, *Hopkins: A Literary Biography* (Oxford: Clarendon Press, 1992), pp. 369–76.
15 L II, p. 74.

the last elaboration of mine' ['The Leaden Echo and the Golden Echo', see Key Poems, **pp. 143–6**], as well as to the sense he got of the poet through the poetry: 'I always knew in my heart Walt Whitman's mind to be more like my own than any other man's living. As he is a very great scoundrel this is not a pleasant confession'.[16] Swinburne was another poet to whom Hopkins's critical thoughts returned at many times in his life and to whom he has been compared by later critics: Swinburne's 'genius is astonishing, but it will, I think, only do one thing'; 'his poetry seems a powerful effort at establishing a new standard of poetical diction, of the rhetoric of poetry; but to waive every other objection it is essentially archaic, biblical a good deal, and so on: now that is a thing that can never last; a perfect style must be of its age'.[17] Hopkins thought of his own poetry as being of its age (though not as perfect) and acquaintance with the work of the poets he admired (including Christina Rossetti, Tennyson and Wordsworth) as well as those such as Whitman and Swinburne about whom he had reservations, helps us to read his poetry in the context in which he himself thought it should be read.

In 1886, three years before his premature death, Hopkins wrote to Bridges: 'I would have you and Canon Dixon and all true poets remember that fame, the being known, though in itself one of the most dangerous things to man, is nevertheless the true and appointed air, element, and setting of genius and its works'.[18] Hopkins's poems are virtually all autobiographical, though except for 'The Wreck of the Deutschland' they mostly present snapshots of an emotion he is currently feeling rather than a narrative of his life. Poetry for Hopkins was never quite a hobby, nor was it a profession: it is one of literary history's tragic ironies that Hopkins died without knowing that his poetry would have an audience and another that his final poem, 'To R. B.' (see Key Poems, **pp. 159–60**) apologizes for having lost the creativity that readers today recognize throughout his work.

---

16 L III, p. 157, p. 155.
17 L I, p. 79; L II, p. 99.
18 L I, p. 231.

Chronology

Bullet points are used to denote events in Hopkins's life and the career of his poetry, and asterisks to denote historical and literary events.

1844
- Gerard Manley Hopkins (GMH) born (28 July) in Stratford, Essex
* Coventry Patmore publishes his first collection, *Poems*

1845
* John Henry Newman converts to Roman Catholicism

1848
* Newman, *Loss and Gain*

1850
* Death of William Wordsworth; Tennyson publishes *In Memoriam A. H. H.*, becomes Poet Laureate

1854
* Patmore publishes the first of his *Angel in the House* sequence of poems, *The Betrothal*; others follow: *The Espousals* (1856), *Faithful for Ever* (1860) and *The Victories of Love* (1863)

1855
* Tennyson, *Maud and Other Poems*; Whitman, first edition of *Leaves of Grass*; Browning, *Men and Women*

1859
* Charles Darwin, *Origin of Species*

1860
- GMH wins poetry prize at Highgate School with 'The Escorial'

1862
* Christina Rossetti, *Goblin Market and Other Poems*

1863
- GMH begins undergraduate studies at Balliol College, Oxford

1864
- GMH meets Christina Rossetti (1830–94)
* Patmore becomes a Roman Catholic

1865
- GMH meets Bridges's relative Digby Dolben (1848–67) in Oxford

1866
- GMH makes decision to become a Roman Catholic (July); John Henry Newman receives GMH into the Roman Catholic Church (21 October)
* Christina Rossetti, *The Prince's Progress and Other Poems*

1867
- GMH graduates from Oxford University with a first-class degree

1868
- GMH decides to become a priest, considers both the Benedictines and the Jesuits (2 May); 'Slaughter of the Innocents': GMH burns copies of his poems and resolves to write no more, thinking poetry writing incompatible with his vocation as a priest (11 May); enters the Jesuit Novitiate in Roehampton, London
* Browning, first instalments of *The Ring and the Book*

1869
* Tennyson, *The Holy Grail and Other Poems*

1870
- GMH takes vows of poverty, chastity and obedience; begins philosophy studies lasting three years at Stonyhurst seminary in Lancashire
* Death of Dickens; First Vatican Council declares the doctrine of Papal Infallibility, precipitating renewed anti-Catholic measures and feeling in many European states

1871
* George Eliot, *Middlemarch* (1871–2); beginning of *Kulturkampf*, the struggle led by Otto von Bismarck, Chancellor of the German Empire, against the Roman Catholic Church's influence in Germany

1873
* Bridges's first collection, *Poems*

1874
- GMH begins theology studies lasting three years at St Beuno's, Wales

1875

*   *Deutschland*, a ship sailing from Germany to America, wrecked off
the Thames estuary. Many passengers drown, including five Franciscan
nuns expelled from Germany by Bismarck's *Kulturkampf* policies (6–7
December); the shipwreck is reported in *The Times* newspaper, 11 and
18 December

- GMH begins to write 'The Wreck of the Deutschland' (December)

1877

- GMH writes 'God's Grandeur', 'As Kingfishers Catch Fire', 'Spring', 'The
Windhover', 'Pied Beauty', 'Hurrahing in Harvest' and other sonnets;
ordained as a priest (23 September)

1879

- While living again in Oxford as curate at St Aloysius's church, GMH writes
'Duns Scotus's Oxford', 'Binsey Poplars', 'Henry Purcell', 'The Bugler's
First Communion', 'Peace' and others; leaves Oxford for post as curate in
Bedford Leigh

1880

- GMH writes 'Felix Randall'
*   Death of George Eliot

1882

- While working as classics teacher at Stonyhurst College, GMH writes 'The
Leaden Echo and the Golden Echo'

1883

- GMH meets Coventry Patmore (1823–96)

1884

- Becomes Professor of Greek and Latin Literature at University College,
Dublin (founded in 1851)

1885

- GMH probably writes most of the 'Terrible Sonnets'.

1886

- GMH finishes 'Spelt from Sibyl's Leaves'
*   Hardy, *The Mayor of Casterbridge*

1889

- GMH writes 'Thou Art Indeed Just, Lord' and 'To R. B.'; dies of typhoid
(8 June)
*   Death of Browning

1892

*   Death of Tennyson; death of Whitman

1912
*   Bridges's *Collected Poems* published

1913
*   Bridges is made Poet Laureate

1916
*   Bridges publishes an anthology, *The Spirit of Man*, which includes six of
       GMH's poems

1918
*   Bridges publishes the first edition of GMH's poems; 750 copies are printed

Contemporary Documents

From **John Henry Newman,** *Loss and Gain: The Story of a Convert*
(1848), 5th edition (London: Burns, Lambert & Oates, 1869), pp. 303–4,
307–8, 382–3

J. H. Newman (1801–90) was among the best known and influential Victorian
religious leaders. One of the founding figures of the Oxford Movement, Newman
was until 1845 a member of the Church of England. His pamphlet *Tract 90*, pub-
lished in 1841, was part of a highly controversial attempt to minimize the distance
between the Church of England and the Roman Catholic Church. So intense was
the hostility arising in Protestant circles to Newman's pamphlet that the series
in which it appeared, *Tracts for the Times*, was forced to cease publication.

After his conversion to Roman Catholicism, Newman became Rector of the
new Roman Catholic university in Dublin, where Hopkins was to spend the last
five years of his life. The relationship between the two men began nearly twenty
years earlier when in 1866 Hopkins wrote to Newman, who was in Birmingham
at the oratory he had founded in 1847. Hopkins asked to see Newman to
discuss his intention to convert: 'I do not want to be helped to any conclusions
of belief, for I am thankful to say my mind is made up, but the necessity of
becoming a Catholic (although I had long foreseen where the only consistent
position wd. lie) coming upon me suddenly has put me into painful confusion of
mind about my immediate duty in my circumstances'.[1]

Loss and Gain is the story of a young man, Charles Reding, a member of the
Church of England, who undergoes a religious crisis which is only relieved by his
conversion at the end of the novel to the Roman Catholic Church. The novel
was published three years after Newman's own conversion. These extracts give
a flavour of the experience of a convert resisting the social and familial pres-
sures to remain within the Anglican Church. At the start of the first extract,
Charles has made the decision to convert but has not yet been received into
the Roman Catholic Church. He and his friend Campbell are discussing the
effect that his decision will have on his family.[2]

---

1   L III, 21–2.
2   For ease of reading I have modernized the layout of this extract.

Campbell did not at once reply; then he said, 'I shall have to break it to your poor mother; Mary thinks it will be her death.'

Charles dropped his head on the window-sill upon his hands. 'No,' he said; 'I trust that she, and all of us, will be supported.'

'So do I, fervently,' answered Campbell; 'it will be a most terrible blow to your sisters. My dear fellow, should you not take all this into account? Do seriously consider the actual misery you are causing for possible good.'

'Do you think I have not considered it, Campbell? Is it nothing for one like me to be breaking all these dear ties, and to be losing the esteem and sympathy of so many persons I love? Oh, it has been a most piercing thought; but I have exhausted it, I have drunk it out. I have got familiar with the prospect now, and am fully reconciled. Yes, I give up home, I give up all who have ever known me, loved me, valued me, wished me well; I know well I am making myself a by-word and an outcast.'

'Oh, my dear Charles,' answered Campbell, 'beware of a very subtle temptation which may come on you here. I have meant to warn you of it before. The greatness of the sacrifice stimulates you; you do it because it is so much to do.'

Charles smiled. 'How little you know me!' he said; 'if that were the case, should I have waited patiently two years and more? Why did I not rush forward as others have done? *You* will not deny that I have acted rationally, obediently. I have put the subject from me again and again, and it has returned.'

'I'll say nothing harsh or unkind of you, Charles,' said Campbell; 'but it's a most unfortunate delusion. I wish I could make you take in the idea that there is the chance of it's *being* a delusion.'

'Ah, Campbell, how can you forget so?' answered Charles; 'don't you know this is the very thing which has influenced me so much all along? I said, "Perhaps I am in a dream. Oh, that I could pinch myself and awake!" You know what stress I laid on my change of feeling upon my dear father's death; what I thought to be convictions before, vanished then like a cloud. I have said to myself, "Perhaps these will vanish too." But no; "the clouds return after the rain;" they come again and again, heavier than ever. It is a conviction rooted in me; it endures against the prospect of loss of mother and sisters. Here I sit wasting my days, when I might be useful in life. Why? Because this hinders me. Lately it has increased on me tenfold. You will be shocked, but let me tell you in confidence, – lately I have been quite afraid to ride, or to bathe, or to do anything out of the way, lest something should happen, and I might be taken away with a great duty unaccomplished.[3] No, by this time I have proved that it is a real conviction. My belief in the Church of Rome is part of myself: I cannot act against it without acting against God.'[4] [. . .]

Charles leapt from the gig with a beating heart, and ran up to his mother's room. She was sitting by the fire at her work when he entered; she held out her

---

3   Charles is afraid to die before he has become a member of the Roman Catholic Church in case his soul should be in jeopardy. Hopkins made a similar point to his father about the urgency of his own conversion: 'if I were to delay and die in the meantime I shd. have no plea why my soul was not forfeit' (L III, p. 92).

4   Hopkins felt similarly: 'I have no power in fact to stir a finger: it is God Who makes the decision and not I' (L III, p. 92).

hand coldly to him, and he sat down. Nothing was said for a little while; then, without leaving off her occupation, she said, 'Well, Charles, and so you are leaving us. Where and how do you propose to employ yourself when you have entered upon your new life?'

Charles answered that he had not yet turned his mind to the consideration of any thing but the great step on which every thing else depended.

There was another silence; then she said, 'You won't find anywhere such friends as you have had at home, Charles.' Presently she continued, 'You have had everything in your favour, Charles; you have been blessed with talents, advantages of education, easy circumstances; many a deserving young man has to scramble on as he can.'

Charles answered that he was deeply sensible how much he owed in temporal matters to Providence, and that it was only at His bidding that he was giving them up.

'We all looked up to you, Charles; perhaps we made too much of you; well, God be with you; you have taken your line.'

Poor Charles said that no one could conceive what it cost him to give up what was so very dear to him, what was part of himself; there was nothing on earth which he prized like his home.

'Then why do you leave us?' she said, quickly; 'you must have your way; you do it, I suppose, because you like it.'

'Oh really, my dear mother,' cried he, 'if you saw my heart! You know in Scripture how people were obliged in the Apostles' times to give up all for Christ.'

'We are heathens, then,' she replied; 'thank you, Charles, I am obliged to you for this;' and she dashed away a tear from her eye.

Charles was almost beside himself; he did not know what to say; he stood up, and leaned his elbow on the mantelpiece, supporting his head on his hand.

'Well, Charles,' she continued, still going on with her work, 'perhaps the day will come' . . . her voice faltered; 'your dear father' . . . she put down her work.

'It is useless misery,' said Charles; 'why should I stay? good-bye for the present, my dearest mother. I leave you in good hands, not kinder, but better than mine; you lose me, you gain another. Farewell for the present; we will meet when you will, when you call; it will be a happy meeting.'

He threw himself on his knees, and laid his cheek on her lap; she could no longer resist him; she hung over him, and began to smooth down his hair as she had done when he was a child. At length scalding tears began to fall heavily upon his face and neck; he bore them for a while, then started up, kissed her cheek impetuously, and rushed out of the room. [. . .]

A very few words will conduct us to the end of our history. It was Sunday morning about seven o'clock, and Charles had been admitted into the communion of the Catholic Church about an hour since. He was still kneeling in the church of the Passionists before the Tabernacle, in the possession of a deep peace and serenity of mind, which he had not thought possible on earth. It was more like the stillness which almost sensibly affects the ears when a bell that has long been tolling stops, or when a vessel, after much tossing at sea, finds itself in harbour. It was such as to throw him back in memory on his earliest years, as if he were really beginning life again. But there was more than the happiness of childhood in his heart; he seemed to feel a rock under his feet; it was the *soliditas Cathedræ Petri*.[5] He went on kneeling, as if he were already in heaven, with the throne of God before him, and angels around [. . .].

From **J. Cumming, 'Ritualism – What is it?'**, from *Ritualism, The Highway to Rome* (London, 1867), extracted in *Anti-Catholicism in Victorian England*, ed. E. R. Norman (London: George Allen & Unwin, 1968), pp. 194–5

The extracts from this mid-Victorian lecture give a sense of contemporary prejudice in some British circles against Roman Catholicism and against the attempts by leaders of the Oxford Movement and others to align faith and practice in the Church of England with those of the Roman Catholic Church. 'Ritualism' refers to the introduction of controversial, often Catholic-inspired, forms and styles of worship into Anglican churches. Cumming's book was dedicated to the profoundly anti-ritualist Protestant Society, with the comment that 'never was our country in greater peril in its highest and holiest interests'. Notice in this extract the association of ritualism and Roman Catholicism with sensuality and theatricalism. Hopkins's father suggested around the time of his son's announcement of his intention to convert that Gerard had been influenced by the visual and sensory appeal of Roman Catholic services and churches, but Hopkins replied: 'I am surprised you shd. say fancy and aesthetic tastes have led me to my present state of mind: these wd. be better satisfied in the Church of England, for bad taste is always meeting one in the accessories of Catholicism' (L III, p. 93).

The subject of my address is, Ritualism; a new name for an ancient, but unhappily not an obsolete heresy. I desire to speak of it not in the faintest feeling of antipathy or dislike to the Church in which it has unhappily broken out, nor indeed in the light of the Articles of that Church; this has been done by others with conclusive effect; but in the light of the inspired and decisive Word of God.[1] Prodigious efforts are being made by the Ritualists to enlist converts, or rather I should say perverts.[2] Young men and young women are captivated and charmed by beautiful music, by a gorgeous ceremonial, by rich and variegated dresses, which also, whether at the ball or at the opera, or in a Ritualistic Church, are no doubt very attractive; and by rites and lights, and attitudes and genuflexions,

5   The solidity of the Chair of Peter – referring to St Peter the Apostle. Jesus said of him 'thou art Peter, and upon this rock I will build my church; and the gates of hell shall not prevail against it' (Matthew 16:18), and the Popes, as leaders of the Roman Catholic Church, are said to be the successors of St Peter. *Cathedra Petri* metaphorically means the Roman Catholic Church.

1   Cumming refers to the Church of England and the Thirty-Nine Articles that make up the core of the doctrinal beliefs of that Church. The Thirty-Nine Articles were laid out as the central beliefs of the Church of England in the sixteenth century. By Hopkins's time they were the object of some controversy within the Church of England but were still upheld for many purposes. They can be found at the back of the Book of Common Prayer.
2   'Pervert' had been used since the seventeenth century to mean an apostate. It did not acquire its sexual meaning until the 1890s.

extremely well done, considering the disadvantages of being performed in a Protestant Church, and the hampering and hostile limits of a communion whose articles and history are intensely opposed alike to the principles, the dogmas, and the ceremonies of Ritualism. [. . .]

The earlier plan of the Ritualists thirty years ago, when Dr Pusey started his system, was to convince the people of the truth of Romish dogmas, and to expect they would afterwards conform to Romish rites.[3] This proved a failure. The intellect and conscience of the nation revolted against it. The new plan is to begin with ceremony instead of ending with it, and through the senses to get at the intellect, the conscience, and the heart of the people. A sceptic writer has said that in nine persons out of ten, if you can only secure their senses, you may calculate upon all the rest. Whether this be true or not, both Rome – the great original, and the Ritualists – the imperfect copyists, are acting upon the principle that if you secure the senses, you may surely calculate you will enlist the mind in their system.

Gerard Manley Hopkins on the language of verse, from letter to A. W. M. Baillie, 10 September 1864, L III, pp. 216–20

In a letter to his college friend Alexander William Mowbray Baillie (1843–1921), the twenty-year-old Hopkins laid out a critical scheme that sorted poetry into three main kinds, depending on whether the poetry was inspired and exceptional, typical of its author, or merely verse rather than prose. The letter begins with the admission 'Do you know, a terrible thing has happened to me. I have begun to *doubt* Tennyson',[1] and goes on to use Tennyson's new poem 'Enoch Arden' (published in 1864, the year Hopkins wrote this letter) as an example of the kind of poetry 'that one could conceive oneself writing [. . .] if one were the poet'. Hopkins's division of poetry into Parnassian, Castalian and Delphic is often referred to by critics of his own work.

I think then the language of verse may be divided into three kinds. The first and highest is poetry proper, the language of inspiration. The word inspiration need cause no difficulty. I mean by it a mood of great, abnormal in fact, mental acuteness, either energetic or receptive, according as the thoughts which arise in it seem generated by a stress and action of the brain, or to strike into it unasked. This mood arises from various causes, physical generally, as good health or state of the air or, prosaic as it is, length of time after a meal. But I need not go into this; all that it is needful to mark is, that the poetry of inspiration can only be written in this mood of mind, even if it only last a minute, by poets themselves. Everybody of

---

3   Romish: a pejorative word for Roman Catholic. Dr Pusey: Edward Bouverie Pusey (1800–82), a professor at Oxford University and a leader of the Oxford Movement. As an undergraduate and while still within the Church of England, Hopkins was much influenced by Pusey and made his confession to him at least once; Pusey disapproved strongly of his conversion (Norman White, *Hopkins: A Literary Biography* (Oxford: Clarendon Press, 1992; paperback edn 1995), p. 128, p. 139).

1   L III, p. 215.

course has like moods, but not being poets what they then produce is not poetry. The second kind I call *Parnassian*.[2] It can only be spoken by poets, but it is not in the highest sense poetry. It does not require the mood of mind in which the poetry of inspiration is written. It is spoken *on and from the level* of a poet's mind, not, as in the other case, when the inspiration which is the gift of genius, raises him above himself. For I think it is the case with genius that it is not when quiescent so very much above mediocrity as the difference between the two might lead us to think, but that it has the power and privilege of rising from that level to a height utterly far from mediocrity: in other words that its greatness is *that it can be* so great. You will understand. *Parnassian* then is that language which genius speaks as fitted to its exaltation, and place among other genius, but does not sing (I have been betrayed into the whole hog of a metaphor) in its flights. Great men, poets I mean, have each their own dialect as it were of Parnassian, formed generally as they go on writing, and at last, – this is the point to be marked, – they can see things in this Parnassian way and describe them in this Parnassian tongue, without further effort of inspiration. In a poet's particular kind of Parnassian lies most of his style, of his manner, of his mannerism if you like. But I must not go farther without giving you instances of Parnassian. I shall take one from Tennyson, and from *Enoch Arden*, from a passage much quoted already and which will be no doubt often quoted, the description of Enoch's tropical island.

> The mountain wooded to the peak, the lawns
> And winding glades high up like ways to Heaven,
> The slender coco's drooping crown of plumes,
> The lightning flash of insect and of bird,
> The lustre of the long convolvuluses
> That coil'd around the stately stems, and ran
> Ev'n to the limit of the land, the glows
> And glories of the broad belt of the world,
> All these he saw.[3]

Now it is a mark of Parnassian that one could conceive oneself writing it if one were the poet. Do not say that *if* you were Shakespear you can imagine yourself writing Hamlet, because that is just what I think you can*not* conceive. In a fine piece of inspiration every beauty takes you as it were by surprise, not of course that you did not think the writer could be so great, for that is not it, – indeed I think it is a mistake to speak of people admiring Shakespear more and more as they live, for when the judgment is ripe and you have read a good deal of any writer including his best things, and carefully, then, I think, however high the place you give him, that you must have rated him equally with his merits however great they be; so that all after admiration cannot increase but keep alive this estimate, make his greatness stare into your eyes and din it into your ears, as it were, but not make it greater, – but to go on with the broken sentence, every fresh

2 A critical term invented by Hopkins; derived from an adjective dating originally from the mid-seventeenth century, meaning 'belonging to poetry'. Parnassus is a mountain in Greece that was believed to be sacred to Apollo and the muses.

3 Alfred Tennyson, 'Enoch Arden', ll. 568–76.

beauty could not in any way be predicted or accounted for by what one has already read. But in Parnassian pieces you feel that if you were the poet you could have gone on as he has done, you see yourself doing it, only with the difference that if you actually try to find you cannot write his Parnassian. Well now to turn to the piece above. The glades being 'like ways to Heaven' is, I think, a new thought, it is an inspiration. Not so the next line, that is pure Parnassian. If you examine it the words are choice and the description is beautiful and unexceptionable, but it does not *touch* you. The next is more Parnassian still. In the next lines I think the picture of the convolvuluses does touch; but only the picture: the words are Parnassian. It is a very good instance, for the lines are undoubtedly beautiful, but yet I could scarcely point anywhere to anything more idiomatically Parnassian, to anything which I more clearly see myself writing *qua* Tennyson,[4] than the words

> The glows
> And glories of the broad belt of the world.

What Parnassian is you will now understand, but I must make some more remarks on it. I believe that when a poet palls on us it is because of his Parnassian. We seem to have found out his secret. Now in fact we have not found out more than this, that when he is not inspired and in his flights, his poetry does run in an intelligibly laid down path. Well, it is notorious that Shakespear does not pall, and this is because he uses, I believe, so little Parnassian. He does use some, but little. Now judging from my own experience I should say no author palls so much as Wordsworth; this is because he writes such an 'intolerable deal of' Parnassian.[5]

If with a critical eye and in a critical appreciative mood you read a poem by an unknown author or an anonymous poem by a known, but not at once recognizable, author, and he is a real poet, then you will pronounce him so at once, and the poem will seem truly inspired, though afterwards, when you know the author, you will be able to distinguish his inspirations from his Parnassian, and will perhaps think the very piece which struck you so much at first mere Parnassian. You know well how deadened, as it were, the critical faculties become at times, when all good poetry alike loses its clear ring and its charm; while in other moods they are so enlivened that things that have long lost their freshness strike you with their original definiteness and piquant beauty.

I think one had got into the way of thinking, or had not got of the way of thinking, that Tennyson was always new, *touching*, beyond other poets, not pressed with human ailments, never using Parnassian. So at least I used to think. Now one sees he uses Parnassian; he is, one must see it, what we used to call Tennysonian. But the discovery of this must not make too much difference. When puzzled by one's doubts it is well to turn to a passage like this. Surely your maturest judgment will never be fooled out of saying that this is divine, terribly beautiful – the stanza of *In Memoriam* beginning with the quatrain

---

4 i.e. as Tennyson.
5 Hopkins is referring to Shakespeare's *Henry IV* Part I, Act 2 Scene 4, where Prince Hal comments of Falstaff's diet: 'O monstrous! but one half-penny-worth of bread to this intolerable deal of sack!'

> O Hesper o'er the buried sun,
> And ready thou to die with him,
> Thou watchest all things ever dim
> And dimmer, and a glory done.[6]

I quote from memory. Inconsequent conclusion: Shakespear is and must be utterly the greatest of poets.

Just to end what I was saying about poetry. There is a higher sort of Parnassian which I call *Castalian*,[7] or it may be thought the lowest kind of inspiration. Beautiful poems may be written wholly in it. Its peculiarity is that though you can hardly conceive yourself having written in it, if in the poet's place, yet it is too characteristic of the poet, too so-and-so-all-over-ish, to be quite inspiration. E.g.

> Yet despair
> Touches me not, though pensive as a bird
> Whose vernal coverts winter hath laid bare.[8]

This is from Wordsworth, beautiful, but rather too essentially Wordsworthian, too persistently his way of looking at things. The third kind is merely the language of verse as distinct from that of prose, Delphic, the tongue of the Sacred *Plain*, I may call it, used in common by poet and poetaster.[9] Poetry when spoken is spoken in it, but to speak it is not necessarily to speak poetry. I may add there is also *Olympian*.[10] This is the language of strange masculine genius which suddenly, as it were, forces its way into the domain of poetry, without naturally having a right there. Milman's poetry is of this kind I think, and Rossetti's *Blessèd Damozel*.[11] But unusual poetry has a tendency to seem so at first.

From **Gerard Manley Hopkins, 'Poetic Diction'**, 1865(?), J, pp. 84–5

In this undergraduate essay Hopkins makes two points that are well worth bearing in mind when reading both his poetry and later criticism of it. The first is the emphasis on parallelism as the heart of poetic technique. Parallelism covers a range of devices, including constructions of meaning and of sound, but is to be seen in a great many instances in Hopkins's poetry: one example is

---

6   Hopkins slightly misquotes Tennyson's lyric 121 in his great elegy *In Memoriam A. H. H.* (published 1850): 'Sad Hesper o'er the buried sun'.
7   Castalia was a spring on Mount Parnassus, again associated with the Muses.
8   William Wordsworth, 'Composed near Calais, on the road leading to Ardres, August 7, 1802' (published 1807).
9   Delphi was a town on Mount Parnassus and the name of a sanctuary dedicated to Apollo where an oracle lived. Poetaster: a petty or paltry poet (*OED*).
10 Olympus was the mountain on which the Greek gods were said to live.
11 Henry Hart Milman (1791–1868): Oxford-educated poet and historian. Dante Gabriel Rossetti's poem 'The Blessed Damozel' was published in 1850. Hopkins admired D. G. Rossetti's poetry but preferred his sister Christina Rossetti's work: in a letter of 1872 he wrote 'I daresay he has more range, force, and interest, and then there is the difference between a man and a woman, but for pathos and pure beauty of art I do not think he is her equal' (L III, p. 119).

'Spelt from Sibyl's Leaves' (see Key Poems, **pp. 152–4**), where construction and meaning are parallel in lines such as 'Her fond yellow hornlight wound to the west, | her wild hollow hoarlight hung to the height'. A less intense example is to be seen in the final line of 'Moonrise' (see Key Poems, **pp. 128–9**) (which coincidentally also uses a caesura mark): 'Parted me leaf and leaf, divided me, | eyelid and eyelid of slumber'. Parallelisms of sound, similarly, are very frequent in Hopkins; as in the first line of 'The Leaden Echo and the Golden Echo' (see Key Poems, **pp. 143–6**), for instance: 'How to kéep – is there ány any, is there none such, nowhere known some, bow or brooch or braid or brace, lace, latch or catch or key to keep'.

The second point of interest in this essay is Hopkins's distinction between 'marked' and 'chromatic' parallelism. In other writings of roughly the same period, he borrowed from music theory the terms 'diatonic' and 'chromatic' to describe the same relations of abrupt and gradual change.[18] Especially in his early years, Hopkins (rather like Shelley and Keats) tended towards synaesthetic expressions, i.e. using terms and metaphors from one kind of sense perception to describe another, as when he described 'a bright rainbow' with 'two, perhaps three complete octaves, that is three, perhaps four strikings of the keynote or nethermost red'.[19] His use of terms borrowed from music to describe two kinds of change is of a part with this. Criticism that focuses on Hopkins's use of sound patterns such as rhyme (see for instance J. Hillis Miller's analysis of rhyme in 'Pied Beauty', in Modern Criticism, **pp. 92–4**) usually takes into some account his own writing on poetic technique.

[. . .] it is plain that metre, rhythm, rhyme, and all the structure which is called verse both necessitate and engender a difference in diction and in thought. The effect of verse is one on expression and on thought, viz. concentration and all which is implied by this. This does not mean terseness nor rejection of what is collateral nor emphasis nor even definiteness though these may be very well, or best, attained by verse, but mainly, though the words are not quite adequate, vividness of idea or, as they would especially have said in the last century, liveliness.

But what the character of poetry is will be found best by looking at the structure of verse. The artificial part of poetry, perhaps we shall be right to say all artifice, reduces itself to the principle of parallelism. The structure of poetry is that of continuous parallelism, ranging from the technical so-called Parallelisms of Hebrew poetry and the antiphons of Church music up to the intricacy of Greek or Italian or English verse. But parallelism is of two kinds necessarily – where the opposition is clearly marked, and where it is transitional rather or chromatic. Only the first kind, that of marked parallelism, is concerned with the structure of verse – in rhythm, the recurrence of a certain sequence of syllables, in metre, the

---

1   'On the Origin of Beauty: A Platonic Dialogue' (probably written in 1865), J, pp. 86–114 (p. 106).
2   J, p. 237 (for clarity I have excised Hopkins's punctuation).

recurrence of a certain sequence of rhythm, in alliteration, in assonance and in rhyme. Now the force of this recurrence is to beget a recurrence or parallelism answering to it in the words or thought and, speaking roughly and rather for the tendency than the invariable result, the more marked parallelism in structure whether of elaboration or of emphasis begets more marked parallelism in the words and sense. [. . .] To the marked or abrupt kind of parallelism belong metaphor, simile, parable, and so on, where the effect is sought in likeness of things, and antithesis, contrast, and so on, where it is sought in unlikeness. To the chromatic parallelism belong gradation, intensity, climax, tone, [. . .] *chiaroscuro*,[20] perhaps emphasis: while the faculties of Fancy and Imagination might range widely over both kinds, Fancy belonging more especially to the abrupt than to the transitional class.

Gerard Manley Hopkins on his conversion, from letter to his father, 16 October 1866, L III, pp. 91–5

Hopkins's decision to convert to Roman Catholicism caused a period of intense family unhappiness. His father and mother wrote to him urging and pleading that he should delay any further action until at least six months had passed; Hopkins refused. In this letter he explains some of his thinking on the matter.

My dear Father,
[. . .]
I cannot fight against God Who calls me to His Church: [. . .]. I have no power in fact to stir a finger: it is God Who makes the decision and not I.

But you do not understand what is involved in asking me to delay and how little good you wd. get from it. I shall hold as a Catholic what I have long held as an Anglican, that literal truth of our Lord's words by which I learn that the least fragment of the consecrated elements in the Blessed Sacrament of the Altar is the whole Body of Christ born of the Blessed Virgin, before which the whole host of saints and angels as it lies on the altar trembles with adoration.[1] This belief once got is the life of the soul and when I doubted it I shd. become an atheist the next day. But, as Monsignor Eyre says, it is a gross superstition unless guaranteed by infallibility.[2] I cannot hold this doctrine confessedly except as a Tractarian

---

3   An Italian word meaning the use of light and shade in painting.

---

1   Matthew 26:26–8; Mark 14:22–4; Luke 22:19–20 (all AV).
2   Infallibility: the exclusive legitimacy of the Roman Catholic Church as the only church founded by Christ. Monsignor Charles Eyre was a Roman Catholic prelate in Scotland who became Archbishop of Glasgow in 1879; infallibility here refers to the infallibility of the church, not of the Pope (papal infallibility was not an official doctrine of the Roman Catholic Church until the First Vatican Council in 1869–70). Christ's words in Matthew 16:18 to the Apostle Peter ('thou art Peter, and upon this rock I will build my church; and the gates of hell shall not prevail against it' – AV) founded the church and were held by Eyre and others to guarantee the legitimacy of its doctrines from Peter through to the popes.

or a Catholic: the Tractarian ground I have seen broken to pieces under my feet.[3] [. . .]

I am surprised you shd. say fancy and aesthetic tastes have led me to my present state of mind: these wd. be better satisfied in the Church of England, for bad taste is always meeting one in the accessories of Catholicism. My conversion is due to the following reasons mainly (I have put them down without order) – (i) simple and strictly drawn arguments partly my own, partly others', (ii) common sense, (iii) reading the Bible, especially the Holy Gospels, where texts like 'Thou art Peter'[4] (the evasions proposed for this alone are enough to make one a Catholic) and the manifest position of St. Peter among the Apostles so pursued me that at one time I thought it best to stop thinking of them, (iv) an increasing knowledge of the Catholic system (at first under the form of Tractarianism, later in its genuine place), which only wants to be known in order to be loved – its consolations, its marvellous ideal of holiness, the faith and devotion of its children, its multiplicity, its array of saints and martyrs, its consistency and unity, its glowing prayers, the daring majesty of its claims, etc etc. [. . .]

You are so kind as not to forbid me your house, to which I have no claim, on condition, if I understand, that I promise not to try to convert my brothers and sisters. Before I can promise this I must get permission, wh. I have no doubt will be given. Of course this promise will not apply after they come of age. [. . .]

You ask me if I have had no thought of the estrangement. I have had months to think of everything. Our Lord's last care on the cross was to commend His mother to His Church and His Church to his mother in the person of St John.[5] If even now you wd. put yourselves into that position wh. Christ so unmistakeably gives us and ask the Mother of sorrows[6] to remember her three hours' compassion at the cross [. . .] this Holy Family wd. in a few days put an end to estrangements for ever. If you shrink fr. doing this, though the Gospels cry aloud to you to do it, at least for once – if you like, only once – approach Christ in a new way in which you will at all events feel that you are exactly in unison with me, that is, not vaguely, but casting yourselves into His sacred broken Heart and His five adorable Wounds.[7] Those who do not pray to Him in His Passion pray to God but scarcely to Christ.[8] I have the right to propose this, for I have tried both ways, and if you will not give one trial to this way you will see you are prolonging the estrangement and not I.

---

3 Tractarian: member of the Church of England who subscribed to the doctrines of the controversially High Church (i.e. Anglo-Catholic) *Tracts for the Times*, a series of pamphlets on religious matters written by John Henry Newman (who later became a Roman Catholic and a cardinal in that church) and others. For discussion of Hopkins and Tractarianism, see Margaret Johnson, *Gerard Manley Hopkins and Tractarian Poetry* (Aldershot: Ashgate, 1997). An extract from the book is included in Modern Criticism, **pp. 67–8**.
4 See fn. 2 above. Peter was the foremost of the apostles.
5 John 19:25–7
      Now there stood by the cross of Jesus his mother, and his mother's sister, Mary the wife of Cleophas, and Mary Magdalene.
      When Jesus therefore saw his mother, and the disciple standing by, whom he loved, he saith unto his mother, Woman, behold thy son!
      Then saith he to the disciple, Behold thy mother! And from that hour that disciple took her unto his own home. (AV)
6 i.e. Mary the mother of Christ.
7 i.e. the wounds sustained by Christ on the cross, to hands, feet and side.
8 The Passion: Christ's suffering and death on the cross.

From **Ignatius Loyola, *The Spiritual Exercises of St Ignatius*** (sixteenth century), transl. by Louis J. Puhl, Jr (Westminster, MD.: Newman Press, 1951), pp. 2–23

> The Society of Jesus, which Hopkins entered as a novice in September 1868, becoming an ordained priest nine years later, was founded by Ignatius Loyola in 1540. Loyola was canonized in 1622, sixty-six years after his death. The Spiritual Exercises he devised are among the key documents of the order, and are designed to be used over a four-week period of intense meditation to help the reader structure his reflection on his faith. Hopkins, like other Jesuits (priests in the Society of Jesus), used the Spiritual Exercises as the basis for profound self-investigations during retreats, and began in the early 1880s to write a commentary on them. The extracts give an outline of the some of the fundamental beliefs and spiritual duties of Hopkins's order.

Man is created to praise, reverence, and serve God our Lord, and by this means to save his soul.

The other things on the face of the earth are created for man to help him in attaining the end for which he is created.

Hence, man is to make use of them in as far as they help him in the attainment of his end, and he must rid himself of them in as far as they prove a hindrance to him.

Therefore, we must make ourselves indifferent to all created things, as far as we are allowed free choice and are not under any prohibition. Consequently, as far as we are concerned, we should not prefer health to sickness, riches to poverty, honor to dishonor, a long life to a short life. The same holds for all other things.

Our one desire and choice should be what is more conducive to the end for which we are created.

[...]

Method of Making the General Examination of Conscience

1. The first point is to give thanks to God for the favors received.
2. The second point is to ask for grace to know my sins and to rid myself of them.
3. The third point is to demand an account of my soul from the time of rising up to the present examination. I should go over one hour after another, one period after another. The thoughts should be examined first, then the words, and finally, the deeds in the same order as was explained under the Particular Examination of Conscience.
4. The fourth point will be to ask pardon of God our Lord for my faults.
5. The fifth point will be to resolve to amend with the grace of God. Close with an *Our Father*.

From **Gerard Manley Hopkins, 'Comments on the Spiritual Exercises of St. Ignatius Loyola'**, August 1880, in Humphry House, ed., *The Note-Books and Papers of Gerard Manley Hopkins* (Oxford: Oxford University Press, 1937)

As part of his life as a Jesuit, Hopkins made regular retreats (i.e. spent periods of time away from his usual duties and surroundings, engaging in prayer, penitence and reflection), during which he worked through and meditated on the Spiritual Exercises. The opening words of this extract, 'Homo creatus est', are quoted from the Latin version of the first sentence of the 'Principle and Foundation' of the Spiritual Exercises (see extract above): 'Man is created to praise, reverence, and serve God our Lord, and by this means to save his soul'. The great Hopkins scholar Humphry House commented that 'No single sentence better explains the motives and direction of Hopkins's life than this "Man was created to praise" '.[1] Poems including 'God's Grandeur' (see Key Poems, **pp. 129–30**), 'Pied Beauty' (Key Poems, **p. 135**) (and 'The Leaden Echo and the Golden Echo' (Key Poems, **pp. 143–6**) explore the relationship of man with God through praise.

'Homo creatus est' – Aug. 20 1880: during this retreat, which I am making at Liverpool, I have been thinking about creation and this thought has led the way naturally through the exercises hitherto. I put down some thoughts [. . .] I find myself both as man and as myself something most determined and distinctive, at pitch, more distinctive and higher pitched than anything else I see; I find myself with my pleasures and pains, my powers and my experiences, my deserts and guilt, my shame and sense of beauty, my dangers, hopes, fears, and all my fate, more important to myself than anything I see. And when I ask where does all this throng and stack of being, so rich, so distinctive, so important, come from / nothing I see can answer me. And this whether I speak of human nature or of my individuality, my selfbeing. For human nature, being more highly pitched, selved, and distinctive than anything in the world, can have been developed, evolved, condensed, from the vastness of the world not anyhow[2] or by the working of common powers but only by one of finer or higher pitch and determination than itself and certainly than any that elsewhere we see, for this power had to force forward the starting or stubborn elements to the one pitch required. And this is much more true when we consider the mind; when I consider my selfbeing, my consciousness and feeling of myself, that taste of myself, of *I* and *me* above and in all things, which is more distinctive than the taste of ale or alum, more distinctive than the smell of walnutleaf or camphor, and is incommunicable by any means to another man (as when I was a child I used to ask myself: What must it be to be someone else?). Nothing else in nature comes near this unspeakable stress of pitch, distinctiveness, and selving, this selfbeing of my own. Nothing explains it

---

1   *The Note-Books and Papers of Gerard Manley Hopkins*, ed. Humphrey House (Oxford: Oxford University Press, 1937), p. 416.
2   Not in any random or haphazard way.

or resembles it, except so far as this, that other men to themselves have the same feeling. But this only multiplies the phenomena to be explained so far as the cases are like and do resemble. But to me there is no resemblance: searching nature I taste *self* but at one tankard, that of my own being. The development, refinement, condensation of nothing shews any sign of being able to match this to me or give me another taste of it, a taste even resembling it.

From **Gerard Manley Hopkins, Sermon for 23 November 1879**, S, pp. 35–8

Hopkins was not a great success as a writer of sermons; neither his congregations nor his Jesuit superiors seem to have thought highly of his. In October 1880 he preached in Liverpool on divine providence and the guardian angels and told his congregation that 'God heeds all things at once. He takes more interest in a merchant's business than the merchant, in a vessel's steering than the pilot, in a lover's sweetheart than the lover, in a sick man's pain than the sufferer, in our salvation than we ourselves' (S, p. 89). His use of the term 'sweetheart' led to his being forbidden to preach until each sermon had been inspected by his superiors. Though this prohibition was not implemented, it was a humiliating episode for Hopkins. But though his flock may not have been much interested in his sermons, they are certainly valuable for the student of Hopkins's poetry, since they sometimes touch on topics and use images that illuminate the poems. In this sermon, given in Bedford Leigh, Hopkins discusses Jesus Christ as 'our hero, a hero all the world wants'. Christ is a 'warrior and a conqueror', 'a king', 'a statesman', 'a thinker', 'an orator and poet' (S, pp. 34–5). Hopkins's description of Christ throws light on figures of Christ in 'The Windhover' (see Key Poems, **pp. 133–5**), 'The Wreck of the Deutschland' (Key Poems, **pp. 113–28**) and other poems, as well as giving evidence of the sexualized quality of Hopkins's faith.

[Jesus Christ] is the true-love and the bridegroom of men's souls: the virgins follow him whithersoever he goes; the martyrs follow him through a sea of blood, through great tribulation; all his servants take up their cross and follow him. And those even that do not follow him, yet they look wistfully after him, own him a hero, and wish they dared answer to his call. [. . .]

There met in Jesus Christ all things that can make man lovely and loveable. In his body he was most beautiful [. . .] his body was the special work of the Holy Ghost. He was not born in nature's course, no man was his father; had he been born as others are he must have inherited some defect of figure or of constitution, from which no man born as fallen men are born is wholly free unless God interfere to keep him so. But his body was framed directly from heaven by the power of the Holy Ghost, of whom it would be unworthy to leave any the least botch or failing in his work. So the first Adam was moulded by God himself and Eve built up by God too out of Adam's rib and they could not but be pieces, both, of faultless workmanship: the same then and much more must Christ have been. His constitution too was tempered perfectly, he had neither disease nor the seeds of any: weariness he felt when he was wearied, hunger when he fasted, thirst when he had long gone without drink, but to the touch of sickness he was a stranger. I leave it to you, brethren, then to picture him, in whom the fulness of the godhead dwelt bodily, in his bearing how majestic,[1] how strong and yet how lovely and lissome in his limbs,[2] in his look how earnest, grave but kind. In his Passion all this strength was spent, this lissomness crippled, this beauty wrecked, this majesty beaten down. But now it is more than all restored, and for myself I make no secret I look forward with eager desire to seeing the matchless beauty of Christ's body in the heavenly light.

I come to his mind. He was the greatest genius that ever lived. You know what genius is, brethren – beauty and perfection in the mind. For perfection in the bodily frame distinguishes a man among other men his fellows: so may the mind be distinguished for its beauty above other minds and that is genius. Then when this genius is duly taught and trained, that is wisdom; for without training genius is imperfect and again wisdom is imperfect without genius. But Christ, we read, advanced in wisdom and in favour with God and men:[3] now this wisdom, in which he excelled all men, had to be founded on an unrivalled genius. [. . .]

Now in the third place, far higher than beauty of the body, higher than genius and wisdom the beauty of the mind, comes the beauty of his character, his character as a man. [. . .] Poor was his station, laborious his life, bitter his ending: through poverty, through labour, through crucifixion his majesty of nature more shines. No heart as his was ever so tender, but tenderness was not all: this heart so tender was as brave, it could be stern. He found the thought of his Passion past bearing, yet he went through with it.[4] He was feared when he chose: he took a whip and singlehanded cleared the temple.[5] The thought of his gentleness towards children, towards the afflicted, towards sinners, is often dwelt on; that of his courage less. But for my part I like to feel that I should have feared him.

From **Gerard Manley Hopkins, 'Author's Preface'** to the manuscript copies of his poems, c. 1883, Phillips, pp. 106–9

Hopkins wrote the 'Author's Preface' when the book he was prefacing was only a volume containing manuscript copies of his poems, written in by hand by Bridges or Hopkins himself. The 'Preface' gives Hopkins's account of the metrical principles of his poems, and a comparative section on what he calls 'common' or 'standard' (not sprung) rhythm. Perhaps the most important general points to be drawn from this extract are that Hopkins believed that sprung

---

1   cf. 'Hurrahing in Harvest', l. 11: 'Majestic — as a stallion stalwart, very-violet-sweet! —' (Key Poems, **p. 136**).

2   cf. 'As kingfishers catch fire', l. 13: Christ is 'Lovely in limbs, and lovely in eyes not his' (Key Poems, **pp. 131–2**).

3   Luke 2:52: 'And Jesus increased in wisdom and stature, and in favour with God and man' (AV); 'And Jesus advanced in wisdom and age and grace with God and men' (DR).

4   cf. Matthew 26.39: 'And he went a little farther, and fell on his face, and prayed, saying, O my Father, if it be possible, let this cup pass from me: nevertheless not as I will, but as thou wilt' (AV).

5   Matthew 21:12–13; Mark 11:15–18; John 2:14–16.

rhythm reflected the rhythms of ordinary English speech, and that he assumed that the poems were to be read aloud. In a letter to Bridges in 1878 Hopkins wrote: 'Why do I employ sprung rhythm at all? Because it is the nearest to the rhythm of prose, that is the native and natural rhythm of speech, the least forced, the most rhetorical and emphatic of all possible rhythms, combining, as it seems to me, opposite and, one wd. have thought, incompatible excellences, markedness of rhythm – that is rhythm's self – and naturalness of expression [. . .] My verse is less to be read than heard [. . .] it is oratorical, that is the rhythm is so' (L I, p. 46).

F. R. Leavis commented on the 'Author's Preface' that it

> will help no one to read his verse – unless by giving the sense of being helped: it merely shows how subtle and hard to escape is the power of habits and preconceptions. The prescription he gives when warm from reading his verse – "take breath and read it with the ears, as I always wish to be read, and my verse becomes all right" – is a great deal more to the point, and if we add "and with the brains and the body" it suffices.[1]

But as an authoritative account of Hopkins's own understanding of his rhythmic innovations, it is useful here.

The poems in this book are written some in Running Rhythm, the common rhythm in English use, some in Sprung Rhythm, and some in a mixture of the two.[2] And those in the common rhythm are some counterpointed, some not.[3] [. . .]

Sprung Rhythm, as used in this book, is measured by feet of from one to four syllables, regularly, and for particular effects any number of weak or slack syllables may be used. It has one stress, which falls on the only syllable if there is only one or, if there are more, then scanning as above, on the first, and so gives rise to four sorts of feet, a monosyllable and the so-called accentual Trochee, Dactyl, and the First Paeon.[4] And there will be four corresponding natural rhythms; but nominally the feet are mixed and any one may follow any other. And hence Sprung Rhythm differs from Running Rhythm in having or being only one nominal rhythm, a mixed or 'logaoedic'[5] one, instead of three, but on the other hand in having twice the flexibility of foot, so that any two stresses may either follow one

1   F. R. Leavis, *New Bearings in English Poetry: A Study of the Contemporary Situation* (London: Chatto & Windus, 1932, repr. with 'Retrospect 1950', 1950; Harmondsworth: Penguin (Peregrine), 1963), p. 136.
2   this book: the manuscript book of Hopkins's poems which Robert Bridges had collected.
3   counterpointed: having a rhythmical pattern set over or against the underlying one. Counterpointing 'supposes a well-known and unmistakeable or unforgetable standard rhythm' (L I, p. 45), to which a contrasting rhythm is added. Many of Hopkins's sonnets are in counterpointed rhythm.
4   Trochee: a metrical foot consisting of a stressed syllable followed by an unstressed one: / x. Dactyl: a foot consisting of a stressed syllable followed by two unstressed ones: / x x. First paeon: a foot consisting of a stressed syllable followed by three unstressed ones: / x x x.
5   Strictly, a metre in which dactyls are combined with trochees; more loosely, a metre in which feet of different kinds are used.

another running[6] or be divided by one, two, or three slack syllables. But strict Sprung Rhythm cannot be counterpointed.[7] In Sprung Rhythm, as in logaoedic rhythm generally, the feet are assumed to be equally long or strong[8] and their seeming inequality is made up by pause or stressing.[9]

Remark also that it is natural in Sprung Rhythm for the lines to be *rove over*, that is for the scanning of each line immediately to take up that of the one before,[10] so that if the first has one or more syllables at its end the other must have so many the less at its beginning; and in fact the scanning runs on without break from the beginning, say, of a stanza to the end and all the stanza is one long strain,[11] though written in lines asunder.[12]

Two licences are natural to Sprung Rhythm. The one is rests, as in music; but of this an example is scarcely to be found in this book, unless in the *Echos*, second line.[13] The other is *hangers* or *outrides*, that is one, two, or three slack syllables added to a foot and not counting in the nominal scanning. They are so called because they seem to hang below the line or ride forward or backward from it in another dimension than the line itself, according to a principle needless to explain here. These outriding half feet or hangers are marked by a loop underneath them, and plenty of them will be found.[14] [. . .]

Note on the nature and history of Sprung Rhythm – Sprung Rhythm is the most natural of things. For (1) it is the rhythm of common speech and of written prose, when rhythm is perceived in them. (2) It is the rhythm of all but the most monotonously regular music, so that in the words of choruses and refrains and in songs written closely to music it arises. (3) It is found in nursery rhymes, weather saws,[15] and so on; because, however these may have been once made in running rhythm, the terminations having dropped off by the change of language, the

---

6 Follow one another running: come one after another with no unstressed or, in Hopkins's term, 'slack', syllables in between. In a letter to his friend R. W. Dixon in 1879, Hopkins wrote 'the word *Sprung* which I use for this rhythm means something like abrupt and applies by rights only where one stress follows another running, without syllable in between' (L II, p. 23).
7 Counterpointing is Hopkins's term, derived from music, for a metre in which some feet are reversed: e.g. an iamb (x /) is used where a trochee (/ x) is expected. Sprung rhythm cannot be counterpointed because the stress *must* fall on the first syllable of each foot.
8 i.e. a foot consisting of four syllables is considered to be no longer or stronger than a foot consisting of just one.
9 Notice how Hopkins relies on the reading voice to make sprung rhythm work.
10 In a letter to Dixon in 1880, Hopkins explained that his preference was for 'over-rove' lines in lyric poetry, but 'for dramatic verse, which is looser in form, I should have the lines "free-ended" and each scanned by itself' (L II, p. 40).
11 strain: Hopkins is borrowing this word from music, where it can mean a melody: in this context, he means a unit, comparable to a section of a piece of music. In some other forms of poetry, each line must be scanned separately, but Hopkins wants each of his stanzas to be scanned as a single unit, ignoring the line-breaks for the purposes of investigating the metre. Compare his use of 'strain' in 'Spring', l. 10: 'A strain of the earth's sweet being in the beginning' (Key Poems, **p. 132**).
12 asunder: separated or divided.
13 'The Leaden Echo and the Golden Echo', l. 2: 'Back beauty, keep it, beauty, beauty, beauty, . . . from vanishing away?' (Key Poems, **pp. 143–6**). The ellipsis marks what Hopkins calls the 'rest' (in music, a period of silence).
14 Hopkins believed that his poetry, if printed, ought to appear complete with his markings indicating how the poems' metrics worked. Very few editions commonly print these markings on the same pages as the poems, though Catherine Phillips, for instance, gives them in the notes on the poems.
15 saws: sayings.

stresses come together and so the rhythm is sprung. (4) It arises in common verse when reversed or counterpointed, for the same reason.

But nevertheless in spite of all this and though Greek and Latin lyric verse, which is well known, and the old English verse seen in *Pierce Ploughman* are in sprung rhythm, it has in fact ceased to be used since the Elizabethan age, Greene being the last writer who can be said to have recognized it.[16] For perhaps there was not, down to our days, a single, even short, poem in English in which sprung rhythm is employed – not for single effects or in fixed places – but as the governing principle of the scansion.

From *The Times,* report of the wreck of the *Deutschland,* 11 December 1875, L III, pp. 442–3

Hopkins explained to his friend Richard Watson Dixon how reading the newspaper reports of a shipwreck stimulated him to return to composing poetry after a long period of writing little:

> for seven years I wrote nothing but two or three little presentation pieces which occasion called for. But when in the winter of '75 the Deutschland was wrecked in the mouth of the Thames and five Franciscan nuns, exiles from Germany by the Falck Laws, aboard of her were drowned I was affected by the account and happening to say so to my rector he said that he wished someone would write a poem on the subject.[1] On this hint I set to work and, though my hand was out at first, produced one.[2]

The wreck was widely reported: the extract is from a detailed report in *The Times,* the most famous English newspaper of the day.

At 2 a.m. [Tuesday, 7 December], Captain Brickenstein, knowing that with the rising tide the ship would be waterlogged, ordered all the passengers to come on deck. . . . Most of them obeyed the summons at once; others lingered below till it was too late; some of them, ill, weak, despairing of life even on deck, resolved to stay in their cabins and meet death without any further struggle to evade it. After 3 a.m. on Tuesday morning a scene of horror was witnessed. Some passengers clustered for safety within or upon the wheelhouse, and on the top of other slight structures on deck. Most of the crew and many of the emigrants went into the rigging, where they were safe enough as long as they could maintain their hold. But the intense cold and long exposure told a tale. The purser of the ship, though a strong man, relaxed his grasp, and fell into the sea. Women and children and

---

16 Now usually spelt *Piers Plowman,* this is an allegorical poem using alliterative verse, written in the 1300s by William Langland. Robert Greene, c. 1558–1592, author of poetry, plays and pamphlets.

---

1   For an explanation of the Falck (or Falk) Laws see **p. 115.**
2   L II, p. 14.

men were one by one swept away from their shelters on the deck. Five German nuns, whose bodies are now in the dead-house here, clasped hands and were drowned together, the chief sister, a gaunt woman 6 ft. high, calling out loudly and often 'O Christ, come quickly!' till the end came. The shrieks and sobbing of the women and children are described by the survivors as agonising. One brave sailor, who was safe in the rigging, went down to try and save a child or woman who was drowning on deck. He was secured by a rope to the rigging, but a wave dashed him against the bulwarks, and when daylight dawned his headless body, detained by the rope, was seen swaying to and fro with the waves. In the dreadful excitement of these hours one man hung himself behind the wheelhouse, another hacked at his wrist with a knife, hoping to die a comparatively painless death by bleeding. It was nearly 8 o'clock before the tide and sea abated, and the survivors could venture to go on deck. At half-past 10 o'clock the tugboat from Harwich came alongside and brought all away without further accident. Most of the passengers are German emigrants, and it is only right to add that they have received here from the first the utmost kindness and sympathy.

.

2

Interpretations

Critical History

During his lifetime, Hopkins's critics were the friends and family members to whom he gave copies of his poems. Because of the circumstances of the publication of his verse, outlined in the Contextual Overview section, professional criticism of his poetry dates only from the early twentieth century, and, as the selection included in this sourcebook indicates, the 1930s saw the first wave of attention from major critics. Hopkins's poetry has never faded from critical view since then. Scholarly interest in him has been fuelled partly by the publication of his letters, journals and sermons during the 1930s and 1950s and the new editions of his work that appeared in 1956, 1967 and 1986. These made it possible to contextualize readings of Hopkins's poems within the evidence of his other literary, religious and social activities. Another important factor in Hopkins's high critical profile is that his life and work have provided useful case studies for a number of influential critical movements of the past six or seven decades.

This is partly because of form. The majority of Hopkins's poems – notable exceptions are 'The Wreck of the Deutschland' (see Key Poems, **pp. 113–28**) and 'The Leaden Echo and the Golden Echo' (Key Poems, **pp. 143–6**) – are lyrics, brief poems (usually sonnets) exploring a particular thought or emotion through powerful imagery. Where other Victorian forms such as the verse-novel and the narrative or epic poem have experienced periods of critical unfashionability and have been comparatively little-used by twentieth-century poets, lyric continues to be a major form for contemporary poetry and to dominate school and university poetry syllabuses, and critical attention to lyric has not lessened.

The brevity, intensity and technical range of most of Hopkins's poems made them eminently suitable for use by proponents of the new developments in English literary studies in the 1920s, a time when the discipline was staking its claim to a major place in the modern academy. The university discipline of 'English Literature' was revolutionized by the development in Cambridge of 'practical criticism', a methodology originally intended to give literary study a quasi-scientific, empirical basis. As it was modified from a pedagogical to a critical activity, practical criticism came to emphasize an imaginative exploration of the interaction of form and content in texts, and continued to privilege the lyric. Hopkins's poetry, then, was ideally suited to adoption by the emerging discipline of English Literature. The American New Criticism of the 1930s and 1940s similarly found Hopkins's poetry congenial to its focus on reading texts as stand-alone complete units. Since then, close reading has continued to be a major and productive strand in Hopkins criticism, as demonstrated by books and essays by Helen Vendler, Eric Griffiths and a number of other critics whose work has avoided the ideological baggage often accompanying New Criticism.

Other critical movements in recent decades have kept Hopkins studies fresh. One of the most important of these is queer studies, which since the 1970s has explored Hopkins's work in terms of his sexuality and the sexual and gender-related themes raised by the poems. When Paddy Kitchen's biography of Hopkins was published in 1978 it addressed for the first time notes he made as an under-graduate about sins he had committed and intended to confess to: these included references to sexual desire for young men, a theme that had been noted in his work before but which had often been denied by respected Hopkins scholars.[1] Almost immediately afterwards followed Michael Lynch's article, excerpted in this sourcebook (**pp. 94–5**), 'Recovering Hopkins, Recovering Ourselves', which claimed Hopkins as a homosexual poet but recognized – as almost all subsequent writers on Hopkins and gender do – that reading Hopkins in this way is compli-cated by his own conflicting attitudes to matters of sexuality. Since then, although a small number of significant Hopkins scholars minimize the evidence of same-sex desire in his work, much new critical writing about Hopkins takes the topics of sexuality and gender into account, even where those are not the main themes of the research. Feminist criticism since the 1970s has tended to agree with queer studies in emphasizing Hopkins's male-centred sexuality. The scarcity of female figures in Hopkins's poetry has drawn a good deal of critical attention, as have the depictions of violence being perpetrated on some of the women who do appear in the poems.[2]

The centenary in 1989 of Hopkins's death gave renewed impetus to critical engagement with his writing, with several international conferences and exhib-itions and the publication of a number of celebratory surveys and collections of essays. Since then, Hopkins studies have continued to flourish. This sourcebook can give only an impression of the breadth and depth of critical and scholarly engagement with the poems. There are some suggestions for further reading at the end of this book; beyond this, a number of print bibliographies are available, and the *Hopkins Quarterly* publishes every year a very useful bibliographical article rounding up each year's Hopkins-related books and articles.[3]

Organization of the Critical Excerpts in this Sourcebook

I have divided the excerpts from post-Second World War criticism of Hopkins in this sourcebook into eight sections, four dealing with thematic or historical

---

1   Paddy Kitchen, *Gerard Manley Hopkins: A Life* (London: Hamilton, 1978).
2   For '(Margaret Clitheroe)' see Phillips, pp. 125–7.
3   Edward H. Cohen, *Works and Criticism of Gerard Manley Hopkins: A Comprehensive Bibliography* (Washington, DC: Catholic University of America Press, 1969); Tom Dunne, *Gerard Manley Hopkins: A Comprehensive Bibliography* (Oxford: Clarendon Press, 1976). Naturally, online bibliographies such as the MLA are invaluable for more recent material.

concerns, and four with readings of particular poems or groups of poems. Some critics' work appears in more than one section. The first section picks up on one of the central questions raised in 1930s Hopkins criticism: how far should we consider Hopkins a Victorian poet, and how far do his innovative practice and the delay of publication of his poems till 1918 mean that he should rather be thought of as a proto-Modernist, better understood in the company of T. S. Eliot and James Joyce than in that of Robert Browning and Matthew Arnold? Compelling recent biographies of Hopkins have done important work in historicizing our understanding of his life; and in the past three or four decades, there has been a general rejection of the implied value-judgement of early twentieth-century criticism that ranked Modernist poetry more highly than Victorian and thus felt it necessary to class Hopkins as a Modernist. The rise of New Historicism as a critical movement has not perhaps affected Victorian studies as profoundly as it has Renaissance and Romantic studies, but it has reinforced in Hopkins criticism a general historicist tendency: Hopkins's poems are rarely now regarded as being so un-Victorian as their first critics considered them. They can be valuably contextualized in various different nineteenth-century groupings (including Tractarian, decadent and late Romantic), and the extracts in this section show how the choice of grouping affects a reading of the poetry.

The next selection in the Modern Criticism section introduces some of the questions raised by queer and feminist criticism of Hopkins. Following that is a group of excerpts addressing topics in Hopkins's use of language. From the earliest Hopkins criticism onward, his intensely imaginative and unconventional linguistic practices have attracted much critical attention. As well as the poetry itself, we have at least two important sources of evidence from Hopkins's own writings that have fed into this critical investigation: one is his essays and discussions in correspondence about poetic diction and the use of language more generally; the other is his diary and journal entries in which he recorded a great array of linguistic phenomena, including dialect words he came on in his travels around the United Kingdom, speculations about the derivations of words, and lists of words with similar sounds.[4] Like many of his contemporaries, Hopkins was deeply interested in the new theories about the development of languages that were emerging in the mid- to late nineteenth century from scholars such as Max Müller, whom Hopkins read as an undergraduate, and in the growing movement for the preservation of local Englishes of which William Barnes (whose poems Hopkins admired) is perhaps the best-remembered exponent today. Hopkins had a lifelong interest in languages: his undergraduate degree was in classics, i.e. Greek and Latin, and he was a sufficiently good scholar to take a first-class degree and to work as Professor of Greek in the Roman Catholic University in Dublin. He also began to learn Welsh while studying at St Beuno's theological college in

---

4   See, for instance, Hopkins's undergraduate essays on 'Poetic Diction' and 'On the Signs of Health and Decay in the Arts' (J, pp. 84–6, 74–80). Examples of journal entries on language include 'Drill, trill, thrill, nostril, nose-thirl [. . .] Common idea piercing' (J, p. 10), 'Fash. Don't fash yourself. Scotch. Connected with *fessus* [Latin: weary, tired], *fatiscor* [Latin: to become weak, to droop]' (J, p. 5), '*Duffer* in Cumberland means ass (literally); in slang parlance metaphorical' (J, p. 15). There is a very useful detailed essay on linguistic entries in Hopkins's diaries by Alan Ward in J, Appendix III, pp. 499–527.

north Wales, and his study of Welsh poetry affected his poetics: he experimented with *cynghanedd*, a technique of complex internal rhyme and consonant patterning. Though he did not master Welsh, he did attempt to write poetry in it: the result characteristically privileged his own sense of poetic rightness over strict conformity to the rules.[5] Somewhat similarly, several Hopkins scholars have shown that his English philological speculations were informed by outdated linguistic theories. As his work in music theory shows, Hopkins rarely allowed expert opinion to deflect him from his own lines of enquiry. Near the end of his life he wrote to Bridges: 'the effect of studying masterpieces is to make me admire and do otherwise. So it must be on every original artist to some degree, and on me to a marked degree'.[6] Hopkins criticism has necessarily devoted a great deal of attention to the effects on his poetry of his deep interest in the underlying systems and the surface variation in phenomena of language.

Originality in language was for Hopkins not a matter of deliberate quirkiness, but was linked to several important philosophical concepts that underpinned his emphasis on uniqueness and individuality in selfhood, whether of people or natural objects. One of the debts that Hopkins criticism owes to the theologically informed specialist work that has been done over the years on his writing is the recognition of the impact of his reading of the medieval theologian John Duns Scotus on Hopkins's thinking about individuality in the human, natural and conceptual worlds. Hopkins's poem 'Duns Scotus's Oxford' (see Key Poems, pp. 136–8) expresses his gratitude and sense of closeness to Duns Scotus, whose work he read during his philosophy studies at the Jesuit training college in Stonyhurst. For Hopkins criticism, the most important Scotian concept is that of *haecceitas*, a medieval Latin word usually translated as 'thisness', signifying the uniqueness of a particular object, experience or person. *Haecceitas* chimed with Hopkins's own concepts of 'inscape' and 'instress', which have been the subject of a great deal of scholarly discussion, and which are discussed in the excerpt from J. Hillis Miller's *The Disappearance of God* in the 'Inscape and Instress' part of the Modern Criticism section (pp. 74–7).

Very broadly speaking, inscape, the fundamental structural pattern supporting the perceptible qualities of any object, is communicated to the viewer by instress, an energy that allows inscape to be perceived. Examples of Hopkins's use of 'inscape' are clearer than those of 'instress', which has a number of not fully distinguished meanings. The branches of an elm tree have 'beautiful inscape', and so have violets: 'even in withering the flower ran through beautiful inscapes by the screwing up of the petals into straight little barrels or tubes'.[7] Inscape is not only visual but can be perceptible by 'every sense', as with bluebells:

> if you draw your fingers through them they are lodged and struggle /
> with a shock of wet heads; the long stalks rub and click and flatten to a
> fan on one another like your fingers themselves would when you passed
> the palms hard across one another, making a brittle rub and jostle like

5   See useful discussion in Norman White, *Hopkins: A Literary Biography* (Oxford: Clarendon Press, 1992; paperback edn 1995), pp. 247–8.
6   L I, p. 291.
7   J, p. 243, p. 211.

the noise of a hurdle strained by leaning against; then there is the faint honey smell and in the mouth the sweet gum when you bite them.[8]

'Inscape' can also be a verb: 'before I had always taken the sunset and the sun as quite out of gauge with each other [. . .], but today I inscaped them together and made the sun the true eye and ace of the whole, as it is'.[9] 'Instress' is also both a verb and a noun; as a verb it appears in a line of 'The Wreck of the Deutschland' about the duty of humans to strive to perceive the presence and goodness of God in the world: 'His mystery must be instressed, stressed'[10] (Key Poems, p. 117). To instress, i.e. to perceive inscape, requires an effort of will and no distractions: 'with a companion the eye and the ear are for the most part shut and instress cannot come'.[11] Considerable amounts of critical effort have been put into the exegesis and analysis of the concepts of 'inscape' and 'instress', and into exploring their role in the poems.

The next part of the Modern Criticism section presents some of the most interesting recent readings of Hopkins's masterpiece, 'The Wreck of the Deutschland'. The following sections, introducing criticism on 'God's Grandeur', 'Pied Beauty' and the 'Terrible Sonnets', sometimes called the 'Sonnets of Desolation', are arranged by chronological order of the poems dealt with. These include some of Hopkins's most important poems, but of course, many poems other than the ones I have selected here have received illuminating and provocative critical attention: indeed so comparatively small is Hopkins's poetic oeuvre that all the complete poems in English have been the subject of valuable readings.

By virtue of its position as the poem with which Hopkins returned to the composition of poetry in English, and because of the unusualness of its form as well as the sheer scale, scope and ambition of its achievement, 'The Wreck of the Deutschland' (see Key Poems, pp. 113–28) is an essential poem for any reader of Hopkins. Criticism of it is represented here by three extracts using very different approaches and finding different qualities in the poem. The most controversial is Thaïs E. Morgan's radical reading (pp. 84–90) which emphasizes the poem's masochistic use of sexual violence. The extract from Helen Vendler's essay (pp. 77–82) on the poem is an example of close reading beautifully making lucidity out of a difficult text, and the piece from Isobel Armstrong's highly influential *Victorian Poetry: Poetry, Politics and Poetics* (pp. 83–4) throws additional light on the central topic of the relationship between Hopkins, the poem's speaker, and the 'tall nun'.

As to the other poems selected for special attention in the Modern Criticism section, 'God's Grandeur' (see Key Poems, pp. 129–30) is one of the most widely written about of Hopkins's sonnets. 'Pied Beauty' (see Key Poems, p. 135) has been a key poem for queer approaches to Hopkins, though two of the three critical extracts printed in this part of the Modern Criticism section examine the poem in other ways. The 'Terrible Sonnets', written eight years after these two poems, are often critically dealt with as a group, as in the extracts in this part

8 J, p. 209.
9 J, p. 196.
10 st. 5, l. 7.
11 J, p. 228.

from W. H. Gardner's (**pp. 96–100**) and J. Hillis Miller's (**pp. 105–6**) work; though the pieces excerpted from Eric Griffiths's (**pp. 102–4**) and Yvor Winters's (**pp. 101–2**) books give readings of a single poem each, it is convenient to place them in the context of criticism of the other sonnets.

Before the Modern Criticism section comes a group of extracts from early critics of Hopkins: the first few are from his friends, Richard Watson Dixon (see Early Critical Reception, **pp. 47–8**), Coventry Patmore (**pp. 48–9**) and Robert Bridges (**pp. 49–52**), all poets and recipients of Hopkins's letters and poems as well as, respectively, an Anglican clergyman, a Roman Catholic convert and an agnostic. The obvious omission here is Bridges' letters to Hopkins about his poetry, but these are unavailable: Bridges destroyed all his half of the correspondence. The extract from Bridges's 'Editor's Preface' (**pp. 49–52**) to the first edition of Hopkins's *Poems* shows Bridges attempting to forestall readers' hostile reactions to the formal experimentation of the verse by pointing out faults of 'Oddity and Obscurity'. Later critics, particularly F. R. Leavis, attacked Bridges for failure to understand and appreciate Hopkins's innovations; but, though his interpretative work has been largely jettisoned by later Hopkins studies, Bridges' work in preserving and publishing the poetry was the basis of all subsequent scholarly and critical work.

Following the extracts from critics in Hopkins's circle come examples of the first wave of Hopkins criticism from the 1920s and 1930s. After the Modernist poetic experimentation of T. S. Eliot, Ezra Pound and a slew of others in the early 1920s, Hopkins's innovations in metrics and diction began to look less dauntingly incomprehensible to readers willing to explore novel forms. Early criticism nonetheless often focused on Hopkins's scansion, as well as on the critics' varying responses to the difficulty of the poems, and on the question of placing Hopkins in an appropriate literary context. The enthusiasm of critics such as I. A. Richards (**pp. 53–4**), William Empson (**pp. 55–6**) and F. R. Leavis (**pp. 59–60** did a great deal to establish Hopkins's place in the canon, a place which (though later criticism has certainly altered the notion of canonicity and Hopkins's relation to it) he has held for the best part of a century.

Early Critical Reception

From **Richard Watson Dixon, letters of 5 April 1879 and 1 March 1880**, L II, pp. 26–7; L II, pp. 32–3

Richard Watson Dixon (1833–1900), a minor Victorian poet and Church of England clergyman, was briefly a master at Highgate School during Hopkins's time there, but their friendship was established in 1878 when Hopkins wrote to him to congratulate him on his 1861 book of poems, *Christ's Company*, of which Hopkins said 'I became so fond of it that I made it, so far as that could be, a part of my own mind'.[1] Dixon was one of the very small number of people to whom Hopkins sent copies of some of his poetry; though his response, like Patmore's (see **pp. 48–9**), was not published until long after both his and Hopkins's death, his comments were among the earliest criticism the poems received.

Dixon wanted Hopkins's poems to be more widely known and attempted to publish Hopkins's 'The Loss of the Eurydice' with an introduction by Dixon in a Carlisle newspaper in 1879. At first Hopkins's response was uneasy ('I am troubled about it because it may come to the knowledge of some of ours [i.e. Jesuits] and an unpleasant construction be put on it'),[2] but shortly afterwards he became extremely anxious and forbade the publication, arguing that appearing in a local newspaper could not win him much attention, that Jesuits were required to submit items for publication to a society censor, and that Dixon, as a clergyman in the Church of England, could not 'stand godfather' to the poem. The friendship survived this incident and Dixon and Hopkins corresponded until the year before Hopkins's death.

Letter of 5 April 1879

Reverend and Most Dear Sir –

I have your Poems and have read them I cannot say with what delight, astonishment, & admiration. They are among the most extraordinary I ever read & amazingly original. [. . .]

It seems to me that they ought to be published. Can I do anything?

1   L II, p. 1.
2   L II, p. 29.

Reverend and Most Dear Sir, –

I return your Poems at last [. . .] I have read them many times with the greatest admiration: in the power of forcibly & delicately giving the essence of things in nature, & of carrying one out of one's self with healing, these poems are unmatched. [. . .]

The Sonnets are all truly wonderful: of them my best favourites are the Starlight Night, the Skylark, Duns Scotus Oxford: and the Windhover. [. . .]

The Deutschland is enormously powerful: it has however such elements of deep distress in it that one reads it with less excited delight though not with less interest than the others. I hope that you will accept the tribute of my deep and intense admiration. You spoke of sending me some more. I cannot in truth say what I think of your work.

From **Coventry Patmore, letter of 20 March 1884**, L III, pp. 352–4

Hopkins met the distinguished poet Coventry Patmore (1823–96) in the summer of 1883, when Patmore visited Stonyhurst, the college at which Hopkins had been teaching classics for a year. Hopkins had been aware of Patmore as an editor since at least his undergraduate days in Oxford: he cites Patmore's anthology of poetry for children, *The Children's Garland*,[1] in his dialogue 'On the Origin of Beauty.'[2] Similarly, he had long admired Patmore's poetry. Patmore had converted to Roman Catholicism in 1864 and was well known as the author of the collections of poetry making up *The Angel in the House* sequence. A few weeks after their meeting, Hopkins began a correspondence with Patmore that lasted until shortly before Hopkins's death. In March 1884 Hopkins sent Patmore some of his own poems; the extract gives Patmore's reactions to them, on the whole not very encouraging. Patmore later wrote to Robert Bridges:

> I wish I had not had to tell Hopkins of my objections [to his poems]. But I had either to be silent or to say the truth; and silence would have implied more difference than I felt. I have seldom felt so much attracted towards any man as I have been towards him, and I shall be more sorry than I can say if my criticisms have hurt him[3]

My dear Mr Hopkins, – I have read your poems – most of them several times – and find my first impression confirmed with each reading. It seems to me that the thought and feeling of these poems, if expressed without any obscuring novelty of

---

1   Coventry Patmore, *The Children's Garland*, London: Macmillan, 1862.
2   J, p. 111.
3   L III, p. 353, n. 1.

mode, are such as often to require the whole attention to apprehend and digest them; and are therefore of a kind to appeal only to the few. But to the already sufficiently arduous character of such poetry you seem to me to have added the difficulty of following *several* entirely novel and simultaneous experiments in versification and construction, together with an altogether unprecedented system of alliteration and compound words; – any one of which novelties would be startling and productive of distraction from the poetic matter to be expressed.

System and learned theory are manifest in all these experiments; but they seem to me to be *too* manifest. To me they often darken the thought and feeling which all arts and artifices of language should only illustrate; and I often find it as hard to follow you as I have found it to follow the darkest parts of Browning – who, however, has not an equal excuse of philosophical system. 'Thoughts that *voluntary* move harmonious numbers' is, I suppose, the best definition of poetry that ever was spoken.[1] Whenever your thoughts forget your theories they do so move, and no one who knows what poetry is can mistake them for anything but poetry. 'The Blessed Virgin compared to the Air we breathe' and a few other pieces are exquisite to my mind, but, in these, you have attained to move almost unconsciously in your self-imposed shackles, and consequently the ear follows you without much interruption from the surprise of such novelties; and I can conceive that, after awhile, they would become additional delights. But I do not think that I could ever become sufficiently accustomed to your favourite Poem, 'The Wreck of the Deutschland' [see Key Poems, **pp. 113–28**] to reconcile me to its strangenesses.

I do not think that your musical signs [. . .] help at all.[2] I fancy I should always read the passages in which they occur as you intend them to be read, without any such aid; and people who would not do so would not be *practically* helped by the notation.

From **Robert Bridges, 'Editor's Preface to Notes'**, first (1918) edition of Hopkins's *Poems*, edited with notes by Robert Bridges (London: Milford, 1918), in *Poems of Gerard Manley Hopkins*, ed. W. H. Gardner (London: Oxford University Press, 1930), pp. 202–9 (pp. 204–9).

Robert Bridges (1844–1930; Poet Laureate from 1913) was Hopkins's closest friend. They met as Oxford undergraduates, probably early in 1863. After Hopkins entered the Jesuit novitiate in 1868 their opportunities to meet were very limited, but they corresponded regularly from 1866 to Hopkins's death, with a hiatus of two and a half years in the early 1870s. Very soon after Hopkins's death in 1889 Bridges set about planning an edition of some of his poems, but it was not until 1918 that Hopkins's *Poems* were published (see Norman White, *Hopkins: A Literary Biography*, pp. 458–65 for a discussion of the

---

1   The quotation is from John Milton, *Paradise Lost* (1667), Book 3, l. 37.
2   A reference to the signs Hopkins drew on the MSS of his poems to indicate how they should be read aloud, and which were one of the main reasons why the editors of the Jesuit journal *The Month* refused to publish 'The Wreck of the Deutschland'.

circumstances surrounding the delay). This first edition of the *Poems* included a lengthy note by Bridges discussing the difficulties a reader was likely to find puzzling in Hopkins's work, but commending the originality and beauty of the more successful of Hopkins's poetic effects.

Apart from questions of taste – and if these poems were to be arraigned for errors of what may be called taste, they might be convicted of occasional affectation in metaphor, as where the hills are 'as a stallion stalwart, very-violet-sweet',[1] or of some perversion of human feeling, as, for instance, the 'nostrils' relish of incense along the sanctuary side',[2] or 'the Holy Ghost with warm breast and with ah! bright wings',[3] these and a few such examples are mostly efforts to force emotion into theological or sectarian channels, as in 'the comfortless unconfessed' and the unpoetic line 'His mystery must be unstressed stressed',[4] or, again, the exaggerated Marianism[5] of some pieces, or the naked encounter of sensualism and asceticism which hurts the 'Golden Echo'. –

Apart, I say, from such faults of taste, which few as they numerically are yet affect my liking and more repel my sympathy than do all the rude shocks of his purely artistic wantonness – apart from these there are definite faults of style which a reader must have courage to face, and must in some measure condone before he can discover the great beauties. For these blemishes in the poet's style are of such quality and magnitude as to deny him even a hearing from those who love a continuous literary decorum and are grown to be intolerant of its absence. And it is well to be clear that there is no pretence to reverse the condemnation of those faults, for which the poet has duly suffered. The extravagances are and will remain what they were. Nor can credit be gained from pointing them out: yet, to put readers at their ease, I will here define them: they may be called Oddity and Obscurity; and since the first may provoke laughter when a writer is serious (and this poet is always serious), while the latter must prevent him from being understood (and this poet has always something to say), it may be assumed that they were not a part of his intention. Something of what he thought on this subject may be seen in the following extracts from his letters. In Feb. 1879, he wrote: 'All therefore that I think of doing is to keep my verses together in one place – at present I have not even correct copies –, that, if anyone should like, they might be published after my death. And that again is unlikely, as well as remote. . . . No doubt my poetry errs on the side of oddness. I hope in time to have a more balanced and Miltonic style. But as air, melody, is what strikes me most of all in music and design in painting, so design, pattern, or what I am in the habit of calling inscape is what I above all aim at in poetry. Now it is the virtue of design,

---

1   'Hurrahing in Harvest', l. 10 (see Key Poems, **p. 136**).
2   From 'The Habit of Perfection', ll. 17–20. This was an early poem (1866) about the sanctification of the senses and body.
3   See 'God's Grandeur', ll. 13–14 (see Key Poems, **pp. 129–30**).
4   'Comfortless unconfessed': 'Wreck of the Deutschland', st. 31; 'His mystery': 'Wreck of the Deutschland', st. 5 (see Key Poems, **pp. 117, 126–7**).
5   Marianism: adoration of the Virgin Mary.

pattern, or inscape to be distinctive and it is the vice of distinctiveness to become queer. This vice I cannot have escaped.'[6] And again two months later: 'Moreover the oddness may make them repulsive at first [. . .]. Indeed when, on somebody returning me the Eurydice,[7] I opened and read some lines, as one commonly reads whether prose or verse, with the eyes, so to say, only, it struck me aghast with a kind of raw nakedness and unmitigated violence I was unprepared for: but take breath and read it with the ears, as I always wish to be read, and my verse becomes all right.'[8]

As regards Oddity then, it is plain that the poet was himself fully alive to it, but he was not sufficiently aware of his obscurity, and he could not understand why his friends found his sentences so difficult: he would never have believed that, among all the ellipses and liberties of his grammar, the one chief cause is his habitual omission of the relative pronoun;[9] and yet this is so [. . .]

This grammatical liberty, though it is a common convenience in conversation and has therefore its proper place in good writing, is apt to confuse the parts of speech, and to reduce a normal sequence of words to mere jargon. Writers who carelessly rely on their elliptical speech-forms to govern the elaborate sentences of their literary composition little know what a conscious effort of interpretation they often impose on their readers. But it was not carelessness in Gerard Hopkins: he had full skill and practice and scholarship in conventional forms, and it is easy to see that he banished these purely constructional syllables from his verse because they took up room which he thought he could not afford them: he needed in his scheme all his space for his poetical words, and he wished those to crowd out every merely grammatical colourless or toneless element; and so when he had got into the habit of doing without these relative pronouns – though he must, I suppose, have supplied them in his thought, – he abuses the licence beyond precedent [. . .]

Here, then, is another source of the poet's obscurity; that in aiming at conden-sation he neglects the need that there is for care in the placing of words that are grammatically ambiguous. English swarms with words that have one identical form for substantive,[10] adjective, and verb; and such a word should never be so placed as to allow of any doubt as to what part of speech it is used for; because such ambiguity or momentary uncertainty destroys the force of the sentence. Now our author not only neglects this essential propriety but he would seem even to welcome and seek artistic effect in the consequent confusion; and he will some-times so arrange such words that a reader looking for a verb may find that he has two or three ambiguous monosyllables from which to select, and must be in doubt as to which promises best to give any meaning that he can welcome; and then, after his choice is made, he may be left with some homeless monosyllable still on his hands. Nor is our author apparently sensitive to the irrelevant suggestions that our numerous homophones cause; and he will provoke further ambiguities or obscurities by straining the meaning of these unfortunate words.

---

6 L I, p. 66.
7 Reference to Hopkins's other shipwreck poem, 'The Loss of the Eurydice', written in 1878.
8 L I, p. 79.
9 Relative pronouns: e.g. who, whom, which, that.
10 Substantive: noun.

Finally, the rhymes where they are peculiar are often repellent, and so far from adding charm to the verse that they appear as obstacles. This must not blind one from recognizing that Gerard Hopkins, where he is simple and straightforward in his rhyme is a master of it – there are many instances, – but when he indulges in freaks, his childishness is incredible. His intention in such places is that the verses should be recited running on without pause, and the rhyme occurring in their midst should be like a phonetic accident, merely satisfying the prescribed form. But his phonetic rhymes are often indefensible on his own principle. The rhyme to communion in 'The Bugler'[11] is hideous, and the suspicion that the poet thought it ingenious is appalling; eternal, in 'The Eurydice', does not correspond with burn all,[12] and in 'Felix Randal' and some and handsome[13] is as truly an eye-rhyme as the love and prove[14] which he despised and abjured; – and it is more distressing, because the old-fashioned conventional eye-rhymes are accepted as such without speech-adaptation, and to many ears are a pleasant relief from the fixed jingle of the perfect rhyme; whereas his false ear-rhymes ask to have their slight but indispensable differences obliterated in the reading, and thus they expose their defect, which is of a disagreeable and vulgar or even comic quality. He did not escape full criticism and ample ridicule for such things in his lifetime; and in '83 he wrote: 'Some of my rhymes I regret, but they are past changing, grubs in amber: there are only a few of these; others are unassailable; some others again there are which malignity may munch at but the Muses love.'[15]

Now these are bad faults, and, as I said, a reader, if he is to get any enjoyment from the author's genius, must be somewhat tolerant of them; and they have a real relation to the means whereby the very forcible and original effects of beauty are produced. There is nothing stranger in these poems than the mixture of passages of extreme delicacy and exquisite diction with passages where, in a jungle of rough root-words, emphasis seems to oust euphony; and both these qualities, emphasis and euphony, appear in their extreme forms. It was an idiosyncrasy of this student's mind to push everything to its logical extreme, and take pleasure in a paradoxical result; as may be seen in his prosody where a simple theory seems to be used only as a basis for unexampled liberty. [. . .] Now since those who study style in itself must allow a proper place to the emphatic expression, this experiment, which supplies as novel examples of success as of failure, should be full of interest; and such interest will promote tolerance. [. . .]

It is lamentable that Gerard Hopkins died when, to judge by his latest work, he was beginning to concentrate the force of all his luxuriant experiments in rhythm and diction, and castigate his art into a more reserved style. Few will read the terrible posthumous sonnets without such high admiration and respect for his poetical power as must lead them to search out the rare masterly beauties that distinguish his work.

11 'The Bugler's First Communion' (in Phillips, pp. 146–8), ll. 5 and 8: Hopkins rhymes 'boon he on' with 'communion'.
12 'The Loss of the Eurydice', ll. 119 and 120.
13 'Felix Randal', ll. 2 and 3 (see Key Poems, pp. 141–2).
14 'Love' and 'prove' do not rhyme when spoken but are spelt as if they do; this is what eye-rhyme means.
15 L I, p. 180.

From **Robert Bridges, 'Our Generation Already Is Overpast'**,
Poems of Gerard Manley Hopkins, 2nd edn (London: Oxford University Press,
1930, repr. 1938), pp. xi–xv

This sonnet appeared before the 'Author's Preface' (see above, **pp. 33–6**), in
Bridges's first edition of Hopkins's poetry. The sonnet was written in 1918,
during the First World War ('Hell wars without'), and the year the first edition
was published. It also appeared in the second edition in 1930.

> Our generation already is overpast,
> And thy lov'd legacy, Gerard, has lain
> Coy in my home; as once thy heart was fain
> Of shelter, when God's terror held thee fast
> In life's wild wood at Beauty and Sorrow aghast;
> Thy sainted sense trammel'd in ghostly pain,
> Thy rare ill-broker'd talent in disdain:
> Yet love of Christ will win man's love at last.
>
> Hell wars without; but, dear, the while my hands
> Gather'd thy book, I heard, this wintry day,
> Thy spirit thank me, in his young delight
> Stepping again upon the yellow sands.
> Go forth: amidst our chaffinch flock display
> Thy plumage of far wonder and heavenward flight!

From **I. A. Richards, 'Gerard Hopkins'**, *The Dial*, 1926, from Gerald
Roberts, ed., *Gerard Manley Hopkins: The Critical Heritage* (London: Routledge
& Kegan Paul, 1987), pp. 140–6

I. A. Richards was one of the founders of the modern discipline of English
Literature. His *Principles of Literary Criticism* (1924) was an attempt to establish a
secure, rational methodological basis for literary criticism, which was respond-
ing to Modernism's programme of objectivity and rigour. His *Practical Criticism*
(1929) initiated the practice of subjecting poems to close reading. Richards was
one of the earliest influential critics to write very favourably about Hopkins's
poetry, and was among the commentators who associated his poetry with
Modernism rather than with the work of his Victorian contemporaries. His
essay on Hopkins in *The Dial*, an American periodical which was by the 1920s an
important supporter of Modernist poetry, gave speculative readings of several
of the major poems. Richards sees Hopkins's priestly vocation as at odds with
his poetic talent.

Modern verse is perhaps more often too lucid than too obscure. It passes through
the mind (or the mind passes over it) with too little friction and too swiftly for the

development of the response. Poets who can compel slow reading have thus an initial advantage. The effort, the heightened attention, may brace the reader, and that peculiar intellectual thrill which celebrates the step-by-step conquest of understanding may irradiate and awaken other mental activities more essential to poetry. [. . .]

Few poets illustrate this thesis better than Gerard Hopkins, who may be described, without opposition, as the most obscure of English verse writers. [. . .] Possibly their obscurity may explain the fact that these poems are not yet widely known. But their originality and the audacity of their experimentation have much to do with the delay. [. . .] The more the poems are studied, the clearer it becomes that their oddities are always deliberate. They may be aberrations, they are not blemishes. It is easier to see this to-day since some of his most daring innovations have been, in part, attempted independently by later poets. [. . .]

It is an important fact that he is so often most himself when he is most experimental. [. . .]

If we compare those poems and passages of poems which were conceived definitely within the circle of Hopkins' theology with those which transcend it, we shall find difficulty in resisting the conclusion that the poet in him was often oppressed and stifled by the priest. In this case the conflict which seems to lie behind and prompt all Hopkins' better poems is temporarily resolved through a stoic acceptance of sacrifice. An asceticism which fails to reach ecstasy and accepts the failure. All Hopkins' poems are in this sense poems of defeat. [. . .]

Meanwhile the lamentable fact must be admitted that many people just ripe to read Hopkins have been and will be too busy asking 'does he scan?' to notice that he has anything to say to them. And of those that escape this trap that our teachers so assiduously set, many will be still too troubled by beliefs and disbeliefs to understand him. His is a poetry of divided and equal passions – which very nearly makes a new thing out of a new fusion of them both. But Hopkins' intelligence, though its subtlety with details was extraordinary, failed to remould its materials sufficiently in attacking his central problem. He solved it emotionally, at a cost which amounted to martyrdom; intellectually he was too stiff, too 'cogged and cumbered' with beliefs, those bundles of invested emotional capital, to escape except through appalling tension.[1]

From **Laura Riding and Robert Graves, A Survey of Modernist Poetry** (London: Heinemann, 1927), p. 90

The American poet and critic Laura Riding (now sometimes known as Laura (Riding) Jackson) and Robert Graves, the British novelist, poet and critic, collaborated on a number of editorial and critical projects through the late 1920s and 1930s. A Survey of Modernist Poetry emphasized a detailed close method for the study of poetry that was enormously influential on twentieth-century criticism, from I. A. Richards (see preceding extract) and the great critic and poet

---

1   'cogged and cumbered': 'The Leaden Echo and the Golden Echo', l. 43 (see Key Poems, **p. 146**).

William Empson through the New Criticism of the 1950s. Riding and Graves defend Hopkins against accusations of over-obscurity with the argument that the task of the poet is 'to remind people what the universe really looks and feels like, that is, what language means. If he does this conscientiously he must use language in a fresh way or even, if the poetical language has grown too stale and there are few pioneers before him, invent new language'.[1]

One of the first modernist poets to feel the need of a clearness and accuracy in feelings and their expression so minute, so more than scientific, as to make of poetry a higher sort of psychology, was Gerard Manley Hopkins, a Catholic poet writing in the 'eighties. We call him a modernist in virtue of his extraordinary strictness in the use of words and the unconventional notation he used in setting them down so *that they had to be understood as he meant them to be, or understood not at all* (this is the crux of the whole question of the intelligibility of 'difficult' poetry).

From **William Empson, Seven Types of Ambiguity** (London: Chatto & Windus, 1930; 2nd edn, Hogarth Press, 1947, repr. 1984), pp. 225–6

William Empson, a very distinguished poet as well as critic, was one of the towering figures of English Literature as it emerged as a university discipline informed by practical criticism (Empson calls his method 'verbal analysis') in the 1930s.[1] *Seven Types of Ambiguity* was (famously) begun while Empson was an undergraduate at Cambridge University; seven decades later it remains an eminently readable and imaginative seminal work in the close reading of poetry. Throughout the book, Empson compares the Metaphysical poetry brought to the foreground of critical attention by T. S. Eliot and others with nineteenth-century poetry, much of which was in 1930 badly out of vogue. Empson's ability to draw multiple meanings from phrases and lines of poetry was very fruitfully applied to Hopkins and has been the basis of a strong strand of Hopkins criticism ever since. This extract centres on a reading of 'The Windhover' (see Key Poems, **pp. 133–5**). Empson acknowledged that he was to some extent reading against the grain: about his analysis of the highly ambiguous word 'Buckle!' in l. 10 he asked

what would Hopkins have said if he could have been shown this analysis? It is, perhaps, the only really disagreeable case in the book. If I am right, I am afraid he would have denied with anger that he had meant "like a bicycle wheel," and then after much

1   Laura Riding and Robert Graves, *A Survey of Modernist Poetry*, London: Heinemann, 1927, pp. 94–5.

1   *Seven Types of Ambiguity*, p. viii.

conscientious self-torture would have suppressed the whole poem.[2]

Words in italics are quotations from the sonnet.

Hopkins became a Jesuit, and burnt his early poems on entering the order; there may be some reference to this sacrifice in the *fire* of the Sonnet. Confronted suddenly with the active physical beauty of the bird, he conceives it as the opposite of his patient spiritual renunciation; the statements of the poem appear to insist that his own life is superior, but he cannot decisively judge between them, and holds both with agony in his mind. *My heart in hiding* would seem to imply that the *more dangerous* life is that of the Windhover, but the last three lines insist it is *no wonder* that the life of renunciation should be the more *lovely*. *Buckle* admits of two senses and two meanings: 'they do buckle here,' or 'come, and buckle yourself here'; *buckle* like a military belt, for the discipline of heroic action, *buckled* like a bicycle wheel, 'make useless, distorted, and incapable of its natural motion.' *Here* may mean 'in the case of the bird,' or 'in the case of the Jesuit'; *then* 'when you have become like the bird,' or 'when you have become like the Jesuit'. *Chevalier* personifies either physical or spiritual activity; Christ riding to Jerusalem, or the cavalryman ready for the charge; Pegasus, or the Windhover.

Thus in the first three lines of the sestet we seem to have a clear case of the Freudian use of opposites, where two things thought of as incompatible, but desired intensely by different system of judgements, are spoken of simultaneously by words applying to both; both desires are thus given a transient and exhausting satisfaction, and the two systems of judgement are forced into open conflict before the reader. Such a process, one might imagine, could pierce to regions that underlie the whole structure of our thought; could tap the energies of the very depths of the mind. At the same time one may doubt whether it is most effective to do it so crudely as in these three lines; this enormous conjunction, standing as it were for the point of friction between the two worlds conceived together, affects one rather like shouting in an actor, and probably to many readers the lines seem so meaningless as to have no effect at all. The last three lines, which profess to come to a single judgment on the matter, convey the conflict more strongly and more beautifully.

The metaphor of the *fire* covered by ash seems most to insist on the beauty the *fire* gains when the ash falls in, when its precarious order is again shattered; perhaps, too, on the pleasure, in that some movement, some risk, even to so determinedly static a prisoner, is still possible. The *gold* that painters have used for the haloes of saints is forced by alliteration to agree with the *gash* and *gall* of their self-tortures; from this precarious triumph we fall again, with *vermilion*, to bleeding.

---

2   Empson, *Seven Types of Ambiguity*, p. 226, n. 1. The note is one of the additions that appear in the second edition.

From **C. Day Lewis, A Hope for Poetry** (Oxford: Basil Blackwell, 1934, repr. 1947), pp. 7–8

Cecil Day Lewis was Professor of Poetry at Oxford University in the early 1950s and became Poet Laureate in 1968. At the beginning of his much earlier book, A Hope for Poetry, he claims that the 'immediate ancestors' of post-First World War poetry are Hopkins, Wilfred Owen and T. S. Eliot.[1] In this extract Day Lewis discusses the contrast between Hopkins's own refusal to be influenced and the influence he has had on later poets.

But, for all this, Hopkins remains without affinities.[2] Poets may be divided into two classes; those who assimilate a number of influences and construct an original speech from them, and those whose voice seems to come out of the blue, reminding us of nothing we have heard before. [. . .] We do not suppose, of course, that any poet can remain entirely unaffected by the work of other poets; or that anyone can produce poetry by however skilful a blending of the best ingredients. The naïf[3] poet, too, may sometimes write sophisticated poetry, or even turn into a sophisticated poet – it seems increasingly difficult, indeed, for him to avoid doing so. But it is possible to put the bulk of a poet's work over a number of years into one class or the other.

Though one or two of Hopkins's mature poems come into the first class [. . .] he is predominantly what I have called a 'naïf' poet. [. . .] It is, therefore, all the more remarkable to find him exerting such an influence on modern verse; for poets of this type do not belong to any 'school' of poetry and are apt not to found one. We admire Blake or Housman[4] from a distance: any closer approach to their technique would lead us into pastiche. This is, perhaps, because their technique springs more immediately and purely from their experience than is the case with the 'sophisticated' writer. Up to a point this is true of Hopkins's also: one is frequently coming across undigested fragments of his style imbedded in post-war verse. But he has had a much more real influence than this mere bequeathing of echoes: and it is due, I think, to the fact that, unlike most naïf poets, he was a technical innovator. Such poets (Blake, Housman, Emily Dickinson) are usually content to work within conventional forms: their daemon[5] does the rest. It may seem contradictory to assert that a technical innovator can be a naïf poet, but I do not believe it is necessarily so. I should even go so far as to call Hopkins an unconscious revolutionary: in other words, his innovations are not due to a deliberate rebelling against the conventional technique of the time, as were those of Wordsworth, but spring from a kind of innocent experimenting with words, as a child of genius might invent a new style of architecture while playing with bricks.

1   A Hope for Poetry, p. 2.
2   Day Lewis may be echoing the structure of l. 9 of Hopkins's 'God's Grandeur': 'And, for all this, nature is never spent' (see Key Poems, **p. 130**).
3   naïf: naïve (not subject to the influence of poetic tradition).
4   William Blake (1757–1827) and A. E. Housman (1859–1936): English poets, among other things.
5   daemon: spirit, or individual genius.

From **W. B. Yeats, 'Introduction',** *The Oxford Book of Modern Verse: 1892–1935* (Oxford: Clarendon Press, 1936), pp. xxxix–xl

> The great Irish poet W. B. Yeats edited one of the major canon-forming anthologies of early twentieth-century poetry, *The Oxford Book of Modern Verse*, a few years before his death in 1939. In his chatty and witty Introduction, Yeats describes the 'revolt against Victorianism' that characterized the young poet of the late nineteenth century: the revolt was 'against irrelevant descriptions of nature, the scientific and moral discursiveness of *In Memoriam* [. . .] the political eloquence of Swinburne, the psychological curiosity of Browning, and the poetical diction of everybody. [. . .] Then in 1900 everybody got down off his stilts; [. . .] Victorianism had been defeated'.[1] Yeats's response to Hopkins's poetry was uneasy, but he included 'Pied Beauty', 'Spring', 'Duns Scotus's Oxford', 'The Leaden Echo and the Golden Echo' and three other Hopkins poems in his anthology.

I read Gerard Hopkins with great difficulty, I cannot keep my attention fixed for more than a few minutes; I suspect a bias born when I began to think. He is typical of his generation where most opposed to mine. His meaning is like some faint sound that strains the ear, comes out of words, passes to and fro between them, goes back into words, his manner a last development of poetical diction. My generation began that search for hard positive subject-matter, still a predominant purpose. Yet the publication of his work in 1918 made 'sprung verse' the fashion, and now his influence has replaced that of Hardy and Bridges. In sprung verse a foot may have one or many syllables without altering the metre, we count stress not syllable, it is the metre of the *Samson Agonistes* chorus and has given new vitality to much contemporary verse. It enables a poet to employ words taken over from science or the newspaper without stressing the more unmusical syllables, or to suggest hurried conversation where only one or two words in a sentence are important, to bring about a change in poetical writing like that in the modern speech of the stage where only those words which affect the situation are important. In syllabic verse, lyric, narrative, dramatic, all syllables are important. Hopkins would have disliked increase of realism; this stoppage and sudden onrush of syllables were to him a necessary expression of his slight constant excitement.

From **Charles Williams, 'Introduction to the Second Edition'**, *Poems of Gerard Manley Hopkins* (London: Oxford University Press, 1930), pp. xi–xv

> Charles Williams took over the task of editing Hopkins's poems from Robert Bridges after the first (1918) edition. Williams was a poet and novelist, an Anglican and worked on the editorial staff at Oxford University Press. His

---

1   Yeats, Introduction, p. ix, p. xi.

edition of Hopkins's poems added sixteen mainly juvenile poems to the canon already established by Bridges. The extract from the 'Introduction' to his edition of the *Poems* begins with an account of the effect of Hopkins's use of alliteration, taking as an example the line 'Thou has bound bones and veins in me, fastened me flesh' ('The Wreck of the Deutschland', st. 11.5; see Key Poems, **p. 115**).

It is as if the imagination, seeking for expression, had found both verb and substantive [i.e. noun] at one rush, had begun almost to say them at once, and had separated them only because the intellect had reduced the original unity into divided but related sounds. [. . .] The very race of the words and lines hurries on our emotion; our minds are left behind, not, as in Swinburne, because they have to suspend their labour until it is wanted, but because they cannot work at a quick enough rate. 'Cast by conscience out' is not a phrase; it is a word. So is 'spendsavour salt'.[1] Each is thought and spoken all at once; and this is largely (as it seems) the cause and (as it is) the effect of their alliteration. They are like words of which we remember the derivations; they present their unity and their elements at once. [. . .]

Alliteration, repetition, interior rhyme, all do the same work [in Hopkins's poems]: first, they persuade us of the existence of a vital and surprising poetic energy; second, they suspend our attention from any rest until the whole thing, whatever it may be, is said. Just as phrases which in other poets would be comfortably fashioned clauses are in him complex and compressed words, so poems which in others would have their rising and falling, their moments of importance and unimportance, are in him allowed no chance of having anything of the sort. They proceed, they ascend, they lift us (breathlessly and dazedly clinging) with them, and when at last they rest and we loose hold and totter away we are sometimes too concerned with our own bruises to understand exactly what the experience has been. [. . .]

The poet to whom we should most relate Gerard Hopkins [is] Milton. The simultaneous consciousness of a controlled universe, and yet of division, conflict, and crises within that universe, is hardly so poignantly expressed in any other English poets than those two. [. . .]

We can find in [Hopkins's work] (*a*) a passionate emotion which seems to try and utter all its words in one, (*b*) a passionate intellect which is striving at once to recognize and explain both the singleness and division of the accepted universe. But to these must be added a passionate sense of the details of the world without and the world within, a passionate consciousness of all kinds of experience.

---

1   Both quotations are from 'The Candle Indoors', l. 14 (Phillips, p. 144).

From **F. R. Leavis, New Bearings in English Poetry: A Study of the Contemporary Situation** (London: Chatto & Windus, 1932, repr. with 'Retrospect 1950', 1950; Harmondsworth: Penguin (Peregrine), 1963), pp. 152, 156

The great critic F. R. Leavis, one of the most influential figures in twentieth-century literary criticism, whose *New Bearings in English Poetry* (1932) and *Revaluations* (1936) contributed enormously to forming a new English poetic canon and set of aesthetic criteria for reading poetry, was an early promoter of Hopkins's poetry. It is largely through Leavis's forceful influence that Hopkins came to be adopted as a 'canonical' writer at a time when other Victorian poets were being dropped from or minimized in the canon. Like Riding and Graves (see Early Critical Reception, **pp. 54–5**), Leavis saw Hopkins's work as having more in common with poetry of the twentieth than of the nineteenth century.

With characteristic force, Leavis wrote: 'we see that it is possible for respected critics, writing about [Hopkins's poems] with the consciousness of authority, to exhibit conspicuously in public a complete and complacent obtuseness, and yet arouse no remark: that is the measure of Hopkins's original-ity'.[1] His chapter on Hopkins opens with an attack on the arguments in Robert Bridges's 'Editor's Preface' (see Early Critical Reception, **pp. 49–52**), though he admits readily that

> 'Hopkins is really difficult, and the difficulty is essential. If we could deceive ourselves into believing that we were reading easily his purpose would be defeated; for every word in one of his important poems is doing a great deal more work than almost any word in a poem of Robert Bridges'.[2]

He takes issue with Charles Williams's argument (often taken up by later critics) that Hopkins's poetry is like Milton's and instead likens his 'imagery, and his way of using the body and movement of the language' to Shakespeare's.[3]

The poems of Hopkins that stand in best hope of general acceptance (after *Margaret*) are the group of intensely personal sonnets that he wrote towards the end of his life.[4] *The Windhover* and *Spelt from Sibyl's Leaves* are in sonnet-form, but the late sonnets are immediately recognizable as such. Moreover they lack anything in the nature of

The roll, the rise, the carol, the creation,[5]

---

1   F. R. Leavis, *New Bearings in English Poetry: A Study of the Contemporary Situation*, London: Chatto & Windus, 1932, p. 130.
2   op. cit. p. 134
3   op. cit. p. 138. For Charles Williams's argument, see Early Critical Reception, **pp. 58–9**.
4   'Margaret': i.e. 'Spring and Fall' (see Key Poems, **p. 143**). The 'intensely personal sonnets' are the so-called 'Terrible Sonnets', including 'To Seem the Stranger Lies My Lot', 'I Wake and Feel the Fell of Dark, Not Day', 'No Worst, There Is None', '(Carrion Comfort)', 'Patience, Hard Thing!' and 'My Own Heart Let Me Have More Pity On' (see Key Poems, **pp. 146–52**).
5   'To R. B.', l. 12 (see Key Poems, **pp. 159–60**).

for the pressure of personal anguish was too strong; and consequently they do not present so formidable an appearance as where the Hopkins technique is more copiously elaborated. As Bridges put it, when Hopkins died 'he was beginning to concentrate the force of all his luxuriant experiments in rhythm and diction, and castigate his art into a more reserved style.'[6] The austerity was rather, perhaps, the effect of that cruel inner friction expressed in *The Windhover* and *Spelt from Sibyl's Leaves*. In spite of the terrible import of these poems there is still a certain magnificent buoyancy in the handling of the technical problems. But when he wrote those last sonnets Hopkins had no buoyancy left. They are the more interesting from the point of view of this study in that they bring out more plainly the relation of his medium to speech. More obviously here than in the more canorous[7] poems the ruling spirit is that of living idiom; we can hear the speaking voice [. . .]

The strength and subtlety of his imagery are proof of his genius. But Victorian critics were not familiar with such qualities in the verse of their time. The acceptance of Hopkins would alone have been enough to reconstitute their poetic criteria. But he was not published in 1889. He is now felt to be a contemporary, and his influence is likely to be great. It will not necessarily manifest itself in imitation of the more obvious of his technical peculiarities (these, plainly, may be dangerous toys); but no one can come from studying his work without an extended notion of the resources of English. And a technique so much concerned with inner division, friction, and psychological complexities in general has a special bearing on the problems of contemporary poetry.

He is likely to prove, for our time and the future, the only influential poet of the Victorian age, and he seems to me the greatest.

---

6   See extract from Robert Bridges' 'Editor's Preface', Early Critical Reception, p. 52.
7   canorous: singing.

Modern Criticism

Victorianism

From **Donald Davie, *Purity of Diction in English Verse*** (London: Routledge & Kegan Paul, 1967), pp. 171–5, 182

In an oft-quoted and controversial judgement, Donald Davie locates Hopkins's Victorianism as characteristic of 'a decadent age'; Davie's work is an early example of a strand in Hopkins criticism that places the poet alongside late nineteenth-century aestheticist and decadent writers including Walter Pater and Oscar Wilde. Comparing his work with Keats's (a comparison many critics have made), Davie finds that Hopkins's language is 'a muscle-bound monstrosity'. Davie uses discourses centring on health and on gender to discuss Hopkins, and thus this extract bears comparison with the critics featured in the Gender section (see below **pp. 64–69**).

Hopkins wrote in a decadent age, and if he is its greatest poet, he may be so because he cultivates his hysteria and pushes his sickness to the limit. Certainly he displays, along with the frantic ingenuity, another decadent symptom more easily recognized, the refinement and manipulation of sensuous appetite. This is an important, perhaps the essential, part of that pure beauty which he recognized in Tennyson and missed in Burns, a quality of hectic intensity. Much of his work, in criticism and poetry alike, is concerned with restoring to a jaded palate the capacity for enjoyment. [. . .]

His earliest work, the school prize-poems, are conspicuously Keatsian, and revel in an excess of sensuous luxury; and of course this luxury is a conspicuous feature of all his verse. It is possible that Hopkins thought to counterbalance this Keatsian effeminacy by the strenuous masculinity of 'inscape'; perhaps for some readers he does so and thereby attains a human mean, not decadent at all. Others again may find the compensating masculinity not in 'inscape' at all but in the taut frame of intellectual argument in all the poems, an important aspect of his poetry which the poet seems to take curiously for granted. (One may suspect that it was this, more than rhythm or diction which baffled Bridges sometimes; if so, neither

Bridges nor Hopkins realized it.) Other readers again may find that 'inscape' and sensuous luxury go together and make the poetry decadent, and that the strict Jesuitical logic, for all its discipline, is not really a sign of health, but only another aspect of that systematizing elaboration which produced the doctrine of 'inscape' and the prosody. One has to leave this margin for difference of opinion, for if 'decadent' occurs in the critic's vocabulary at all, it comes at the point where criticism is not distinguishable from moral philosophy. [. . .]

We applaud him, and rightly, for making his language current and refusing archaism.[1] But again that is only the start; the language is anything but current by the time Hopkins has finished with it. [. . .]

'The naked thew and sinew' is not enough for Hopkins.[2] It has to be crammed, stimulated and knotted together. He has no respect for the language, but gives it Sandow-exercises until it is a muscle-bound monstrosity.[3] It is the Keatsian luxury carried one stage further, luxuriating in the kinetic and muscular as well as the sensuous. Word is piled on word, and stress on stress, to crush the odours and dispense a more exquisite tang, more exquisite than the life. To have no respect for language is to have none for life; both life and language have to be heightened and intensified, before Hopkins can approve them. He has been praised more warmly still; and it is contended that his use of language is Shakespearean. Certainly Shakespeare shows similar audacity. But the cases are not parallel. For Shakespeare there was not, in this sense, a language to respect. It was still in the meltingpot, fluid, experimental and expanding rapidly. Even in their speaking, Shakespeare's contemporaries were at liberty to coin, convert, transpose and cram together. Hopkins [. . .] treats nineteenth-century English as if it were still unstable and immature.

From **Alison G. Sulloway,** *Gerard Manley Hopkins and the Victorian Temper* (London: Routledge & Kegan Paul, 1972), pp. 1–5

Later twentieth-century critics have frequently revisited the question raised by several 1930s Hopkins critics of whether his poetry is more characteristic of Victorian or Modernist styles (see extracts from Riding and Graves, **pp. 54–5**, and Leavis, **pp. 59–60**). Alison G. Sulloway, a major Hopkins scholar, complicates what is understood by 'the Victorian temper' and identifies Hopkins as exploring the characteristic concerns of his age, particularly in relation to religion and selfhood.

---

1 Hopkins wrote to Bridges in 1879 that 'it seems to me that the poetical language of an age shd. be the current language heightened, to any degree heightened and unlike itself, but not (I mean normally: passing freaks and graces are another thing) an obsolete one' (L III, p. 89).

2 Quoting Hopkins: Dryden 'is the most masculine of our poets; his style and his rhythms lay the strongest stress of all our literature on the naked thew and sinew of the English language' (L I, pp. 267–8). The phrase has often been picked up by critics.

3 Sandow-exercises: early twentieth-century body-building exercises popularized by the strongman Eugene Sandow (1867–1925).

Gerard Manley Hopkins has not always been considered a conspicuous example of the Victorian temper. But that temper itself is an elusive mood, shifting all the way from unqualified optimism to the blackest distress, and its prismatic quality may be one of its most distinguishing features. In some quarters it appeared in almost buoyant guises: men thought of themselves as bearers of a new science, a new renaissance hellenism, or an invigorated hebraism.[1] In other quarters men feared that the breakdown in faith and in the remnants of the ancient feudal order presaged the end of England as a civilized power.

Under these conditions many of the most sophisticated Victorians who interest us today found themselves attempting to reconcile polaric attitudes so that they might look out upon their new world without falsifying it and at the same time achieve some sort of moral poise. Inevitably these Victorian humanists, struggling to discern what Matthew Arnold called the spirit of the whole, were victims of the same mood swings that characterized the age itself. And it is this shifting spirit, now exuberant, now tentatively hopeful, or at least reconciliatory, now gloomy, if not actually apocalyptic, that places Hopkins so firmly in the centre of the Victorian tradition. He suffered the classic religious traumas for which the age was famous. In his case he resolved his religious crisis by submission to Rome. As an undergraduate Hopkins had soaked himself in Ruskin's works; Ruskin had reassured his disciples that nature's bounty was an earnest of God's concern, and Hopkins gratefully rejoiced in that bounty. Ruskin had warned his disciples that the foul towns, the ravaged countryside, and the starving citizenry were all symbols of England's moral decay, and Hopkins's own warnings on the condition of England paraphrase Ruskin's where they do not paraphrase Carlyle's. Ruskin, Carlyle, Thomas Arnold, and innumerable other Victorians had preached that to work is to pray, and that only a working Christian had the right to call himself a gentleman; almost a third of Hopkins's mature poems deliver the same sermon. He was as ambivalent about art, nature, and the aesthetic life as many of his contemporaries, and he shared with the gloomier Victorian prophets a sense of impending doom, so that art seemed frivolous at times, if not actually immoral, and nature no longer a comfort.

But we are bound to ask ourselves very precisely how this prismatic Victorian mood differs from the transitional mood of earlier centuries. It did differ sharply in certain ways, and we ought to let a few literate Victorians tell us how. That they do so in chorus, from the eighteen-thirties onward, suggests something about the mood itself. For these Victorians saw themselves as creatures of a particular self-consciousness quite new in Christendom. They were peculiarly and often painfully aware of the self and its tentative place in a society undergoing radical changes. Sometimes they analysed the self and all its properties and its settings with cool detachment. At other times they behaved as though they were trapped alone in a room full of mirrors on all sides, so that no matter how long and how honourably they tried, they could not rid themselves of the vision of their fragmented selves. [. . .]

Hopkins was as ambivalent about the rights and the duties of the self as any other Victorian. He had dedicated himself with joyous abandon to his Maker. Yet

---

1 i.e. a new cultural flowering in the tradition of Ancient Greece or the ancient Jewish nation.

not only was he profoundly aware that artists cannot function without valid and realized selves, and that England needed artists, but by the eighteen-eighties he had tortured himself into an admission that it was not at all easy for any human being to get rid of the self's imperious clamour [. . .].

Many of Hopkins's complaints about his fellow poets centred upon what he considered their archaic language and their thoroughly outmoded treatment of outmoded subjects. But it was largely their style, the symbol of spiritual laziness, that engaged his criticism. 'A perfect style must be of its age' (CD, 99, 1881), he confided to Dixon, and by a perfect style, fit to mirror such a tumultuous age, Hopkins meant something fresh and startling, no matter how much it borrowed from the past, a style able to encompass a poet's feelings and his beliefs, and much of the heterogeneous stuff of his own times. To be sure, Hopkins also asserted over and over the right of the artist to a highly personal style, capable of doing justice to the assertive self; and critics and literary historians have given him his due here, as he would have wished them to do. They have analysed his sprung rhythm, his word coinings, and his alliterative techniques. They have recognized as well the role of the past in his rich prosody, from the classical, medieval, and metaphysical strains to the pastoral lyricism of the Romantic poets. But as yet Hopkins's critics have only partially taken him at his word, and there have been very few to suggest that his manner as well as his matter is more often than not a reflection of self-conscious Victorian England. He fashioned his style according to his own critical canons—no man more so; and his poetry contains the stamp of Victorian England as well as of England's past. Highly idiosyncratic as it is, it transcends private idiosyncrasy to speak of Victorian concerns.

Gender

From **Sandra M. Gilbert and Susan Gubar, The Madwoman in the Attic: The Woman Writer and the Nineteenth-Century Literary Imagination** (New Haven, Conn.: Yale University Press, 1979, repr. 1984), pp. 3–7, 10–11, 96

> Gilbert and Gubar's The Madwoman in the Attic was one of the most influential works in the 1970s' wave of feminist criticism. Here they cite Hopkins ('that apostle of aesthetic virility'[1]) as an example of the attitude that associates poetic creativity with masculinity, and in so doing they set in motion the critical interest in Hopkins's complex responses to gender. The quotations from poetry are all from 'To R. B.' (see Key Poems, **pp. 159–60**).

Is a pen a metaphorical penis? Gerard Manley Hopkins seems to have thought so. In a letter to his friend R. W. Dixon in 1886 he confided a crucial feature of his theory of poetry. The artist's 'most essential quality,' he declared, is 'masterly

---

1   Gilbert and Gubar, *The Madwoman in the Attic*, p. 96.

execution, which is a kind of male gift, and especially marks off men from women, the begetting of one's thought on paper, on verse, or whatever the matter is.'[2] In addition, he noted that 'on better consideration it strikes me that the mastery I speak of is not so much in the mind as a puberty in the life of that quality. The male quality is the creative gift.'[3] Male sexuality, in other words, is not just analogically but actually the essence of literary power. The poet's pen is in some sense (even more than figuratively) a penis.

Eccentric and obscure though he was, Hopkins was articulating a concept central to that Victorian culture of which he was in this case a representative male citizen. [. . .]

In patriarchal Western culture [. . .] the text's author is a father, a progenitor, a procreator, an aesthetic patriarch whose pen is an instrument of generative power like his penis. More, his pen's power, like his penis's power, is not just the ability to generate life but the power to create a posterity to which he lays claim [. . .]. In this respect, the pen is truly mightier than its phallic counterpart the sword, and in patriarchy more resonantly sexual. Not only does the writer respond to his muse's quasi-sexual excitation with an out-pouring of the aesthetic energy Hopkins called 'the fine delight that fathers thought'—a delight poured seminally from pen to page—but as the author of an enduring text the writer engages the attention of the future in exactly the same way that a king (or father) 'owns' the homage of the present. No sword-wielding general could rule so long or possess so vast a kingdom.

[. . .] if a woman lacks generative literary power, then a man who loses or abuses such power becomes like a eunuch—or like a woman. [. . .] when Hopkins wanted to explain to R. W. Dixon the aesthetic consequences of a *lack* of male mastery, he seized upon an explanation which developed the implicit parallel between women and eunuchs, declaring that 'if the life' is not 'conveyed into the work and . . . displayed there . . . the product is one of those *hens' eggs* that are good to eat and look just like live ones but never hatch' (italics ours). And when, late in his life, he tried to define his own sense of sterility, his thickening writer's block, he described himself [. . .] both as a eunuch and *as a woman*, specifically a woman deserted by male power: 'the widow of an insight lost,' surviving in a diminished 'winter world' that entirely lacks 'the roll, the rise, the carol, the creation' of male generative power, whose 'strong/Spur' is phallically 'live and lancing like the blow pipe flame.'

---

2   This is a slight misquotation: Hopkins wrote (about visual artists): 'Now this is the artist's most essential quality, masterly execution: it is a kind of male gift and especially marks off men from women, the begetting one's thought on paper, on verse, on whatever the matter is; the life must be conveyed into the work and be displayed there, not suggested as having been in the artist's mind: otherwise the product is one of those hen's-eggs that are good to eat and look just like live ones but never hatch [. . .]' (L II, p. 133).

3   'on better consideration it strikes me that the mastery I speak of is not so much the male quality in the mind as a puberty in the life of that quality. The male quality is the creative gift [. . .]' (L II, p. 133).

From **Alison G. Sulloway, 'Gerard Manley Hopkins and "Women and Men" as Partners in the Mystery of Redemption'** (1989) *Texas Studies in Literature and Language, 31(1)* pp. 44–5

Sulloway argues that Hopkins's female characters are not realistically imagined, but she emphasizes the emotional impact of images of nurturing that she identifies as feminine.

Hopkins's imagination seemed to admit only the possibility of two roles for women, the unearthly woman, silent wife or heroic martyr, or the Medusa, the monster, the slut. It may be that the actual world of women offered him few other models.

Hopkins's benign prosodic woman was sometimes a warrior woman in Christ's camp and sometimes a nurturing mother figure, a blooming Virgin Mary serenely awaiting her child's birth. [. . .] the dichotomous warrior-mother does not represent complex women as they are, but women as Hopkins needed to see them. But this feminine figure does represent some of Hopkins's poetry at its finest, when the poet's craft mirrors his various moods without any sense of disjunction.

It is paradoxical that Hopkins's constraining images of the opposite sex, which are merely fiercer, more doctrinally explicit than his quarrel with all human sinners, including himself, should have produced some of his most tender and most skillful poetry. His anguished battles between himself and his beloved Creator are justifiably admired both as poetry and as the record of a suffering creature caught in a trap and struggling to maintain fidelity to the Creator's principles. But the drama of this poetry has been admired at the expense of the poetry that records a more subtle human drama, perhaps a more feminine drama. In the archetypal poems about women, the speaker is expressing some very human needs and yearnings, the need of the child in every human being for comfort, for maternal compassion rather than paternal justice. Hopkins may have invented archetypal figures who could provide these reassurances for him, if only in his imagination, but it is just this imagination that allows Hopkins's readers to rejoice in one lovely and felicitous poetic moment after the other, in these very poems that are the magic fruit of deep human distress.

'In the Valley of the Elwy' is one of those moments when Hopkins's anima served his muse most graciously:

> I remember a house where all were good
>   To me, God knows, deserving no such thing:
>   Comforting smell breathed at very entering,
>   Fresh fetched, as I suppose, off some sweet wood.
>
> That cordial air made those kind people a hood
>   All over, as a bevy of eggs the mothering wing
>   Will, or mild nights the new morsels of Spring:

> Why, it seemed of course; seemed of right it should.[8]
> [. . .]

The poet includes 'the lovely . . . woods, waters, meadows, combes, vales, / All the air things wear that build this world of Wales' in the benevolent feminine gifts created for human comfort. But the speaker cannot fully avail himself of this world of loving things and people. His cry that God would extend a mother's comfort to him, a 'creature dear O,' is met by his own courageous acceptance that God holds the scales of judgment. Yet these archetypal symbols of male authority are tempered by female compassion: they are 'considerate scales.' God is 'master' but he is also a 'father and fond,' and his fatherhood includes what Hopkins usually thinks of—or rather feels archetypally about—as mother love.

From **Margaret Johnson, *Gerard Manley Hopkins and Tractarian Poetry*** (Aldershot: Ashgate, 1997), pp. 94–6, 98–9, 110–17

Johnson's study of Hopkins places him in the context of other poets influenced by the High Church theology of the Oxford Movement (or Tractarianism), of whom Christina Rossetti is probably the best-known example. Hopkins had read both Christina Rossetti's poetry and that of her brother Dante Gabriel Rossetti. In this extract Johnson compares Hopkins's and Rossetti's writing about women.

There is a marked contrast between [Christina] Rossetti's women, bound to wait until they are fetched, and Hopkins' women, whose martyrdom brings them directly to Christ or even calls him to them, as happens with the nun in *The Wreck of the Deutschland*. The difference indicates a fundamental difference in the perception the two poets have of the participation of women in religious affairs. Rossetti, who daily lived with the constraints imposed on the middle-class Victorian spinster, held a far less sanguine view of the possibilities available to women than Hopkins did. The male-dominated world he inhabited from the time of his education at Highgate School, through his Oxford and Tractarian years and into his Jesuit vocation, offered him little encouragement to consider the inequities which attended women's attempts to move out of the domestic spheres into which social expectations had forced them. This did not prevent him from holding opinions on the matter, however. They were typical of the opinions of many middle-class men of his age, and were shared by many women also. [. . .]

Rossetti's own awareness of 'the difference between a man and a woman' permeates much of her poetry, to the extent that her examination of the need to remember her place points out just how far she was from living the ideal or being able to accept it. [. . .] The cumulative effect of the tensions between the ideal and the reality permit readings of her poetry to range from the Ruskinian to the recent perception of subversive depths. There is no parallel awareness of any similar

---

1   For the complete sonnet, see Key Poems, p. 133. The Gardner and MacKenzie and the Phillips editions render line 4 as 'Fetched fresh, as I suppose, off some sweet wood'.

operation in those works of Hopkins which deal with women; it is an area in which his work lacks subtlety.

Hopkins' own view of women had much to do with his personal decision not just to remain single, as Rossetti did, but to be a celibate and take religious orders. His constant reworking of the Dorothea and Winifred tales shows an interest in the virgin martyr; as does his unfinished poem on St. Thecla.[1] [. . .]

Where virgin deaths in Rossetti's works tend to suggest opportunity wasted or at best deferred, Hopkins, silently subscribing to the contemporary concept of woman as simultaneously more spiritual and more physical than men, sees virgin death as spiritual life. That this was a position difficult to maintain, in relation to his own life and to the lives of women whom he actually knew, may account for his constant reworking of the Dorothea poem, and the abandonment unfinished of Thecla, Winifred and Margaret Clitheroe: the ideal was too far from the reality.[2]

From **Julia F. Saville, A Queer Chivalry: The Homoerotic Asceticism of Gerard Manley Hopkins** (Charlottesville, Va.: University Press of Virginia, 2000), pp. 120–2

Saville's book offers a mediation between what she describes as two extremes in attitudes in Hopkins criticism to his sexual attraction to men. As part of this mediation she uses the term 'queer', denoting 'an energetic resistance to the inertia of sexual conformity coupled with a commitment to articulating and negotiating innumerable differences – ethnic, religious, political, and so on – constellated around sexuality'[1] rather than 'gay' or 'homosexual' in her account of the way sexuality manifests itself in Hopkins's poems. Michael Lynch's controversial article (**pp. 94–5**) was not the first recognition of Hopkins's male-centred sexuality but it did open up the field for an argument between those who rejected the validity of a 'gay' or 'queer' reading of Hopkins and those who accepted – to varying degrees – that reading Hopkins did indeed involve attention to male homosexual desire and identity.[2] Saville brings gender-related

1 Thecla was said to have been converted to Christianity on hearing St Paul preach; she later rejected the advances of a would-be lover and experienced several miraculous escapes from death at the hands of persecutors.
2 For Winifred, see 'The Leaden Echo and the Golden Echo' (**pp. 143–6**), and annotations. Margaret Clitheroe was put to death for her Roman Catholicism in 1586. Unlike Winifred and Thecla, she was a married woman with children. Hopkins began a poem about her around the mid-1870s.

1 Julia F. Saville, A Queer Chivalry: The Homoerotic Asceticism of Gerard Manley Hopkins, Charlottesville, Va.: University of Virgina, 2000, p. 6.
2 In rebuttal of the insistence on Hopkins's male-centred sexuality, particularly his intense friendship with Digby Dolben, put forward by Robert Bernard Martin in his 1991 biography, Gerard Manley Hopkins: A Very Private Life (London: HarperCollins), see for instance Justus George Lawler's Hopkins Re-Constructed: Life, Poetry, and the Tradition (New York: Continuum, 1998), esp. pp. 77–8. Lawler argues: 'The historical reality is, again, that very little distinguishes Hopkins from his celibate or noncelibate, married or unmarried, homo- or heterosexual predecessors or contemporaries except his lyric genius, and his all-redemptive slightly zany sense of the comical and the whimsical.' For criticism that locates Hopkins in various kinds of nineteenth-century homosocial and homosexual contexts, see for instance Richard Dellamora, Masculine Desire: The Sexual Politics of Victorian Aestheticism (Chapel Hill, NC: University of North Carolina Press, 1990).

readings together with detailed investigations of Hopkins's poetics and argues that 'his poetics requires the reader to appreciate fine differences (not only sexual but religious, aesthetic, and class, among others) while living with ambiguity and ambivalence; therefore, to say he is a queer poet is to resist his more reductive (if perhaps forceful) appropriation as either gay or homosexual'.[3]

Hopkins is never comfortable on the subject of heterosexual eros. 'Spring' suggests that Christ is the only figure who can legitimate sexuality for him without its becoming the site of corruption, anxiety, and guilt. Hopkins's unease with sexual difference, yet his delight in a more general category of heterogeneity and nonconformity, has prompted the claim that he belongs to those Victorian sexual dissidents such as Wilde, Symonds, and Whitman who are today considered the founders of a specifically gay or male-homosexual literary discourse. [. . .]

All critics who recognize the sensuality of Hopkins's poetry, and are thereby led to consider his treatment of sexuality, must confront his ambivalence toward the male body. On the one hand, he documented his attractions to young men [. . .], celebrated male beauty, and alluded to Christ as 'the only person that I am in love with' [L I, p. 66]. On the other hand, he regarded his homosexual attractions as sins worthy of formal confession, considered physical beauty – specifically, the beauty of the male body – 'dangerous' [. . .] and distanced himself from figures such as Wilde [. . .] and Whitman [. . .].

But if the inextricable linking of the corporeal and the spiritual or psychic [. . .] permits Hopkins's profoundly tactful figurations of Christ as sublime lover to bring him a small measure of erotic satisfaction, if he derives psychic solace from what I have called his queer chivalry, this is only through the mediation of a painstakingly constructed barrier of poetic language. Hopkins never feels at liberty to celebrate his love of Christ without paying for that pleasure in heavy ascetic coin. So, to celebrate him as gay in the spirit of an outing, for all the cathartic payoff this may yield, is misplaced. [. . .]

It would be more accurate to say that Hopkins finds within a tradition of Christian devotional rhetoric and chivalric discourse a space in which he can develop his peculiarly ascetic poetics that, operating at its best, explores new dimensions in chivalric manliness that nonetheless conforms to the most scrupulous standards of moral purity. This poetics allows him both to articulate and to distance himself from a polymorphous desire (for love from a man and for punishment for that love) that is by definition unconscious. It is at those moments in Hopkins's verse when rhetoric acceptable to traditional Christian doctrine registers an unsettling erotic charge – and the critic must confront the difficult question of whether the poet could be conscious of such an effect – that the term *queer* comes into its own as more suggestive and accurate than the term *gay*.

---

3   op. cit. p. 6.

Language

From **James Milroy, *The Language of Gerard Manley Hopkins***
(London: Andre Deutsch, 1977), pp. 154–6

> One aspect of Milroy's linguistic approach to Hopkins's writing that has been influential for other critics is its exploration of Hopkins's preference for English words derived from Anglo-Saxon rather than from Latin and Greek, and in his tracing of Hopkins's interests in philology (the study of the history and structures of language). *The Language of Gerard Manley Hopkins* includes an extremely useful 'Commentary on Words Used in Rare, Special or Non-Standard Senses in Hopkins's Poetry'.

In our discussion of the formative influences on Hopkins's concept of 'current language', we gave considerable attention to the nature and sources of this vocabulary. Hopkins favours monosyllabic words of early English origin (usually Anglo-Saxon, Scandinavian or early Norman French), which are currently or potentially used in two or more parts-of-speech classes (*catch, coil, comb, ruck*). Many have phonaesthetic or etymological associations within connected series (*st-, sk-, fl-, gr-* series and others are listed in the diaries; *trod* and *trade* are etymologically connected; *dew: degged* is an etymological doublet).[1] In their form, some of these words are not standard English (*pash, mammock, slogger*), but more often words which are standard in form are used in senses which are not the normal standard ones. Sometimes a dialectal sense must be invoked [. . .] and this is often difficult to separate from the usage of traditional crafts and trades [. . .]. Yet others (*pitch, sake, -scape*) have developed specific Hopkinsian usages, usually in the prose of the journal. [. . .] Hopkins's exploitation of etymology (even though it sometimes becomes a language-game) is also part of his purism and *in-earnestness*. It is not undertaken for the sake of resuscitating obsolete meanings (any more than his dialectal uses are motivated by a desire to 'preserve' dialect), but because it enables him to exploit and draw attention to patterns and relationships that actually do exist in the language and to return to literal rather than metaphorical senses of many words (thus, *trade* implies the act of treading as well as the derived sense: 'commerce'). [. . .]

Overwhelmingly, the sources of Hopkins's lexicon lie, not in the classics, but in his observation of the patterns of current language, aided by knowledge derived from dictionaries and language scholarship.

But the relation of Hopkins's poetic uses of this vocabulary to its sources in the language is complex and difficult to explain. Every reader of Hopkins experiences difficulty in knowing the precise meaning of a word in a given context. Some ordinary words, like *buckle* in 'The Windhover',[2] are notorious cruxes, but many others which have been less often discussed, are equally troublesome. What

---

1 phonaesthetic: relating to phonemes (very small sounds or clusters of sounds in a language) that tend to occur in words of similar meaning, for example: 'gl' in glimmer, glint, glisten.
2 See Empson's comment on 'buckle', Early Critical Reception p. 55.

precisely does the poet mean by *pied and peelèd May* or *belled fire* or *disseveral*?[3]
[. . .] When the word is not a normal standard word at all (*brandle, sloggering*),
we may think we have found the answer by tracing a dialectal or historical origin,
only to discover that the dialectal or 'original' meaning does not quite fit the use in
context. There is also a set of favourite Hopkinsian words, which constitute his
basic vocabulary for describing inscape (*skeined, rope, comb, rack, bow* and
others). These stand out because they often depart from expected norms and,
although we usually understand them in an obvious sense, we do not fully grasp
or 'catch' them unless we are aware of a complex set of semantic associations
which they usually carry. [. . .]

We do not *explain* the special effect of this rich language by merely stating that
individual words are of provincial or early English origin. We must also ask why
he uses these words and not others, and consider them in relation to his methods
of heightening language in context in the poetry. [. . .] The kinds of example we
must bear in mind as we discuss his lexical usage are these: why does the poet
prefer *braids of thew* to, for example, 'cords of muscle'; or *of a fourth the doom
to be drowned* to 'of a quarter the fate to be drowned'?[4] It is less relevant to
suggest that Hopkins might be conditioned by metre and rhythm than it would be
to suggest it of other poets: sprung rhythm gives freedom. Other phonetic devices
such as alliteration and vowelling may be more important, but they are only part
of an explanation (*fate* is indeed a puny word beside *doom*), since semantic
associations are relevant too. The obvious preference in these passages for Anglo-
Saxon words (*braids, thew, fourth, doom*) is hardly more of an explanation, since
we must further ask *why* Anglo-Saxon words should be preferable. The answer to
this is broadly a semantic one. Native English words contract much more com-
plex, subtle and far-reaching networks of relationship within the language than
do Classical borrowings, and that is so whether the relationships are grammat-
ical, semantic or phonaesthetic. Such words can be said to have more 'meaning' in
the sense that they have more associations, and one word from the set (e.g. *stal-
wart*, from the *stand, stall, stallion, stead, steady* set) suggests the 'meaning' of
one or more of the others and partakes of some of their 'meanings' by association.

From James Milroy, 'Hopkins the Purist (?): Some Comments on the Sources and Applications of Hopkins's Principles of Poetic Diction', in John S. North and Michael D. Moore (eds), *Vital Candle: Victorian and Modern Bearings in Gerard Manley Hopkins* (Waterloo, Ont.: University of Waterloo Press, 1984), pp. 150–1

Milroy sees Hopkins's Anglo-Saxonisms as an instance of a widespread ten-
dency among Victorian poets and contrasts Hopkins's diction with that of
Algernon Swinburne, a poet with whom he is often compared and whom

---

3   The first two quotations are from st. 26 of 'The Wreck of the Deutschland', the third from 'That
     Nature is a Heraclitean Fire', l. 14 (see Key Poems, **p. 125, p. 157**).
4   'Braids of thew': 'Wreck of the Deutschland', st. 16; 'of a fourth the doom to be drowned': st. 12.
     (See Key Poems, **pp. 120, 121**.)

Hopkins read and cautiously admired, for example, in a letter to Dixon of 1881:

> Swinburne is a strange phenomenon: his poetry seems a power-
> ful effort at establishing a new standard of poetical diction, of
> the rhetoric of poetry; but to waive every other objection it is
> essentially archaic, biblical a good deal, and so on: now that is a
> thing that can never last; a perfect style must be of its age.[1]

The anti-classicism of nineteenth-century language scholars is sometimes extreme: they express annoyance when they discover some word of Latin origin in use amongst the peasantry; they complain about 'foreign' inroads into English; they admire the fossil poetry stored up in Anglo-Saxon dialect words; they even try to restore English to an Anglo-Saxon type of language. Morris writes his Icelandic saga translations in a kind of modern Anglo-Norse; Barnes suggests *folkwain* for 'omnibus,' *soaksome* for 'bibulous' and *pitches of suchness* for 'degrees of comparison.'[2] Henry Sweet, the greatest and most influential phonetician of the century, recommended that schoolchildren should learn German, Anglo-Saxon and the history of English: he appears to have thought that contact with the classical languages would deprave the youth of England.

The preference for Anglo-Saxon (or at least non-Latin) vocabulary is exhibited by other Victorians besides Hopkins. The difference, however, is that Tennyson, Swinburne and others show this preference while retaining a much more conventional model of diction. Consider the opening lines of Swinburne's Chorus from 'Atalanta in Calydon:'

> When the hounds of spring are on winter's traces,
>   The mother of months in meadow or plain
> Fills the shadows and windy places
>   With lisp of leaves and ripple of rain;
> And the brown bright nightingale amorous
> Is half assuaged for Itylus,
> For the Thracian ships and the foreign faces
> The tongueless vigil, and all the pain.

The vocabulary of this is largely Anglo-Saxon or of early French origin, but the differences in the underlying model (as compared with Hopkins) are evident. The most obvious difference is the preference for elaborate periphrasis ('hounds of spring . . . winter's traces . . . mother of months'), and the referential meanings of these periphrases are not actually self-evident. Clearly, Hopkins's preference for a different kind of diction is partly conditioned by his different choice of subject-matter. Hopkins's poems deal mainly with personal experiences and current

1   L II, p. 99.
2   William Barnes (1801–86), philologist and poet using Dorset dialect. Hopkins admired Barnes's work. William Morris (1834–96), poet, immensely influential writer on design and craft, and co-translator with Eiríkr Magnússon of works such as *The Story of Grettir the Strong* (1869) and the multi-volume *Saga Library* (1891–1905).

events, Swinburne's with classical mythology. Hopkins is also concerned with specificity and detailed descriptions of everyday objects, events and processes: as a result his poetry tends to be semantically dense – its information content is high and the circumstances surrounding the events are carefully specified. [. . .] Hopkins requires a new diction because his purpose is to figure forth his perceptions and observations in a language that is appropriate; he is not interested in adorning well-known and conventional motifs with elegant periphrases.

From **Isobel Armstrong, Victorian Poetry: Poetry, Poetics and Politics** (London: Routledge, 1993), pp. 427–30

Isobel Armstrong has written on Hopkins elsewhere, including particularly in *Language as Living Form in Nineteenth Century Poetry*.[1] This later book, *Victorian Poetry: Poetry, Poetics and Politics*, has been a major influence on recent criticism of nineteenth-century verse. Armstrong's identification of what she calls the 'double poem', a kind of poem which is self-conscious, ambiguous and sceptical and, she argues, characteristic of Victorian poetry, has very wide critical currency. She sees Hopkins as 'both a revolutionary and a reactionary poet' whose innovative contribution to the Victorian problem of understanding 'the relationship between subject and object and the representation of this relationship' was his emphasis on linguistics as a possible solution.[2]

Hopkins seems to yearn for a primitive condition which he knows to be fallacious – that words might be so individuated and concrete that they will be closely related to the things they represent in almost unmediated unity with them. If they cannot do this they will possess the quality of the things themselves, having a physicality, substantiveness and materiality which almost turns them into solids. Hopkins's early preference for an onomatopoetic account of language in which the sounds of words participate in the things which originate them is related to this desire. [. . .]

Even though he abandoned it, we can see how this atavistic strain in Hopkins's thought shapes both his theory and his poetry and makes it linguistically a throng of highly individuated particularities, straining against the cohesive predications which achieve structural wholeness. [. . .]

The spoken word guarantees a presence, an immediacy of utterance which minimises the gap between speaker and listener and foregrounds the specificity of every statement. When using 'current language heightened' he aims not for a mimesis of speech but for an inscape of its improvised, living structure.[3] Exclamations, imperatives and interrogatives break into his condensed and often incomplete sentences. The sudden interruptions and changes between sentence

1   Isobel Armstrong, *Language as Living Form in Nineteenth Century Poetry*, Brighton: Harvester, 1982.
2   Armstrong, *Victorian Poetry: Poetry, Poetics and Politics*, p. 420.
3   Hopkins used this phrase in a letter to Bridges of 1879, indicating an ideal for poetic diction (L I, p. 89).

types, the paratactic,[4] co-ordinative grammar, the elliptical compression and embedding of clauses, are all ways of creating the structure of living speech and from which we can infer a syntactic order from the unfinished grammatical forms. The disparate and often incompatible dialect – slang, archaism, neologising compounds – which coexist in his work are for him permissible because they are all ways of producing, in their arresting oddness, the distinctiveness of inscaped speech. [. . .]

Not only does Hopkins's language come to the verge of collapsing into discrete entities: it also risks nonsense by inventing metaphorical forms so tenuously related to an originary meaning that they push comprehension to the limit. 'Spare' and 'fickle' would be examples from 'Pied Beauty', for they cannot easily exclude their conventional associations (economical, unfaithful), and the effort to create new ones is almost an act of will. Paradoxically, one is back with Humpty Dumpty's assertion: it all depends who's master-poet.[5] In Hopkins's work the language celebrating God's mastery often cuts across a cultural agreement about meaning.

The curiously coercive nature of Hopkins's vocabulary discloses the paradox of his revolutionary language – or perhaps one should say, the paradox of his conservative language. His desire to individuate words [. . .] and to form the exact, the 'proper' meaning, so that the word is as close as possible to the thing it represents, actually has the consequence of dislodging the referent.[6] [. . .] in practice the attempt to treat the word as if it were the thing it represents has the effect of detaching it from reference as the idiosyncratic substitution (for instance, 'spare' for 'exceptional') is made. It is as if the substitutive nature of language intervenes at the very moment when the word appears to be in identity with the thing [. . .]. And so the 'fixed points' of Hopkins's language enter an ungrounded economy of signification in spite of his attempt to refuse this abstraction and flux. The word/thing relationship, a kind of use value of language, actually creates the conditions of ungrounded exchange value and 'flux' of meaning.

Inscape and Instress

From **J. Hillis Miller, *The Disappearance of God*** (Cambridge, Mass.: Belknap Press of Harvard University Press, 1963), pp. 288–93, 295

An early exponent of post-structuralist criticism, J. Hillis Miller is one of the most influential critics of the past three decades and has published important and innovative studies of Victorian and twentieth-century poetry and prose. In this book, Miller focuses on five nineteenth-century writers whose work, he argues, deals with the absence of God from the world. He suggests that

---

4   Parataxis is the technique of setting clauses one after another without using conjunctions or other words to indicate the connection between them.

5   Reference to Lewis Carroll, *Through the Looking Glass* (1871), chapter 6. Alice asks Humpty-Dumpty how words can be made to mean many different things; Humpty-Dumpty replies that it is simply a question of who is to be master.

6   I.e. the thing being referred to.

> Hopkins has, beyond all his contemporaries, the most shatter-
> ing experience of the disappearance of God', because despite a
> middle period in which he was able to celebrate the presence of
> Christ in the created world of nature, by the end of his life,
> '[Hopkins] believes in God, but is unable to reach him. Deserted
> by his nature, he is left with a blind violence of will toward a
> God who keeps himself absent.[1]

In this extract Miller describes Hopkins's concepts 'inscape' and 'instress'
and connects them with his use of rhyme in the poems. In an undergraduate
essay Hopkins wrote 'all beauty may by a metaphor be called rhyme', because
'the principle of beauty [is] a combination of regularity with disagreement': this
fundamental aesthetic judgement connects Hopkins's practice in use of rhyme
(and other effects such as alliteration and parallelism) with his theories about
the perception of form, including inscape and instress.[2]

Each thing in Hopkins' world has the utmost freshness or sharpness of outline,
and this distinctiveness of pattern is carried down to the tiniest detail. There is no
blurring or softening of edges. Each thing stands out vividly as though it were
surrounded by perfectly translucid air, and air can reach all the surfaces of even
the smallest and most intricate object, so abrupt is the frontier between the object
and its surroundings: [. . .]

Color, texture, pattern – all are evidence of the energy of instress which upholds
the world. Perhaps even more important is Hopkins' sense of what might be
called inner texture, the interior structure and grain of a thing. The inner quality
of each thing is just as distinctive as is its exterior pattern or surface. Each object is
held in being by a system of strands, ropes, or sinews, lines of force which reach
everywhere from the center to the surface, organize the thing, and make it one.
The unity of an object lies not so much in its exterior pattern or texture, as in the
way every morsel of it is strung together and held in tension by an intertwined
pattern of bones, muscles, and veins.

Hopkins sees even the most apparently slack and unstructured objects, like
clouds or water, as roped and corded together by a tense network of lines of
energy. The image of strands, wires, stems, or veins recurs in his work. [. . .]

Burliness and ropes of energy within, color, texture, and pattern without – these
make up each created thing for Hopkins. If instress is the pervasive energy of
being, upholding all things equally, inscape is the name for this energy as it
manifests itself in the distinctive structure of things, both inner and outer. [. . .]
His own word inscape always implies the sense of a skeletonlike structure which
captures and encloses an inner principle of life, as a basket or cage may imprison a
wild bird of the air. The inner pressure of instress, permeating nature, is the true
source of inscape, and brought into the open by it. The word is *in*-scape, the outer
manifestation or 'scape' of an inner energy or activity not external pattern which

1   Hillis Miller, *The Disappearance of God*, pp. 352-3, 359.
2   J, p. 102.

is pleasing to the eye as design: 'All the world is fall of inscape and chance left free
to act falls into an order as well as purpose: looking out of my window I caught
it in the random clods and broken heaps of snow made by the cast of a broom'
[J, p. 230]; 'Fineness, proportion, of feature comes from a moulding force which
succeeds in asserting itself over the resistance of cumbersome or restraining mat-
ter' [L, III, p. 306]. Inscape is the expression of a force which lives in change, and
waterfalls which flow or clouds which are 'moulded ever and melted across skies'[3]
[. . .] as much possess inscape as a tree of distinctive pattern. [. . .]
   All things have instress and inscape. If instress makes things alike, the fact that
all things are full of inscape means that things are alike in being unlike. But
though this seems to permit nothing in nature analogous to the relation of rhyme
in poetry and music, rhyming can actually be found everywhere in Hopkins'
nature. [. . .]
   Hopkins' nature is not made up of groups of the same thing side by side in
helter-skelter disorder. Each thing is echoed by other examples of the same thing,
and these exist not at random but in a patterned field, spaced at regular intervals,
like notes on the diatonic scale.[4] [. . .]
   It may be true that each thing has its *haecceitas*,[5] the individualizing form which
distinguishes it from all other members of the same species, but this is not what
most interests Hopkins, neither in his journals nor in his nature poems. What
fascinates him is the inner law or pattern which any one oak tree, cloud, or flower
shares with similar trees, clouds, or flowers. This is its inscape. Though any
member of the species possesses its inscape, this pattern is most easily detached to
the mind when we can see a large number of individuals side by side in echoing
order. The inscapes of nature are in this exactly like the inscapes of rhythm and
rhyme in poetry. [. . .]
   Even with the most ideal conditions the catching of inscapes is no 'ecstasy,' no
merging of seer and thing seen in which all distinction is lost. Hopkins' description
of the proper relation between self and world is another version of rhyming. The
interior and exterior inscapes must echo one another, not merge. The stem of stress
is not a current of force which unifies subject and object. It is the reverberation
which shows that two separate things, the mind and what it knows, are in
resonance.
   This echoing of mind and world Hopkins calls a 'canon of feeling.' The mind
and its object sing the same tune, but at a distance. The mind protects its integrity
by taking a shape of feeling which is like the inscape it sees, and yet holds it at
arm's length. If it cannot do this it may either be unable to feel the inscape, or, at
the opposite extreme, the inscape may rush into the mind and carve out its own
pattern there with painful precision, threatening the distinctiveness of the specta-
tor's selftaste. The awareness of the need for a canon of feeling usually comes to
Hopkins when there is a failure of correspondence between mind and world, a

---

3   See Key Poems, p. 136: 'Hurrahing in Harvest', l. 4.
4   Hopkins was very interested in the theory of music, in which the diatonic is just one of many ways
    of organizing notes in a regular ordered scale.
5   See Headnote to 'Duns Scotus's Oxford', Key Poems, p. 137, for information on Scotus and
    haecceitas.

time when, like Coleridge in 'Dejection: An Ode,' he sees, not feels, how beautiful things are:[6]

> . . . the warm greyness of the day, the river, the spring green, and the cuckoo wanted a canon by which to harmonise and round them in – e.g, one of feeling. [J, p. 135] [. . .]

When the canon of feeling exists there is a perfect echo in the mind for the inscape outside, and the empire of rhyme has been pushed one step further – from chiming of similar trees, clouds, or flowers to a chiming of the mind with what it beholds.

'The Wreck of the Deutschland'

See Key Poems pp. 113–28 for 'The Wreck of the Deutschland'.

From **Helen Vendler, 'The Wreck of the Deutschland'**, in Anthony Mortimer (ed.), *The Authentic Cadence: Centennial Essays on Gerard Manley Hopkins* (Fribourg: University Press of Fribourg, 1992), pp. 38–9, 46–51

> Helen Vendler is one of the most authoritative close-reading critics of American, British and Irish poetry. Among her many books, *The Music of What Happens: Poems, Poets, Critics*[1] and *The Breaking of Style: Hopkins, Heaney, Graham*[2] have been very widely influential. In this essay extract, Vendler addresses some of the key critical issues in reading 'The Wreck of the Deutschland', including Hopkins's relation to the nun and his expressive grammatical and lexical choices.

I would like to emphasize here two things: first, the intimate connection between the two parts of the poem, the 'lyric' first part and the 'narrative' second part; and second, the theological intent of the poem, which is, as I see it, to assert a faith in God's literal power to alter, or 'cure', physical reality. 'The Wreck of the Deutschland' is, as has often been said, a theodicy, in which Hopkins justifies God's way of bringing good out of evil; but I think readers on the whole have not seen it as a modern assertion of the possibility of physical miracle. The poetic weight in the poem falls not on the question (which Hopkins knows the answer to), 'Is the shipwrack then a harvest?' but rather on the intention of the nun's outcry. Hopkins has overheard, through the newspapers, an enigmatic utterance – 'O Christ, Christ come quickly!' – which he feels called upon to interpret, and the whole poem is his act of interpretation. I will return to this question.

The connections between Parts I and II of the poem are intense, reiterated, and

6   Miller quotes the end of the second section of Coleridge's 1802 poem: 'I see them all [natural things], so excellently fair; / I *see*, not *feel*, how beautiful they are!'

1   Helen Vendler, *The Music of What Happens*, Cambridge, Mass.: Harvard University Press, 1988.
2   Helen Vendler, *The Breaking of Style: Hopkins, Heaney, Graham*, Cambridge, Mass.: Harvard University Press, 1995.

emphasized. [. . .] Many of the words that will reappear in Part II have already appeared more than once in Part I, as if Hopkins wished to foreground them for us even before we re-encounter them. We are made to believe in the resemblance between the poet's experience in Part I and the nuns' experience in Part II by the overlap of vocabulary between them, since in poetry two things equal to the same thing are equal to each other. The lexical resemblances are too great to be accidental: we must believe that Hopkins felt the two experiences to be somehow the same experience. As we know, Hopkins wrote the narrative portion of the poem first, saying in his letter to Bridges of August 21, 1877, 'The *Bremen* stanza[3] . . . was, I think, the first written after 10 years interval of silence.' (L I: 44) After establishing his narrative, Hopkins then used the key words from his narrative to write his short lyrical overture. He could not have devised this tactic without a startling moment in which he realized that in retelling the story of the tall nun, as he began his poem, he had revealed to himself the core of his own inner story. The poem as we have it is, I believe, presented backwards in terms of its own generation; but it makes a powerful aesthetic point by introducing us first to its tortured but redeemed protagonist before beginning the ode on the shipwrecked but victorious nuns.

And what is the essence of the inner story of the protagonist? It is that of being imperiled; and in that danger, calling on Christ to intervene and *change* one's fate. Because the poet is convinced – irrationally, perhaps – that if he understands the nun's cry he will understand his own situation and how it should be 'worded', the heart of the poem is found in the poet's effort to guess at, and then decide firmly on, the nun's intention when she called out, 'O Christ, Christ, come quickly!'

Hopkins' decision on her intention has, I think, often been misinterpreted either as a desire for death or [. . .] as the assertion of the nun's actual vision of Christ. As I understand the poem, Hopkins says that the nun called on Christ with the firm intention that He should end the storm and save her from death. The gospel incident on the stormy lake of Gennesareth when the disciples woke Jesus saying, 'Lord, save us ere we perish!' and He calmed the waves with 'Peace, be still',[4] served the nun, Hopkins believed, as the biblical type which she believed could be fulfilled and repeated in the moment of her own distress. In deciding on the nun's intention, Hopkins says that Christ 'was to *cure* the extremity where he had cast her' (italics mine). Hopkins probably had in mind not only the biblical Deluge and the rescue of the disciples at Gennesareth, but also St. Paul's miraculous rescue from shipwreck recounted in Second Corinthians,[5] since St. Paul's forcible conversion is mentioned in the first part of the 'Deutschland'.[6] He also had in mind, as we know from the close of the poem, the Harrowing of Hell, the miraculous rescue of 'the past-prayer, pent in prison.' [. . .]

3 i.e. st. 12.
4 Mark, 4:39: 'And he arose, and rebuked the wind, and said unto the sea, Peace, be still. And the wind ceased, and there was a great calm' (AV). 'And rising up, he rebuked the wind, and said to the sea: Peace, be still. And the wind ceased: and there was made a great calm' (DR).
5 2 Corinthians 11: 25: 'Thrice was I beaten with rods, once was I stoned, thrice I suffered shipwreck, a night and a day I have been in the deep' (AV). 'Thrice I was beaten with rods: once I was stoned: thrice I suffered shipwreck: a night and a day I was in the depth of the sea' (DR). A fuller account of the rescue is given in Acts 27:40–4.
6 In st. 10 l. 5.

The 'Deutschland' owes various poetic debts, notably to Herbert, Keats, and Swinburne;[7] in its final effect it sounds only like itself; and perhaps it is not accidental that its talismanic number is five, an uneven prime. Through its meditation on the number five, it discovers suffering and sacrifice as God's written ciphering and (in the best sense) stigmatizing; it brings God the utterer, uttered, and uttering Logos of speech into the realm of inscription, scarring, and lettering – the modern world of printed, rather than oral, enunciation. Everything in the poem about suffering, utterance, and inscription is many times over-determined, and this thematic richness matches Hopkins' phonetic over-determination, in which there is scarcely a word that is not phonetically related, in ways that reinforce meaning, to several of its neighbors.[8]

The poem is especially concerned with doubling. It possesses a divided and anguished double protagonist, priest and nun. The single male poet matches the single female nun; the name 'Deutschland' is 'double a desperate name'[9] since it refers both to the criminal nation and to the shipwrecked vessel of incarnation; the double-sided country of Germany is the home of both St. Gertrude and the heretic Luther; and our double-sided human nature gives birth to both Cain and Abel – 'Abel is Cain's brother and breasts they have sucked the same.'[10] This emphasis on doubleness suggests that identity for Hopkins is always dangerously double, and that a personal choice for one's better self, after the manner of the Ignatian exercises, is imperative for authenticity and salvation. The 'lyric plot' is precisely an account of the repudiation of the 'wicked' self, hateful to the father, in order to find one's 'good' self in the person of the incarnate Son, the 'heart of the Host',[11] or Jesus in his continuing presence in sacramental form.

We may, if we wish, secularize the ethical choice between 'good' and 'bad' selves by using psychological words like 'authenticity' in place of theological words like 'salvation.' In this vein, we may remind ourselves that shipwrecks had a powerful family connection for Hopkins: his father, who had bitterly disapproved of Hopkins' conversion to Roman Catholicism and ordination as a Jesuit priest, was a marine insurance adjuster, the author of *A Manual of Marine Insurance* (1867), and also of a book called *The Port of Refuge, or advice and instructions to the Master Mariner in situations of doubt, difficulty, and danger* (1873). Both of these books preceded the wreck of 'The Deutschland' by less than a decade, and the second was written just two years before the event. Hopkins' father was also a poet; and we might say, therefore, that Hopkins grew up thinking that poetry and shipwrecks both belonged to his father. In claiming this shipwreck and its poetry for himself, significantly after his father superior suggested to him that someone should write a poem about the event, Hopkins was, we may speculate, affirming a symbolic adulthood, emancipating his own voice, but still apprehensive of the father's retribution ('the frown of his face'[12]). In finding in

---

7 George Herbert (1593–1633), poet, most famously on religious subjects; John Keats (1795–1821) and Algernon Swinburne (1837–1909), both poets with whom Hopkins is often compared for the luxurious sensuousness of their verse.
8 Over-determined: having excessive numbers of explanations and meanings attached.
9 st. 20 l. 3.
10 st. 20 l. 8.
11 st 3. l. 5.
12 st. 3 l. 1.

Christ an image of sonship that was identical with the father, Hopkins found a way 'to flash from the flame [of wrath] to the flame [of love] then, tower from the grace [of repentance] to the grace [of forgiveness]:'.[13] The poet's symbolic partner in finding this authentic cadence for his words is a female; he borrows her enigmatic but faith-filled words and confers on them his own intuited and decided-upon meaning, incorporating her suffering and his own into Christ's passion as the type of all pain, enfolding her rescue and his own within several biblical types of faith – the obedience of Noah's building the ark, the confession of Peter, and the cry of the disciples at Gennesareth. Hopkins' androgynous identification with the towering and victorious nun is, it seems, a condition for the successful melting joy that begins in the poet as tears and words together, and broadens into a 'never-eldering revel and river of youth.'[14] The poetic nexus between the two protagonists comes as stanza 17 joins stanza 18, as 'A virginal tongue told' passes immediately into 'Ah, touched in your bower of bone / Are you!' Hopkins attempts similar identifications with a variety of other female saints, among them Saint Dorothea, Saint Winefred, and Blessed Margaret Clitheroe, but these were all martyred victims. It was only when he found a victorious, rather than a victimized, female self that he could use a powerful voice in the process of the identification.[15] The male sailor who attempts to rescue the women passengers is, necessarily for the triumphing of the lioness/prophetess/nun, haplessly unsuccessful, and is drowned. The newspaper accounts of the shipwreck told of the failure of the sailor's attempt; but Hopkins' insertion into his poem of this small narrative of male defeat has a thematic importance in stressing the contrasted power of the nun.

But an equally important nexus in the poem is the stanza that is the hinge between Part I and Part II. This stanza (11) belongs to a personified Death, who speaks the first lines and so inaugurates, *in propria persona*, the narrative plot. To Hopkins, death is an unmaking, the opposite of creation. The person who unmakes unmaking, who turns death into an occasion of grace, is Christ. The poem travels from Death's triumph, where 'storms bugle his fame' to Christ's triumph; as the Father turns from wrath to compassion, there arrives 'our passion-plungèd giant risen / The Christ of the Father compassionate, fetched in the storm of his strides.'[16] What is enabled, psychologically, by the symbolic integration of father, son, nun, and poet is an androgynous power over death resulting in a strengthened (ultimately immortal) voice; linguistically, what is enabled is a renaming of reality. The 'double-naturèd name'[17] of the 'Deutschland' – 'O Deutschland, double a desperate name!' – is 'new born to the world'[18] by the nun's utterance – the 'heaven-flung, heart-fleshed, maiden-furled / Miracle-in-Mary-of-flame;'[19] that 'heart-throe, birth of a brain, / Word that heard and

---

13 st. 3 l. 8.
14 st. 18 l. 7.
15 Compare with Margaret Johnson's argument about Hopkins and virgin saints in the extract from *Gerard Manley Hopkins and Tractarian Poetry*, Modern Criticism, p. 68.
16 st. 33 ll. 7–8.
17 st. 34 l. 2.
18 st. 34 l. 1.
19 st. 34 ll. 3–4.

kept thee and uttered thee outright.'[20] At the end of the poem, the nun is trans-
formed into a saint who can be invoked to intercede for the conversion (and
consequent spiritual immortality) of England, which will occur through the
agency of the Son, who, in the pun attendant on his role, becomes the day-spring,
a crimson-cresseted east who will 'easter in us.'[21] We may see this convergence of
interceding nun and salvific son in the redemption of England as Hopkins' wish
for reconciliation with his estranged Protestant family. (It can be compared with
his wish for a merciful afterlife for the Protestant Henry Purcell, and with his
sonnet on estrangement, 'To seem the stranger lies my lot': 'Father and mother are
in Christ not near.')[22]

The poem ends in the first-person plural, a form that entered the poem briefly at
the end of Part 1, forecasting the collective and even national salvation hoped for
at the end of the ode. The extraordinary final grammatical arrangement that
Hopkins adopts to present his redemptive Jesus is the figure of partitive nesting:
Jesus is the fire *of* the hearth *of* the charity *of* our hearts, the Lord *of* the throng *of*
the chivalry *of* our thoughts – or, as Hopkins phrases it, 'Our hearts' charity's
hearth's fire, our thoughts' chivalry's throng's Lord.'[23] The first thing to be said
about this double phrase is that it embraces both the affections and the intellect,
as had the earlier formulation for utterance, 'heart-throe, birth of a brain.' Christ
does not reside exclusively either in the will's love or in the intellect's thoughts: as
feudal Lord, he is attended by a throng of chivalry, our thoughts, his knights; as
sun/son, he has been domesticated as the fire of our hearth, the fuel of our love of
others. The ostentatious nesting figure signifies that at the bottom of any
affectional or intellectual reality one comes upon Christ. Look at our hearts; look
into the charity within them; look to the hearth where charity dwells; look to the
fire that animates that love; it is Christ. Look at our thoughts; look at their
knightly attention; look at them thronged around their Lord at the center; that
Lord is Christ. Something like this penetration from circumference to center,
finding the kernel always to be Christ, underlies the use of grammatical nesting.

Hopkins' passionateness of character is certainly felt as much in the closing
stanzas of the 'Deutschland' as it is throughout the poem. Yet we may legitimately
ask where in the poem his passionateness finds its best poetry. There is common
agreement that the poetry of natural reality in the 'Deutschland' is irreproachable,
from the 'wiry and white-fiery and whirlwind-swivellèd snow'[24] to the 'lush-kept
plush-capped sloe.'[25] There is also agreement on the vividness of the psychological
drama of the poem, whether that of the poet quailing in fear or that of the terrified
passengers on the ship. The meditation on the necessity of human suffering is
equally gripping: the poet experiences his Keatsian burst of the sloe-berry on the
tongue when he understands suffering as a consequence of personal sin and as a
means toward salvation through its participation in the Passion of Christ. What
seems, by contrast, least successful in the poem is the recurrent use of specifically

20 st. 30 ll. 7–8.
21 st. 35 l. 5.
22 Both poems are given in Key Poems, **pp. 139–40 and 146–8.**
23 st. 35 l. 8.
24 st. 13 l. 7.
25 st. 8 l. 3.

Roman Catholic diction, whether in the Marian interludes in stanzas 30 and 34, the Franciscan vignette in stanza 23, or the exaggerated remarks on Luther in stanza 20:

> But Gertrude, lily, and Luther, are two of a town,
> Christ's lily and beast of the waste wood.

The sincerity of Hopkins' devotion, whether to the Virgin Mary or to Saints Francis or Gertrude is indubitable, but he had not been raised in the language of Roman Catholic devotional practice and institutional belief, and it sits uneasily in his lines. Its Counter-Reformation iconographical and allegorical pieties are not quite at home with Hopkins' characteristic personal intensities, which tended rather to be psychological, physiological, and visual.

As a psychological document of spiritual guilt, terror, and weakness and subsequent adult reintegration, as a historical narrative, as an *ars poetica*, and as a reinterpretation of Pindaric practice in English, the 'Deutschland' remains a powerful piece of writing.[26] Historically, it reflects both the moment of the forcible secularization characteristic of modern states, and the reaction to this cultural change in the heart of an ex-Protestant, himself an exile in his own culture, concerned to repudiate an authoritarian Protestantism in Germany and in England. It was not the realist social transcription of modern writing but the collective social ritual of Pindar, celebrating a hero, that Hopkins took as a model for his celebration of the nun and Christ as contemporary redemptive heroes, thereby introducing a new Pindaric excitability to English verse. It took many years for the Hopkinsian excitability of temperament, plot, and language to see print, but once it was common property it was widely imitated by poets as diverse as Auden, Lowell, Bishop, Moore, Thomas, and Berryman – in fact, by almost every poet who came across Hopkins' lines.[27] 'The Wreck of the Deutschland' stands for us now not as the dragon folded at the gate (Robert Bridges' words) but rather as the poem in which Hopkins discovered his mature power, and became one of those individual talents (to use Eliot's words) that force the whole poetic tradition in English into its rare historic realignments.[28]

---

26 The original *Ars Poetica* was a poem by the classical writer Horace outlining rules for poetry; Vendler uses the term to mean a text that deals with the writing of poetry. Pindar: ancient Greek lyric poet whose 'epinicion' odes celebrated the victories of athletes. Pindaric: an ode roughly in the manner of Pindar, with varying line lengths and using rhyme. Wordsworth's 'Ode: Intimations of Immortality' (publ. 1807) is an example of a Pindaric ode.

27 W. H. Auden (1907–73), Dylan Thomas (1914–53): British poets; Robert Lowell (1917–77), Marianne Moore (1887–1972), John Berryman (1914–72): American poets.

28 dragon at the gate: see headnote to 'Wreck of the Deutschland', Key Poems, **p. 115**. Eliot's words: reference to T. S. Eliot's hugely influential critical essay 'Tradition and the Individual Talent', published in *The Sacred Wood* (1920).

From **Isobel Armstrong, *Victorian Poetry: Poetry, Poetics and Politics*** (London: Routledge, 1993), pp. 433–4, 436

In this extract, Armstrong focuses, like Vendler, on the central relationship of Hopkins and the nun, particularly exploring the breakdown of language in stanza 28, which she attributes to Hopkins's response to his concept of God who is momentarily both male and female.

['The Wreck of the Deutschland'] celebrates the call of the nun in the sinking ship, who 'rears' herself like the Pegasus heart in 'Hurrahing in the Harvest'.[1] She calls 'O Christ, Christ, come quickly'[2] and experiences, it seems, a direct vision of Christ or union with Him. But Hopkins asks, 'What did she mean?' (stanza 25) and the syntax of the poem breaks down in stanza 28. 'But how shall I . . . make me room there: / Reach me a . . .'. Hopkins's language is nowhere so bold, so innovative and so confident, and yet the poem seems to falter. The first ten stanzas, in which Hopkins meditates on the personal relationship with Christ and the significance of the Incarnation, are very successful.[3] They are actually the *result* of his response to the wreck but are placed prior to the narrative in an effort to withstand the flux of the storm before it is described, to prevent it from dissolving value and significance. It is an effort to transfer the model of a redeeming personal union with Christ to the fate of the 'two hundred souls' lost in the wreck who are redeemed by the nun's utterance. But the model cannot bear the 'stress' of this effort.

'Thou mastering me / God!'[4] God in this verbless sentence is a mastering me God, a God who includes all objects within Himself. He is subject and predicate. The Incarnation, which Hopkins celebrates in language of a virtuosity he hardly reached again, is the guarantee of this inclusion. It enables man to take God into himself just as God takes man into Himself. The language here is oral, sexual, orgasmic. It is only in union with God through the Incarnation that Hopkins's troubled homosexual passions could find release, perhaps because it is a union which transcends gender (stanza 8).

> How a lush-kept-plush-capped sloe
> Will, mouthed to flesh-burst,
> Gush! – flush the man, the being with it, sour or sweet
> Brim, in a flash, full!

Taste, always Hopkins's sense for the most immediate experience of identity, makes taster and thing tasted inseparable. The resistant sloe, its selfidentity, 'kept' single by its 'capped' defensive skin will 'flush' the man, organically penetrating

---

1 See Key Poems, **p. 136**: 'Hurrahing in Harvest' l. 13.
2 st. 24 l. 7.
3 Incarnation: God becoming man in Christ.
4 st. 1 ll. 1–2.

his being. The 'flesh-burst' is its breaking open of separateness and also the mouth of the man himself in sensuous union with what he takes into himself. [. . .]

The poem's troubled sexuality is perhaps an index to its problems. Earlier poems generalise sexuality and Eros as stress, rejoicing in the leaping of the gap between beings, even while these are gendered as the same sex, and the desire for union is a generalised desire. The nun, however, accepting God's mastery, 'keeping' Christ in gestation and experiencing union without 'stain', is emphatically placed as feminine: the sea, paradoxically, has not 'unmothered' her in her virginity. Yet, in the traditional ecclesiastical pun on erection and resurrection, she 'rears' herself towards Christ, and becomes androgynous in taking on His qualities, so that the Christ who is asked to 'come', reciprocally takes on hers. Hopkins is staggered at the revolutionary meaning of this reading (a male *and female* God) and the breakdown or gap in syntax at this point of the poem indicates that aporia, and the temerity of this idea.[5] But, as in the dream work, this is a *signifying* gap: it 'means', signifying the constitutive 'gap' of feminine sexuality and the gap of sexual difference, which would dissolve if the 'saltus' or leap of union between nun and Christ were fully achieved. There would be a dissolution of traditional meaning and perhaps of meaning itself. The pun on the meaning of 'wreck' – to *regard, take notice* (or 'read' for meaning) or to *destroy* – is cruelly preserved in the poem, as Hopkins's solutions to the dissolution of meaning actually recreate it.

From **Thaïs E. Morgan, 'Violence, Creativity, and the Feminine: Poetics and Gender Politics in Swinburne and Hopkins'**, in Anthony H. Harrison and Beverly Taylor (eds), *Gender and Discourse in Victorian Literature and Art* (DeKalb, Ill.: North Illinois University Press, 1992), pp. 85–96

> This controversial and influential essay gives a radical reading of 'The Wreck of the Deutschland' as expressive of a violent eroticism or eroticized violence. Morgan's dual argument is summed up in the first paragraph of the extract.

Through an analysis of the structures of representation in Hopkins's 'The Wreck of the Deutschland' [. . .] I will argue that the foregrounding of violence to the feminine is the effect of misogynistic premises [. . .]. At the same time, the focus on violating the feminine [. . .] serves another purpose, acting as a defensive detour around the dangers of homoerotic desire and the concomitant homophobic fear of the 'effeminate.'

[. . .] In Hopkins's poetics, erotic violence is the precondition for inspiration. Thus, the speaker can even take pleasure in the pain God administers because being 'almost unmade' by His 'touch'[1] is a sign of grace, both spiritual and artistic. In exchange for poetic power, then, the speaker is willing to inscribe his own

---

5   aporia: gap or failure in expression.

1   st. 1 ll. 6 and 7.

body and voice in the 'feminine' – a cultural construct [. . .] that, in theology as well as in art, positions the subject as 'object' or 'vessel' to mediate the Word/ words of a more powerful other.

At the same time, Hopkins's use of the epithet 'master' and the poetic speaker's utter submission to God also suggest a sadomasochistic relation of power between worshiper and divinity, who here, are both male. The eroticization of grace through Hopkins's metaphors invites a reading of the experience of inspiration as 'feminine' in the psychoanalytic sense of masochistic but also implies a homoerotic relation between Christ and the male Christian. In this double reading, the masochistic joy that characterizes the poet-priest's ecstatic cry during his calling to God – 'I did say yes / O at lightning and lashed rod'[2] – parallels the nun's acceptance of her 'unchancelling'[3] by God – 'O Christ, Christ, come quickly!'[4] [. . .]. The action of the divine Word is unmistakably phallic, not to say physically threatening. Before he identifies himself with the martyred nun directly in part 2 of the poem, therefore, Hopkins's speaker has already been feminized in the very act of seeking poetic inspiration from God. [. . .]

By making the present moment of his religious and creative inspiration repeat as well as anticipate the nun's erotic and fatal encounter with the godhead, Hopkins sets up a revisionist Christian typology that serves to destabilize the boundaries of sexual difference.[5] The male artist is most creative precisely when he is most feminized. The 'swoon' of the speaker's 'heart' as he recalls how God 'trod / Hard down'[6] on him in the moment of inspiration both prefigures and postfigures the martyred nun's fatal ecstasy in part 2 of the poem. Hopkins emphasizes the concurrence of sadomasochism and homoeroticism involved in the ascetic assumption of a 'feminine' role in relation to the deity's powers. Perhaps it is his fear of becoming fully feminine that prompts the poetic speaker to express 'dread' as his body is 'touch[ed]' by God: 'Over again I feel thy finger and find thee'.[7] The speaker himself draws our attention to his precarious state: 'almost unmade,' he has become dangerously like a woman, specifically like the nun whose mystical violation the speaker keeps constantly before his memory during this dramatic monologue, and as if dead to himself as a man or 'unmade' in the sense of unmanned and effeminized. [. . .]

Given the strain between genders in part 1 of 'The Wreck of the Deutschland,' the speaker's identification with the martyred nun in part 2 can only be problematic. Above all, it is clear that Hopkins, despite his attraction to the feminine, does not view the feminine as a desirable subject position. Instead, Hopkins is exploring the homoeroticism latent in Christianity in general and in his own poetics in particular *through* the central feminine figure in the text. [. . .]

As he tries to imagine the actual scene of her martyrdom, the speaker identifies passionately with the nun's physical sensations as well as with her spiritual revelation. God's 'touch' is 'an exquisite smart' that 'turns'[8] or brings her out of herself,

---

2   st. 2 l. 1–2.
3   st. 21 l. 6.
4   st. 24 l. 7.
5   Typology: the study of Scriptural symbols.
6   st. 2 ll. 6–7.
7   st. 1 ll. 6–8.
8   st. 18 ll. 1–2.

just as the speaker had felt God's 'finger' in stanza 2. The imagined sight of the play of pain and pleasure across the nun's body as she unites with Christ causes the excited speaker to forget the poetic mastery he claimed for himself in stanza 6 and to ejaculate, '[M]ake words break from me here all alone / Do you!–'[9] [. . .]. Interestingly, during this moment, the tables seem to be turned and the power of inspiration falls to the nun, not to the poet: if she must submit to Christ, the speaker must submit to her and, through her, to Christ. But the nun's mediation of Christ's presence again emphasizes her role as *ancilla dei*,[10] and the speaker's ultimate goal is less to reexperience her martyrdom imaginatively than to experience his own union with Christ, in both the erotic and spiritual senses, through the relatively safe medium of the feminine figure represented in his text.

Yet when he asks, 'What can it be, this glee? the good you have there of your own?'[11] [. . .], the speaker's question implies his recognition that sexual difference still separates the quality of the nun's inspiration from his own. These questions have a double purpose: he wants to know not only what martyrdom is like generally but also what martyrdom in the feminine might be like. Precisely because she is 'mastered' by Christ, his own object of desire, the speaker urgently wants to feel, to know, to appropriate the nun's experience of martyrdom. He questions the nun almost as a jealous lover would, suspecting that, as a woman, she retains for herself a form of divine knowledge and prophetic utterance higher than the male speaker can ever obtain. Later, in stanza 25, Hopkins is still worrying this point: 'The majesty! what did she mean? / . . . Is it love in her of the being as her lover had been?' [. . .]. Ironically, despite his frantic attempts to cross over into the feminine by inscribing the female body at the center of his text, Hopkins's persona remains excluded from the nun's uniquely female knowledge of Christ, or her *jouissance*.[12] The best that he can do is to masquerade in the feminine at several points throughout the poem by taking up the "feminine" position in relation to Christ: passivity, receptivity, and submission. [. . .]

Because of the differences he has marked between himself and the nun–the difference between the 'prophetess' 's receptivity and the poet's creativity, for instance – the speaker's identification with the nun's erotic union with Christ here appears voyeuristic rather than sympathetic. His ventriloquism of her ecstatic cries at the moment of *jouissance* – ' "O Christ, Christ, come quickly" ' – is spoken in a falsetto that mocks as much as records her ecstasy, which, pathetically, she has achieved only through her death.

The speaker's fundamentally misogynistic attitude toward the martyred nun in 'The Wreck of the Deutschland' emerges even more strikingly in stanza 28 [. . .]. Here, his attempted identification with the feminine produces a rape fantasy, in

---

9 st. 18 ll. 3–4.
10 *ancilla dei*: literally 'the handmaid of God', as the Virgin Mary calls herself in Luke 1:38. Also a term for a dead and holy woman, usually a virgin, often, though not necessarily, a nun.
11 st. 18 l. 8.
12 *jouissance*: term used by French post-structuralist theorist Roland Barthes, psychoanalyst Jacques Lacan, psychoanalytical feminist theorist Julia Kristeva and others, and now in wide circulation, indicating extreme and liberating pleasure, which may be found in reading or other kinds of experience (in this instance the nun finds it in martyrdom), but which has at least some sexual connotations.

which the central female figure is violently taken by the male divinity while the speaker looks on:

> But how shall I . . . make me room there:
> Reach me a . . . Fancy, come faster –
> Strike you the sight of it? look at it loom there,
> Thing that she . . . There then! the Master . . .
> Do, deal, lord it . . .
> Let him ride, her pride, in his triumph, despatch and have done . . .
> [. . .]

The nun's encounter with Christ is modeled after the Annunciation, but as revised through Hopkins's violent eroticism.[13] In his role as holy Bridegroom, Christ enters the nun to make her 'bear' the Word. Hopkins's peculiar 'Fancy' of this major Christian story entails a triangulation of desire and power in which the divine male 'Master' 'ride[s]'[14] the nun and, as spectator, the poetic speaker projects himself into both the sadistic/active and masochistic/passive roles of the central pair. On the one hand, the speaker seems to egg Christ on from the sidelines, like a vicarious participant in a gang rape of a woman who got what she was asking for – 'Let him ride, her pride . . . despatch and have done.' On the other hand, as the metaphorical equivalences posited between the speaker and the nun earlier make clear – 'A master, her master and mine!'[15] [. . .] – the speaker cannot but see his own desire for Christ's 'mystery' of 'mastery' in the nun's subjection and also in her *jouissance*.

Arguably, the violence against the central feminine figure in 'The Wreck of the Deutschland' is all the more intense because the poetic 'I' is divided or conflicted, taking on the roles of desired object and desiring subject, or alternating feminine and masculine gender identities throughout the text. Another reason for the connection between misogynistic violence and creativity in Hopkins's poetics must be considered, too. Through a revisionist use of typology, Hopkins in stanzas 20 through 23 shifts the poem's focus from memorialization of the martyred nun to an ecstatic personal vision of 'Lovescape crucified'[16] [. . .] or a palimpsest of the tortured bodies of male martyrs. As a devotional conceit, 'Lovescape crucified' calls to mind the way in which Christ's Passion (stanza 22) prefigures St. Francis's stigmata or the *imitatio Christi* (stanza 23).[17] Similarly, this conceit reinforces the typological parallels between the nun, who stands in for her 'coifed sisterhood'[18] or the other four nuns who died with her, 'father Francis,' and 'suffering Christ.'[19] On the structural level of the poem, then, the conceit of 'Lovescape crucified'

---

13 Annunciation: the angel Gabriel's announcement to Mary of Jesus's conception. See Luke 1:26–38.
14 st. 28 l. 8.
15 st. 19 l. 2.
16 st. 23 l. 4.
17 St Francis of Assisi is said to have developed marks on his hands, feet and side similar to the wounds on Christ's body resulting from crucifixion. These marks or stigmata signify his extreme piety and devotion to Christ. *Imitatio Christi*: literally, imitation of Christ: in this sense, referring to St Francis's devotion to Christ.
18 st. 20 l. 2.
19 st. 23 l. 1; st. 22. l. 2.

works as does the holy number five, through which the speaker moves from admiring the 'five' nuns to imagining the 'five' wounds of Christ and, after Him, the 'five' stigmata of St. Francis.

However, the near identity of Francis's and Christ's martyrdoms contrasts sharply with the manner of the nun's death: her 'virginal' body and its 'exquisite smart' differ significantly from the 'man's make'[20] of Christ's and St. Francis's bodies.[21] Their special 'Mark' differentiates these male martyrs from the female version but also makes them comparable to another splendidly suffering male body – the body of the brave sailor, whose heroic but ultimately futile self-sacrifice, described in stanza 16, ironically prefigures the nun's heroism, depicted in stanzas 17 and 18. If Christ and St. Francis are legitimate objects of devotional contemplation, Hopkins's fantasy about the tragic sailor, 'handy and brave,' who attempts 'to save' the 'women kind below' during the shipwreck, is illicitly homo-erotic in the context of religious worship. Furthermore, even in terms of Victorian typology, Hopkins's inclusion of the sailor in the company of canonical male martyrs (Christ and St. Francis) is a daring move. Of course, the sailor represents a traditional heterosexual ideal of male prowess and chivalry; at the same time, though, he represents a Victorian homosexual ideal of the working-class man's beauty, with 'all his dreadnought breast and braids of thew' [. . .].[22] In the actual event, this sailor was decapitated in his struggle to save others, symbolically los-ing his manhood for Christ – a fate that Hopkins, who confesses himself 'almost unmade' by his devotion to God, both desires and fears.

The specularization of three male bodies in suffering – the sailor's, Christ's, and St. Francis's – competes with the specularization of the female body in the nun's martyrdom. Subtly but unmistakably, Hopkins here shifts from an inscription of the feminine to an inscription of the effeminate at the center of his text. Yet, significantly, the violence in this section of 'The Wreck of the Deutschland' is directed not only at the nun but also at the male martyrs. Hopkins's fascination with male martyrdom or 'Lovescape crucified' is not an untroubled one, and his repetitive focus on the public exhibition or 'Stigma, signal, cinquefoil token'[23] of these three men's exemplariness as religious icons borders on the obsessive. For, paradoxically, their holy status depends on Christ's and Francis's willingness, *as* men, to submit to God as a superior masculine force in the way that a woman, like the nun, would – that is, without reserve but with 'Joy.'[24] Besides its proper Christological meaning, then, the 'Mark' of the male martyrs' bodies here may be read as the poet's attempt to inscribe an emergent homosexual identity into his text – one that still represents itself as improperly effeminate and as exceptional in its mediacy between masculinity and femininity, hence exceptionally vulnerable and fearful of a public martyrdom in the form of a homosexual scandal.[25] Con-sidering this complex interplay of genders in Hopkins's poetics, violence to the feminine in 'The Wreck of the Deutschland' may thus stem from a combination of

---

20 st. 22 l. 3.
21 St Francis of Assisi died of natural causes rather than suffering a violent death but might be said to be a martyr in that he worked himself to death for his faith.
22 st. 16 l. 5.
23 st. 22 l. 7.
24 st. 23 l. 1.
25 Christology is the theological study of Christ.

internalized homophobia and gynephobia, in which the male poet both envies the feminine and fears the feminine as that Other he himself already has become through his homoerotic desire.[26]

> Away . . .
> On a pastoral forehead of Wales,
> I was under a roof here, I was at rest . . .
> No, but it was not these . . .
> Not danger, electrical horror . . .
> The appealing of the Passion is tenderer in prayer apart;
> Other, I gather, in measure her mind's
> Burden . . .[27]

In a recoil that is motivated by an outward-directed gynephobia and an inward-directed homophobia, Hopkins's persona insists upon his distance from the central feminine figure in the poem – geographically, temporally, physically, and spiritually. He rejects identification with the algolagniac spectacle of the nun, or the 'appealing of the Passion' in the feminine.[28] Instead, he asserts his preference for a less sensual, less threatening, more 'manly,' and more conventional 'measure' of showing his devotion to Christ. He also draws an absolute distinction between his relation to Christ and hers: as a woman, the nun is 'Other' and therefore not to be imitated by the male-identified poetic persona. Her grotesque *jouissance* must be set safely in perspective as an example of an extreme, almost grotesque, relation to God. In other words, the central feminine figure in the poem must be suppressed, lest the speaker himself become too feminized or effeminate by imitating a woman's improper way rather than a man's proper way to God.

In the final movement of 'The Wreck of the Deutschland' (stanzas 32–35), Hopkins returns to the standard worship of Christ as carried on 'between men.' Through the body of the nun, the solidarity of the Jesuit community and the larger homosocial community of which it is a part has been assured. Addressing a prayer to Christ – 'I admire thee, master of the tides'[29] [. . .] – the poetic speaker praises His 'mercy,' a mercy evident in his own case but hardly so in the nun's. From the poet-priest's point of view, Christ is 'Kind but royally reclaiming his own'[30] [. . .]: although she has died heroically for her faith, it is the speaker who lives on to benefit from Woman's sacrifice, which has revealed to him Christ's 'mystery' and has granted him a new power to understand the sources of his own inspiration. In effect, by appropriating her direct knowledge of God for his own but rejecting the pathetic vulnerability of her 'body of lovely Death'[31] as wholly 'Other,' the speaker reviolates the nun in order to reassert a masculinist order of power and knowledge – 'prayer apart'[32] – over that weaker vessel, the feminine body of desire. The feminine has served Hopkins's poetics as a mediator for his

---

26 gynephobia: fear of women.
27 st. 24 ll. 1–3, st. 27 l. 1, l. 5, ll. 6–8.
28 algolagniac: sadomasochistic.
29 st. 32 l. 1.
30 st. 34 l. 7.
31 st. 25 l. 4.
32 st. 27 l. 6.

creativity, but his gender alignment is finally, as always, with the masculine. [. . .] Femininity, especially as invested in Christian theology, may enable Hopkins to articulate the fundamental homoeroticism of his religion and his poetics, but this indebtedness to the feminine is transformed, through the poet's own homophobic fear of becoming effeminate, into disdain for and violence to the central feminine figure in his poem.

'God's Grandeur'

See Key Poems, pp. 129–30, for 'God's Grandeur'.

From **Alison G. Sulloway, 'Gerard Manley Hopkins and "Women and Men" as Partners in the Mystery of Redemption'** (1989) *Texas Studies in Literature and Language*, 31(1), pp. 44–5

> Sulloway's reading of this sonnet interprets Nature as gendered feminine and both the Holy Ghost and the forces that threaten the world (industrialization and perhaps Protestantism) as masculine.

Another poem that marvelously blends male and female archetypes without positing hostility between them and dominion of the legally enfranchised over the disenfranchised is 'God's Grandeur' [. . .]. The cosmic quarrel is not between the male principle and the female, but between two male symbols, one benevolent though characterized by 'grandeur' and the other the foulness that was 'seared,' 'bleared,' and 'smeared' with the industrial rape of the countryside. The octave describes this battle between God and the human pillagers.

The sestet contrasts 'the dearest freshness deep down things' – archetypal symbols of women whose gifts to men are mysterious and hidden – with the degradation of dirty and dangerous masculine 'trade' and 'toil,' a symbol of industrial greed out of control. In the first line of the sestet, there is a sudden shift in mood, created by the modifying adjectival phrase, 'And for all this'. The shift of mood suggests not only nature's sweetness compared to the greed of the rich and powerful, but almost a smile or a kind act of a comforter, since 'nature' in its benevolent role is always the comforting mother to Hopkins, a presence whose goodness 'is never spent.'

The 'dearest freshness deep down things' also evoke the earth, comfortably pregnant with hidden riches and gifts as fine as those in Eden. The receding terror of 'the last lights off the black West,' possibly renegade Anglican England as well as industrial England, is imaginatively banished by the brown brink of the rising sun or the Mediterranean east, where Christianity sprang up.

From **James Olney, The Language(s) of Poetry: Walt Whitman, Emily Dickinson, Gerard Manley Hopkins** (Athens, Ga.: University of Georgia Press, 1993), pp. 80–1

Olney's book reads poems by Hopkins, Emily Dickinson and Walt Whitman in an investigation of what he considers to be the three characteristic features of poetic language: heightened rhythm, heightened figuration or metaphoricity, and a defamiliarization of language that reflects the poet's individuality.[1]

'The world is charged with the grandeur of God,' the first line of 'God's Grandeur,' is a characteristic expression of Hopkins's sense of unfailing spiritual presence in the early poems. All of creation is energized as with an electrical charge that is none of humankind's doing though it is there as pulse and impulse for humans too if they do not refuse (or defuse) it. Hopkins developed the same idea in some spiritual notes written some four years after 'God's Grandeur': 'All things therefore are charged with love, are charged with God and if we know how to touch them give off sparks and take fire, yield drops and flow, ring and tell of him' (*The Sermons and Devotional Writings of GMH*, p. 195). It is a sense of the ubiquity and unfailingness of God's presence, in spite of the perversity of the human will, that animates these early poems as in the sestet of 'God's Grandeur'[.] [. . .]
    In the single word 'bent' and in the subtle interplay of *b*'s and *w*'s in these last lines Hopkins suggests the charged and fecund richness of nature, as a result of God's presence, that is the poem's theme. The way in which Hopkins bends the word 'bent' over the enjambed line, pointing simultaneously to the world as morally bent, to the physical bend of the earth's curvature, and to the Holy Ghost's couvadelike bending in concern over the human world; the double sense of 'broods' in the last line as both incubating and worrying over; and the *w/b*'s of 'World broods' and 'warm breast' that are chiasmatically[2] reversed in the *b/w* of 'bright wings' after the release of wonderment in 'ah!' – in all these Hopkins is technically imitating the charged richness of God's presence throughout creation.

From **Eric Griffiths, The Printed Voice of Victorian Poetry** (Oxford: Clarendon Press, 1989), pp. 281–4

Griffiths's book reads Tennyson, Browning, Hardy and Hopkins through the creative tensions built into poetry by its attempts to turn voices into writing. In this extract Griffiths explores the layers of rhythm in 'God's Grandeur'.

The world is not only invigorated or fuelled ('charged') with God's grandeur, it is accused ('charged') with it because the world, and particularly man in the world, has the responsibility ('is charged with') to meet and manifest that grandeur but

---

1   Olney, *The Language(s) of Poetry*, p. 4.
2   chiasmus: repetition of a structure but with the order of its elements reversed.

often fails to live up to its responsibilities. Hence, the 'want of witness' in creation. This reflective wealth of sense in 'charged' comes out of the line gradually, though the line itself strikes out with an axiomatic suddenness and boldness. We might say that the first line has the relation to the body of the sonnet of a text to a sermon, but saying that with assurance would involve a decision about how to voice the line which the line does not itself support; it would ascribe an act of pronouncement to the opening which would then be followed by explication or brooding.[1] Yet the sonnet broods from beginning to end. [. . .]

The sestet does imagine an eco-catastrophe, for in 'though the last lights off the black West went' the verb is a subjunctive, and the line should be paraphrased as 'if the Sun were to be extinguished'. However, the end of man's world is not God's end of the world, as Hopkins makes out in the most astonishing moment of this great sonnet – the moment of the turn at 'went / Oh, morning'. What that moment says is that even were the earth as we know it to be destroyed, there would be a new dawn 'Because the Holy Ghost over the bent / World broods', because God's care for the world exceeds ours, because our destruction of the world could not impair his power to contemplate his creation and hatch ('broods') something more from it. The astonishing thing in the final tercet is Hopkins's audacity in using the natural rhythm of sunset and sunrise to stand for the recovery of creation by its creator even when all the creaturely rhythm that could be known to a man such as Hopkins had stopped, a recovery and perpetuation in the new significance of eternity according to Hopkins and which he yet pictures as the absolute type of temporality as he knows it, the turns-about of night and day. [. . .] The sonnet's exultant agility, its affording to be rash, and its security of mind amidst melodic extravagance [. . .] attune it to ancient and orthodox traditions, for that entirely individual and syntactic move – 'went / Oh, morning' – with its arch of human concept and experience from their setting in temporal existence across to the eternal and transcendent recovers the words of Revelation: 'And I saw a new heaven and a new earth' (21: 1; Douay Bible).

'Pied Beauty'

See Key Poems, p. 135, for 'Pied Beauty'.

From **J. Hillis Miller, *The Disappearance of God*** (Cambridge, Mass.: Belknap Press of Harvard University Press, 1963), pp. 299–303

'Pied Beauty' belongs to the middle period of Hopkins's poetic career which Miller identifies as the time during which Hopkins felt closest to God and wrote his most celebratory poetry. Here Miller argues that 'Pied Beauty' explores a rhyme or resemblance between God's creation and the creative patterns of poetry.

---

1 Sermons traditionally begin with a quotation ('text') from the Bible, which the preacher then elucidates or explores.

Nature in 'Pied Beauty' lives in movement and change. The sky's pattern of couple-color is only momentary; the trout are swimming; the chestnuts have fallen, and are like that evanescent and glowing thing, a fresh firecoal, perfect image of a dynamic energy which is spending itself by its very act of being itself. The finches fly; the landscape is plotted and pieced – what is fallow one year is 'plough' or 'fold' the text; and each trade, with its special gear and tackle and trim, is an activity of making and changing the world.

Though nature here lives in dynamic change it never repeats itself. Like the lark's song it 'goes on . . . through all time, without ever losing its first freshness, being a thing both new and old' (L I, 164). No two couple-colored skies, trout, or finches' wings are alike. They are counter to one another, original, 'spare,' in the sense that a spare part stands by itself, and strange, in the sense that they cannot be wholly known in terms of past experience. Though the poet can recognize that it is a cow, a trout, or a sky, to some degree it evades his categories and appears strange, a strangeness which makes him recognize that he does not understand how it is what it is. 'Who knows how?' he asks, which may mean both: 'How can I tell you all the ways in which things can be fickle or freckled?' and also: 'It is impossible to understand how this comes about.' This failure to understand the thing fully, though it registers on the senses, opens up the gap between sensation (or 'simple apprehension') and perception (or 'understanding') which is so important to Hopkins as a Scotist [. . .]. When a thing appears strange, man becomes aware that to place it in a concept does not do justice to its uniqueness and originality. He comes to see the coarseness of such words as 'cow,' which must do duty for all cows, though each cow, as can be seen in the case of brinded cows, is in some sense original and strange. To name a thing rightly the poet must go beyond nouns, for the noun will tell how a thing is like other things of the same species, but not how it is different from them. Beauty lies in the copresence of the two, unlikeness with likeness, sameness with difference. [. . .]

Hopkins wants us to think that all words have this intimate participation in the nature of what they name. Reality has simultaneously the dynamic activity and instress of verbs, the solidity and substantiality of nouns, and the sensible vividness of adjectives. Signs of this are his fondness for participles, and his use of one part of speech in place of another. He likes to build up groups of words which form a single linguistic unit combining adjective (often as participle), verb, and noun. Sometimes nouns are turned into adjectives. The whole compound forms one word possessing the powers of all the major parts of speech. In 'Pied Beauty' we have 'landscape plotted and pieced' and 'fresh-firecoal chestnutfalls.' The phrases are dappled or pied and express in their structure the fact that the world is made up of groups of dissimilar things which are nevertheless similar and rhyme. [. . .]

It is not an accident that two of the examples (sky and landscape) are universal in scope, for clearly the whole world, taken as a unit, is a case of pied beauty. The poem includes the four universal elements: earth, water, air, and fire. The fields, trout, skies, and firecoals are synecdoches, and the poem is cosmic in scope.[1] Every piece of nature is in itself pied, and at the same time it is part of a larger and

---

1   synecdoches: metaphors in which a thing is called by the name of a part of itself: here, the four nouns Miller lists stand for the four elements.

more inclusive piedness. The relation of sameness and difference, of the one and the many, of general and specific, pervades the whole universe.

The structure of the universe is echoed and imitated by the sound and structure of the poem. The relation of sound between the pairs of quality-words ('swift, slow'; 'sweet, sour'; 'adazzle, dim') is one of piedness. The pairs of words are opposite in meaning, and yet similar in sound, and this similarity in sound leads us to seek a relation of meaning. The poem's structure of sound, like its structure of meaning, and like the universe it imitates in little, is a complex network of relations of likeness in difference – pied beauty within pied beauty, and larger cases of pied beauty embracing smaller. [. . .] The poem's structure of rhythm and sound seems to be all for the purpose of making the poem a model in little of the universe it names.

What of the first line of the poem and the last two? The poem describes the universe as a total harmony of pied beauty, but only as a way of praising God, its creator. What is the relation here between God and nature?

At first it appears that the first line of the poem and the last say much the same thing: a pious thanks to God for having provided this wonderful world of linked multiplicity: 'Glory be to God for dappled things,' and 'Praise him.' But at the end of the poem the statement relating the pied universe to God has a new meaning, for the poem has shown that the most inclusive case of the relation of sameness and difference is the relation of God to the universe. The creator and the creation rhyme.

From **Michael Lynch, 'Recovering Hopkins, Recovering Ourselves'** (1979) *Hopkins Quarterly,* 6, pp. 107–17

Michael Lynch was one of the first critics to 'recover Hopkins as a gay poet'; the questions this article poses about ways in which criticism can connect Hopkins's sexuality with his poetic practice have been to a significant extent answered by later scholars including Julia Saville and Richard Dellamora, but as an early and influential example of (not so named) queer theory applied to Hopkins studies, the article continues to merit attention. Lynch's argument takes up points made by Alison G. Sulloway and others about Hopkins's 'dehumanizing' writing about women and his enthusiasm for the male bodies of Christ, bathing boys[1] and working-class men.[2] But the essay centres round a reading of 'Pied Beauty' as expressive of Hopkins's 'gay aesthetic'.[3]

The *gloria*[4] which opens the poem energizes the first period,[5] beginning almost

---

1 In 'Epithalamium', Phillips, pp. 179–80.
2 'dehumanizing': Lynch, 'Recovering Hopkins', p. 111.
3 op. cit, 113.
4 The 'Gloria' is a section of the Introductory Rites of the Roman Catholic mass, beginning 'Gloria in excelsis Deo et in terra pax hominibus bonae voluntatis', or (in the English version) 'Glory to God in the highest, and peace to his people on Earth' (*Pope John Sunday Missal*, ed. by Mgr. Michael Buckley (Essex: Mayhew, 1978), p. 514).
5 i.e. first sentence; ll. 1–6.

casually with 'dappled things' and moving through particulars that span the four elements as well as animal, vegetable, and mineral realms. [. . .] The human enters only indirectly, first by the farmer's alterations of the landscape and then by the impersonal tools of 'all trades.' Would not the logical next step be to praise the piedness of humankind? Or at least – since Hopkins tends to slight women – the variegations among men? And might not these variegations include sexual ones? Would not, that is, the logical next step involve a *gloria* that would include the very gayness this *style* is already echoing?

I think it would, and that to understand the leap to contrariety in the next line is to understand Hopkins's ambivalence regarding his homosexuality – and the spiritual coordinates of this ambivalence. 'All things counter' is a withdrawal from the expectable human object into all *things*: but it is also an engagement of an unexpected contrariety. Could this not be the only way of accommodating the fully human by one whose own best artistic and spiritual impulses are so closely linked to the *peccatum contra naturam*?[6] The very generality of this formula, in contrast to the specificity of the preceding catalogue, invites us so to read the accommodation.

Especially when the paired opposites that follow are by no means ultimate contraries – 'swift, slow; sweet, sour; adazzle, dim,' and the poem ends with a unisexual fathering-forth that illuminates the association of 'things . . . original' with spareness and strangeness. On this basis, one must argue with Hillis Miller's reading of the poem as affirming a deity who transcends and reconciles contraries. There simply are no ultimate contraries here, and the affirmation is a hesitant one. The second period of the poem [. . .] is far less energized in its movement, far less convincingly specific in its catalogue. It is hesitant, as if reluctant to unfold in language the specific sensual implications of 'all things counter.' The parenthetical '(who knows how?)' is a wondering, in both senses: an awe-full exclamation, but also a question about the etiology of variance.[7] And the poems shrinks from an answer, shrinks by withdrawing to its original subject. And then it shrinks into a line and a half of silence before the minimal amen-like articulation: 'Praise him.'

From **Isobel Armstrong, *Victorian Poetry: Poetry, Poetics and Politics*** (London: Routledge, 1993), pp. 426–7

> Armstrong, like Miller, foregrounds the way that the doubleness of pied things (being two colours, being both like and unlike one another) resolves into a kind of unity, but where Miller sees this unity as ultimately having its roots in an identification of nature with Christ, Armstrong reads the poem politically as proposing outdated or static class and gender categories.

In the plenitude of 'dappled things' in 'Pied Beauty', despite the insistent parallelism of alliteration and rhyme, the world seems to be breaking down into a discontinuous, dappled series of discrete objects and attributes without a principle

---

6   Sin against nature (i.e. homosexuality).
7   etiology: Causation.

of unity. It is 'spare' (unique, like something left over, the exception), 'fickle' (inconsistent) and 'freckled', full of variety. And yet it is a world unified 'past change' because it is precisely the dissimilarity, dappledness, stippledness, piecedness, precisely a relationship of difference, which is the source of relationship. It 'couples' things, not by consisting of mere variety and contrast but by *constituting* relationships. 'Couple-colour', significantly leaping the gap between noun and adjective by being compounded and almost allowing 'couple' to act as a verb, means not only *two colours*, disjunct parts side by side, but *coupled or coupling colour*, acting as copula, establishing Being or stress, and moving to that structure which we can conceptualise through difference.[1]

So far the poem seems unthreatened by problems. Perhaps a hint of trouble can be seen in the fact that this celebration of difference can operate best through the pastoral or the rural. The 'trades' with their differentiated skills are apparently rural trades, that world which Hopkins himself admitted was becoming obsolete and forgotten: it is 'spare', left over, the exception. [. . .] The poem arrests us in a lost history and social order to demonstrate the lost understanding of relation through difference, a history where individuals were defined through their uniqueness, and the uniqueness of their language, and not in terms of an aggregation of parts. It seems that we *need* an undemocratic social order to understand true uniqueness and true form and the uniqueness of language. It also suggests that 'couple-colour', the compound acting as a verb or copula, with its intimation of sexual union and copulation, a world coupling in an infinite series of ordered marital unions, can only occur in a world of fixed gender relations. The strictness of this position is particularly striking when one remembers Hopkins's own sexual longing for his male friends.

The 'Terrible Sonnets'

See Key Poems, pp. 146–52, for the poems.

From **W. H. Gardner,** *Gerard Manley Hopkins: A Study of Poetic Idiosyncrasy in Relation to Poetic Tradition* (London: Secker & Warburg, 1948), 2 vols, Vol. 1, pp. 174–9, 252–3

Gardner was one of the great Hopkins scholars of the twentieth century. His editorial work with N. H. MacKenzie resulted in the publication in 1967 of the highly regarded and authoritative fourth edition of Hopkins's poems. His Penguin collection of the *Poems and Prose of Gerard Manley Hopkins* has been very frequently reprinted since it came out in 1953. This extract is from an earlier book, one of the first studies to be dedicated entirely to Hopkins. Gardner reads the 'Terrible Sonnets' in the light of Shakespearean tragedy. Later in this extract he goes on to consider Hopkins's use of the sonnet form.

---

1   copula: a link or connection.

An underthought derived from *Job* and from the highly charged world of Shakespearian tragedy helps to give poignancy and universality to Hopkins's intensely personal later sonnets.[1] That he had been deeply impressed by the power of the heath-scenes in *King Lear*[2] is suggested by the opening of one four-lined fragment:

> 'Strike, churl; hurl, cheerless wind, then;'[3]

But just as great representative characters like Job, Jeremiah, Hamlet and Lear seem to endure and epitomize in their little world of man a whole macrocosm of suffering, so these sonnets of Hopkins [. . .] are welded by the evocative quality of their imagery into a great disjointed soliloquy, the utterance of a protagonist comparable in tragic significance to those mentioned above. These sonnets are cries 'like dead letters'[4] from man to God, cries which

> 'huddle in a main, a chief
> Woe, world-sorrow; on an age-old anvil wince and sing –'[5]

This latter image is the tragic echo of that eager plea made ten years earlier:

> 'With an anvil-ding
> And with fire in him forge thy will.'[6]

The man who desired to be hammered into shape now complains that he is being hammered *out* of shape, destroyed by the weight of the blows. And as the tempest in Lear's mind was caused by *filial* ingratitude, so this priest's turns of tempest were partly induced by what he (after Jeremiah) virtually describes as divine ingratitude:

> 'Wert thou my enemy, O thou my friend,
> How wouldst thou worse, I wonder, than thou dost,
> Defeat, thwart me?'[7]

In Hopkins's 'winter world',[8] as in the tragic worlds of Lear, Hamlet and Macbeth, all is cheerless, dark and deadly because it is the antithesis of his imagined spring world of productiveness and righteous self-fulfilment

---

1   underthought: allusion beneath the surface of the text.
2   i.e. Act III Scenes 1, 2 and 4, Act 4 Scene 1 of *King Lear*. Act 3 Scene 2 opens with Lear's speech beginning 'Blow, winds, and crack your cheeks! rage! blow!'
3   'Strike, churl; hurl, cheerless wind, then; heltering hail / May's beauty massacre and wispèd clouds grow / Out on the giant air; tell Summer No, / Bid joy back, have at the harvest, keep Hope pale' (Phillips, p. 167).
4   'I wake and feel', l. 7.
5   'No worst, there is none', l. 5.
6   'The Wreck of the Deutschland', st. 10, l. 1.
7   'Justus quidem tu es', ll. 5–7. Jeremiah: see *Key Poems*, p. 158, n. 3.
8   'To R. B.', l. 13.

'See, banks and brakes
Now, leavèd how thick! lacèd they are again
With fretty chervil . . .'[9]

Like Hamlet, he is worried about the definition and performance of his heaven-appointed duty. It is the lot of both men 'to seem the stranger', partly through intellectual idiosyncrasy, partly through religious or moral persuasion. Even the rare cynical mood of ['My own heart let me have more pity on'] may be matched not only by Hamlet but also by certain utterances of Lear and Macbeth.

Several times, in the *Letters*, Hopkins speaks of his own 'blackguardly nature'; and his abnormal sense of personal imperfection was comparable, in its effects, to the stricken conscience of a Macbeth. As Macbeth murdered sleep, so Hopkins suffered night-terrors for what seemed, to his scrupulous mind, commensurate crimes. We can never read the first line of ['I wake, and feel the fell of dark'] —

'I wake and feel the *fell of dark*, not day' —

without associating this hairy beast of darkness with another memorable phrase – the 'fell of hair' which would rouse and stir at a dismal treatise and at the phantoms of guilt.[10]

Small wonder if Hopkins, like Lear, felt the approach of madness. [. . .]

But the most striking expression of this *underthought* or disguised reference is in the sestet of the sonnet which speaks of world-sorrow – ['No worst, there is none']. In an early encounter with God, Hopkins, looking *upwards*, had been overawed by His majesty, trodden 'hard down by the horror of height'.[11] Now, after his encounter with the world, and bruised by God's buffeting, thwarting hand, he must look *downwards* into a bottomless pit of evil, doubt and despair

'O the mind, mind has mountains; cliffs of fall
Frightful, sheer, no-man-fathomed. Hold them cheap
May who ne'er hung there.'[12]

Obsessed with the thought of human vice, the deranged Lear cries

'There's hell, there's darkness, there is the sulphurous pit.';[13]

but a more significant association of height and danger begins when Gloucester says to Edgar

'There is a cliff whose high and bending head
Looks fearfully in the confined deep;'[14]

---

9 'Justus quidem tu es', l. 9–11.
10 *Macbeth*, 5.5.11–13: 'my fell of hair / Would at a dismal treatise rouse and stir / As life were in't: I have supp'd full with horrors'.
11 'The Wreck of the Deutschland', st. 2 l. 7.
12 'No worst, there is none', ll. 9–11.
13 *King Lear* 4.6.129–130.
14 *King Lear* 4.1.73–74.

and the amazing visual efficacy of Edgar's description of the vertiginous height as seen from the brink is among the unforgettable things in all poetry. So Keats testified, when he spoke of himself as 'one who gathers samphire, dreadful trade!'[15] The spiritual counterpart of such a precarious occupation is easily imagined: it is the tension between the upward pull of high principles and aims and the downward pull of physical and moral weakness – the flesh and the Devil. The life-line attaching man to God cuts across the horizontal of his daily needs, and at the point of contact (and greatest tension) he must gather his 'samphire', perform his pre-ordained task. With Keats it was to glean his brain, to express himself through poetry; with Hopkins it was the more complex task of self-expression in art and self-effacement in his vocation. Hopkins 'translates' the precipice into the supernatural order by adding the epithet 'no-man-fathomed'; and the words 'hung there' suggest the daring climber who, his life-line broken, is left clinging to the sheer cliff-face with no help from above and certain destruction below.

In 'Spelt from Sibyl's Leaves,' regarded usually as a predecessor to the 'terrible' sonnets, Hopkins takes his mechanical solution of expanding and slowing his sonnet lines to its outermost limits: 'my long sonnet, the longest, I still say, ever made; longest by its own proper length, namely by the length of its lines; for anything can be made long by eking, by tacking, by trains, tails and flounces' [L I, p. 246]. Hopkins's claim to have written 'the longest sonnet' might better be described as the widest sonnet. In this poem, the possible displeasure of losing the end-rhyme, upon which the sonnet form depends, is naturally most pronounced. For example, 'Earnest, earthless, equal, attuneable, vaulty, voluminous, . . . stupendous' must match three lines later with 'Waste; her earliest stars, earlstars, stars principal, overbend us' (1, 4). Whatever else might be said of this extraordinary poem, it is hard, I think, to argue its success as a sonnet.

In 'Carrion Comfort' the walls move back in, as it were, to form a conventional structure. Hopkins resorts to the more sensible use of alexandrines, which he had used elsewhere in imitation perhaps of Sidney who began his sonnet sequence with this technique.[16] In any case the moderate mechanical solution which Hopkins had elsewhere employed works magnificently:

> Not, I'll not, carrion comfort, Despair, not feast on thee;
>   Not untwist – slack they may be – these last strands of man
> In me or, most weary, cry *I can no more*. I can;
> Can something, hope, wish day come, not choose not to be.

In the remaining of the so-called 'terrible' sonnets, the walls are narrowed to their most conventional confinement. Hopkins returns to the standard sonnet form, 14 lines, 10 syllables each, and this time without the complex metaphors, compound nouns, and inversions which lengthened his earlier sonnets so

---

15 Keats's letter to Benjamin Haydon, 10–11 May 1817, applies Edgar's description of a person harvesting samphire, an edible plant, by clinging to a cliff-face, to his own situation fighting off despondency and anxiety.
16 alexandrines: lines of six iambic feet. Sir Philip Sidney's sequence of 108 sonnets, *Astrophil and Stella*, was composed in 1582 but not published until nine years later.

successfully. Mechanically, he relies only upon syntactical breaks and pauses, and monosyllabic language. It would seem then, in light of his earlier successes, that as the content of his poetry turns most grave, the chosen form puts them at risk of being 'light,' 'tripping,' and 'trifling.' They, of course, are not so, and what keeps them from being so is the same quality which earned them the name 'terrible.' 'The mere gravity of the thought,' Hopkins observed in his earlier discussion of the sonnet's length, 'compels a longer dwelling on the words' [L II, p. 86]. Consider, as a sampling of this theory, the opening lines of these sonnets: 'No worst, there is none. Pitched past pitch of grief'; 'To seem the stranger lies my lot, my life'; 'I wake and feel the fell of .dark, not day'; 'Patience, hard thing! the hard thing but to pray'; 'My own heart let me more have pity on; let . . .'. The graveness or 'gravity' of these thoughts – involuntary or 'unbidden' as it may have been – saves these sonnets from the hazards of their shortness. The lyrical success of these poems, in other words, relies to a very large extent upon their emotional weight, which must lengthen, just as surely as extra syllables and inversions do, the reading of each line.

It may also be that Hopkins, by this time, had discovered the error of his earlier thinking that the English sonnet was substantially shorter than the Italian. His observation of the difference in the number of individual syllabic sounds in a given line is quite true. However, what he does not observe in his remarks to Dixon is something which his contemporary, Dante Gabriel Rossetti (moving between Italian and English), seems to have known intuitively, namely, the semantic efficiency of the English language when compared to that of the Italian. While an Italian sonnet may contain thirteen syllables in a line, the line likely says only as much as, or even less, than a ten-syllable English rendering of the same thoughts. Since English says more with fewer sounds, one might argue that conversion of the sonnet from Italian to English presents the problem opposite to that of which Hopkins complains – that there is, after translating what Petrarch said, room left over. There is room for more sound, but not more thought. The key then is to slow, as it were, the sounds one has. One can do this, as Hopkins's suggests, with gravity – weightier words.

For even with periodic and syntactical breaks within the lines and some eccentric enjambment like 'wear / y' in [. . .] ('To seem the stranger . . .') and 'smile /'s not' in [. . .] ('My own heart . . .'), these sonnets are nonetheless more conventional in their form than anything else the mature Hopkins wrote, and therefore depend upon weighty emotional content to 'lengthen' them satisfactorily. Hence, the despair with which they are wrought was apparently not only an unnerving fact of Hopkins's life, but also, by his own expressed critical standards, an essential ingredient in the poems' artistic success. This is not to discount at all the apparent personal turmoil which the poet experienced, but to point out his certain consciousness, as he wrote and revised these poems, that unlike his earlier efforts, these sonnets relied upon emotional gravity and even despair for their artistic success.

From **Yvor Winters, *The Function of Criticism: Problems and Exercises*** (London: Routledge & Kegan Paul, 1962), pp. 104, 107–8, 113, 145

> Yvor Winters' attack on Hopkins depends on a rejection of what Winters sees as the Romantic valorization of self-expression, expression of selfhood, at the expense of clear, rational, 'exact' language and thought.[1]
> Winters was a highly regarded poet as well as a critic, and besides both of these things, a breeder of Airedale dogs. Of 'The Windhover' he wrote
>
>> At the present time I own a young dog who seems to me exceptionally beautiful [. . .] No less than Hopkins's falcon, he is one of God's little creatures [. . .] I am fairly certain that his moral character is more admirable than that of the bird. Yet it would never occur to me to write a poem describing his beauty and then stating that the beauty of Christ was similar but merely greater. To do so would seem to me ludicrous, and to many it would seem blasphemous. Yet there is no essential difference between my dog and Hopkins's bird; the bird has the advantage merely of the Romantic and sentimental feeling attached to birds as symbols of the free and unrestrained spirit, a feeling derived very largely from Shelley's *Skylark* and from a handful of similar – and similarly bad – poems of the past century and a half.[2] Hopkins' poem employs a mechanical and a very easy formula [. . .] To defend this sort of thing with pretentious remarks about the "sacramental view of nature" is merely foolish [. . .].[3]
>
> The poem Winters is dealing with in the extract below is 'No Worst, There is None'. See Key Poems, **pp. 149–50.**

It is the business of the poet [. . .] to make a statement in words about an experience; the statement must be in some sense and in a fair measure acceptable rationally; and the feeling communicated should be proper to the rational understanding of the experience. [. . .] But with the development of romantic theory in the eighteenth, nineteenth, and twentieth centuries, there has been an increasing tendency to suppress the rational in poetry and as far as may be to isolate the emotional. This tendency makes at best for an incomplete poetry and makes at worst for a very confused poetry. [. . .]

This is not a poem about the effects of violent emotion in general; it is a poem about a particular violent emotion experienced by the poet. The nearest thing to a statement of motive occurs in the first line and a half of the sestet; but what are these mountains of the mind?[4] One does not enquire because one holds them

---

1   Winters, *The Function of Criticism*, p. 105.
2   Percy Bysshe Shelley's 1820 poem 'To a Skylark' begins: 'Hail to thee, blithe spirit / Bird thou never wert – / That from heaven, or near it, / Pourest thy full heart / In profuse strains of unpremeditated art.'
3   Winters, *The Function of Criticism* pp. 133–4.
4   'O the mind, mind has mountains: cliffs of fall / Frightful, sheer, no-man-fathomed.'

cheap, but because one has hung on so many oneself, so various in their respective terrors, that one is perplexed to assign a particular motive. One is inclined to ask: 'What do you know of these matters? Why are you so secretive? And above all, why are you so self-righteous in your secretiveness?' [. . .]

[S]ince he cannot move us by telling us why he himself is moved, he must try to move us by belaboring his emotion. He says, in effect: 'Share my fearful emotion, for the human mind is subject to fearful emotions.' But why should we wish to share an emotion so ill sponsored? Nothing could be more rash. We cannot avoid sharing a part of it, for Hopkins has both skill and genius; but we cannot avoid being confused by the experience and suspecting in it a fine shade of the ludicrous. Who is this man to lead us so far and blindfold into violence? This kind of thing is a violation of our integrity; it is somewhat beneath the dignity of man. [. . .]

If [. . .] we have a poet who is concerned with the expressions of his own inscape (self-expression) and with the inscapes of natural objects and with little else, we may expect him to produce poems which are badly organized, and loosely emotional, and which endeavor to express emotions obscure in their origins and to express those emotions in terms of natural details of landscape to which the emotions are irrelevant. And poems of this kind are what Hopkins most often wrote. [. . .] Hopkins is a poet of fragments for the most part, and it is only if one can enjoy a chaos of details afloat in vague emotion that one can approve of the greater part of his work.

From **Eric Griffiths, *The Printed Voice of Victorian Poetry***
(Oxford: Clarendon Press, 1989), pp. 298–313

Griffiths's reading of 'To Seem the Stranger Lies My Lot' explores the emotional significance of the sounds of the poem. See Key Poems **pp. 146–8**.

It is poignant how 'Father and mother dear' may sound at first like the poeticized opening of a letter ('Dear father and mother'), as if it were going to have that 'strain of address, which writing should usually have' [L III, p. 380] according to Hopkins's ideal. Address has broken under strain, though; the 'Father and mother dear' turns out to be only the third-personal subject of an indicative sentence, the poem being not directly addressed to his parents or anyone else. The poignancy it has is like that of a letter that was never sent. The unspeakable gravity of what conversion meant for him can be seen in the oblique which cuts the line at 'And he my peace / my parting'. Had he put a comma there, it would have seemed as if Christ were simply and cumulatively these two distinct things (compare 'Pass me my coat, my umbrella, and my gloves'); had he put a hyphen, it would have looked as if it was always Christ's nature to split families in this way (he often used a hyphen to express paradoxes which he considered permanent, especially the paradoxes of Christ's nature as 'God-made-flesh'[1]). But it was Hopkins's experience as a Catholic convert to live a life whose essence hung on a contingency, a

1   In '(The Soldier)', in Phillips, p. 168.

blunt, historical fact which had assumed for most of his countrymen the status and potency of a spiritual truth: the schism from Rome. The impact of Christ on that life was then neither a revelation of the essential nature of Christ's bearing on His world, but nor was it possible to extricate the peace Hopkins found in Christ from 'moral and social severance'. The circumstances compounded the essential and the extrinsic in a manner wonderfully linked together so that it was hard to speak without becoming contentious and even keeping silence could not preserve neutrality. The 'I' in 'my peace / my parting' replies to such a situation; it cannot be spoken and yet it is that in the line which most needs to be said.

He had not at first imagined that things had to be this way with his family. He had urged his father to call on Joseph, Mary, and Jesus in the confidence that 'the prayers of this Holy Family wd. in a few days put an end to estrangements for ever' [L III, p. 94] – the conjunction of 'in a few days' and 'for ever' hopes for too much too quickly, as he was to learn. In the poem, he sustains an instant of hope through the ambiguity which arises from a poetic inversion: 'Father and mother dear, / Brothers and sisters are in Christ' says, under its breath, as it were, before the impetus of syntactic completion takes the hope away, that his relations *are* 'in Christ', though Hopkins knew that orthodox Catholic doctrine on the absence of salvation outside the Church had by some Catholics been interpreted as contradicting such hopes. The syntax of the hope approaches spoken English, the curb to the hope turns the poem's syntax away from speech: 'Brothers and sisters are in Christ not near' (rather than the more idiomatic 'Brothers and sisters are not near in Christ') – the line makes a tentative approach to a returned language of domestic ease, but the words for a rapprochement are askew and escape from what he might personally like to say, turning into a poetic conventionality, a discipline beyond him, which breaks up the nearest and dearest by laying stress through the rhyme on the fact that the 'dear' are 'not near'. The poeticality of the line then flushes with just that impetus to plain speaking which it thwarts. 'Near and dear', 'nearest and dearest' – when he wrote this sonnet, these had long (for at least a century) been common reflexes of the language to refer to one's family. [. . .] The rhyme has behind it an amassed force of habitual usage which presses on Hopkins's lines, which they long to accommodate, but which they turn from as the emphatic, alliterating 'not' snatches away the chime of 'near' back to 'dear'; the proximity in sound of the words makes only the more resonant the fact of separation. Such moments recur in the mature Hopkins, moments which gauge the distance of his poetry, his created self, from the habitual readiness of the English language to a native speaker's hand and mouth, moments at which across that elected distance he recovers the possibility of a distinct utterance.

The language stands for his family, and he can do in it what he could not do for them – bring it over to himself without fracturing its identity. His style here is not 'at home with' the English language, nor is it homely, but it 'comes home', though Hopkins's sense of where his home lay, in his art as in his calling, was not with his parents or with their ideas. It was where all surrenders come home: 'As we drove home the stars came out thick: I leant back to look at them and my heart opening more than usual praised our Lord to and in whom all that beauty comes home'.[2]

---

2   J, p. 254.

His style lies, with minute consistency, along that oblique, unvoiceable line between 'peace' and 'parting', a line which marks the substance of his plight and the grounds of his achievement. [. . .]
When the Society of Jesus sent Hopkins to Ireland, they put on the map for him a condition of exile he already knew. The opening lines of 'To seem the stranger . . .' tell the loss, the rest of the poem goes on to discover the gain in that loss, a gain he described to Patmore as the taking of an 'external survey' of English political self-confidence: 'It is good to be in Ireland to hear how enemies, and those rhetoricians, can treat the things that are unquestioned at home'[3] [. . .]
Given Hopkins's nationalistic ardour, calling England the 'wife' to his thought was more than a colour of rhetoric; a professed celibate, he used the word 'wife' with some emphasis. [. . .]
The vow of celibacy could look like the sour grapes of a rejected suitor; the England he wooed would not hear him. He was bound to sympathize with the Irish as a Catholic people, yet he disliked the nationalist agitation; he was a faithful servant of the Church but gravelled by the involvement of brother-priests with illegal organizations in the cause of Irish independence. The grinding of religious on political loyalties – 'thóughts agáinst thoughts ín groans grínd' and 'We hear our hearts grate on themselves'[4] – works into his verse, into its endured torsions, its composed recoil: 'pleading, plead', 'I: I', 'now; now'. The richness of the euphony that he creates in the internal chimes of his lines looms up against a reader-aloud as a thicket of vocal hurdles, of impacted felicities which baffle themselves and make euphony itself a dilemma for the voice – is one to try to preserve the flow or to bring out these small eddies of the sounds in the verse? There is, for example, almost no possibility of elision between words in the closing lines; the verse compels the voice to make a considerable severance between the words if they are to be distinctly audible. Try saying 'hell's spell': the discrimination asked between voiced and unvoiced 's' gives you pause. The style is remarkably achieved as a supreme dexterity which is the opposite of fluent; it is truly a cutting and straining of the windpipe. You are asked to feel the stretching of grammatical units across line-ends both as a racking and as a perseverance, to see the lineation as shredding the continuity of phrases, collapsing the verse into wrecked utterances like 'Only what word', cries which search out an eloquence and then, around the line-end, are given hardly foreseeable sustenance.
The writing, though, contains these implicit requests for hearing and vocalization in order to convey the fact that these are things Hopkins says to no human being ('this to hoard unheard') and that when they are heard by God in the silence of His knowledge, they appear to be 'unheeded'; the poem is a supplication for hearing rather than an oratorical performance before an audience of whose attention the poet is sure. The cadence of its final line, that extremely beautiful sound of longing and anticipation which he procures by supplying the English with a new noun, 'a . . . began' (something which was begun in the past, his discipline of self-perfection, but which has lost the novel charm a 'beginning' might have for him), feels the texture of religious waiting, its tremors and its impatiences held within the security of a pattern whose completion is trusted in but which will

---

3 L III, p. 367.
4 'Spenl from Sibyl's Leaves', l. 14, 'Patience, hard thing', l. 9, in Phillips, p. 170.

settle itself not quite as might have been expected, just as the closing rhyme of 'ban'/ 'began' in this sonnet, rhyming a monosyllable and a disyllable, stays slightly out of kilter, off-key.

From **J. Hillis Miller, *The Disappearance of God*** (Cambridge, Mass.: Belknap Press of Harvard University Press, 1963), pp. 352–5, 359

Miller puts Hopkins's 'Terrible Sonnets' into the context of what he sees as a characteristic late nineteenth-century experience of spiritual desolation.

Hopkins wavers neither in his faith nor in his vocation. His experience is not incompatible with Catholicism. It is spiritual desolation, a vanishing of God from the soul which, as St. Ignatius said, is God's way of testing the soul, and showing it how powerless it is by itself. But though the inner experience of Hopkins' last years is perfectly compatible with Catholic tradition, it is also to be understood in the context of the spiritual history of the nineteenth century. The experience recorded in the 'terrible' sonnets, and in the late letters and retreat notes, is a striking example of the way the nineteenth century was, for many writers, a time of the no longer and not yet, a time of the absence of God. Hopkins has, beyond all his contemporaries, the most shattering experience of the disappearance of God.

Spiritual desolation as Hopkins knows it means first of all an isolation like that the poet suffered at the time of his early poems. The self is cut off from everything outside and shrinks into the impenetrable enclosure of itself. To find oneself in this imprisonment is like being suddenly awakened in the middle of a night so dark that the darkness seems to press in on all sides like the fell of some furry beast [. . .].[1] This darkness is both natural and transnatural, a dark night both of the soul and of the body. The self is cut off from God's sustaining power and dries up like a choked well or fountain. No vein of the gospel proffer feeds it.[2] The self also ceases to participate in the on-going vitality of nature. [. . .] Cut off from its own inscape, the self no longer shares in the pied beauty of the inscapes of nature. In Hopkins' last poems natural images appear only as indirect metaphors for an experience which is transnatural. It is as if the poet were blind and dying of thirst, but it is a spiritual blindness and a spiritual thirst, for which physical blindness and thirst are mere figures [. . .]. The basis of these last poems is no longer an experience of nature, as in 'The Windhover,' but an experience taking place in the *ultima solitudo* of the self.

This isolation of the self from nature and God generates an acutely negative experience of space and time. In place of the constructive natural time of 'Hurrahing in Harvest,' or the fiercely disintegrative time of nature's bonfire, the sonnets of desolation describe time as a vertical fall.[3] There is a complete absence of any

---

1   'I wake, and feel the fell of dark', l. 1.
2   'The Wreck of the Deutschland', st. 4 ll. 7–8.
3   Nature's bonfire: 'That Nature is a Heraclitean Fire'.

sustaining pressure, and time is experienced as the plunge of the unsupported self into the chasm of its own nothingness. Each moment reproduces the nonentity of the one before, and since there are no distinguishable surroundings it is as if the self were pitching with infinite speed into an unfathomable gulf:

> O the mind, mind has mountains; cliffs of fall
> Frightful, sheer, no-man-fathomed.[4] [. . .]

Insomnia is a direct experience of time as a fall. The man who is pitched past pitch of grief into the abysses of the mind has but one comfort in the whirlwind: each day ends in a rehearsal of death, sleep. But suppose sleep will not come? Then the 'black hours'[5] of the night lengthen out until the sufferer is left at an infinite distance from the daylight time in which nature is visible, and in which the moments are a measure of change and growth. The moments of insomnia measure nothing, nothing but the repeating nothingness of the self in its endless fall. [. . .]

The most painful characteristic of this infinite space and time is the breakdown of language. Words are the meeting-place of self, nature, and God the Word. These three have split apart, and as a result language loses its efficacy. Words, instead of reaching out to touch things and give them over to man, no longer have strength enough to leave the self at all. Thwarted by some mysterious decree of heaven or hell, words become the opaque walls of the poet's interior prison. His speech becomes a stuttering staccato of alliterative monosyllables, each word thrown out despairingly in a brief spasm of energy, and each word closing in on itself with explosive or hissing consonants, as if to express, in its isolation from the words around it, the poet's failure to escape from his solitude:

> Only what word
> Wisest my heart breeds dark heaven's baffling ban
> Bars or hell's spell thwarts.[6] [. . .]

Cast outward by the mind to reach nature or God, words fall endlessly through a shadowy void and touch neither things nor the God who made them. Abandoned by God, Hopkins cries out for grace, but his words have lost their virtue and cannot reach their destination. No human words can reach a God who has withdrawn to an infinite distance:

> And my lament
> Is cries countless, cries like dead letters sent
> To dearest him that lives alas! away.[7] [. . .]

Language, nature, space, time – with the failure of grace all the ways fail in

---

4   'No worst, there is none', ll. 9–10.
5   'I wake and feel', l. 2.
6   'To seem the stranger', ll. 11–13.
7   'I wake and feel', ll. 6–8.

which the self can escape from itself and establish connections, with nature or with God. [. . .]

Hopkins, who seems so different from other nineteenth-century writers who suffered the absence of God, in reality ends in a similar place.

3

Key Poems

Introduction

Hopkins insisted that his poems were for reading aloud. He was very concerned that they should be understood by his readers: the notations he wanted printed with the poems (and which contributed to the poems' rejection by editors) were designed to show the reader how to say the lines. The accents that appear on some of the vowels in the poems are Hopkins's marks indicating where stresses should fall when the poem is read out: in some cases readers will disagree with Hopkins's sense of the scansion, and should feel at liberty to voice the lines as they think best. Hopkins supplied the notations because he thought they helped with clarity. When Bridges and Dixon failed to understand some of his poems Hopkins was concerned and sometimes hurt. 'Obscurity I do and will try to avoid so far as is consistent with excellences higher than clearness at a first reading. As for affectation I do not believe I am guilty of it.'[1] But he recognized that the originality of his poetry, the qualities that make it unmistakeable for any other Victorian poet's work, could develop into faults. 'Design, pattern or what I am in the habit of calling "inscape" is what I above all aim at in poetry. Now it is the virtue of design, pattern, or inscape to be distinctive and it is the vice of distinctiveness to become queer. This vice I cannot have escaped'.[2] Towards the end of his life he realized that his poetry had become so full of linguistic coinages and syntactical and metrical innovations that it was becoming too difficult for even a sympathetic reader to understand, and decided characteristically to remedy the situation not by changing his poetry but by adding a prose explanation to the poems:

> one thing I am now resolved on, [. . .] is to prefix short prose arguments to some of my pieces. [. . .] Plainly if it is possible to express a sub[t]le and recondite thought on a subtle and recondite subject in a subtle and recondite way and with great felicity and perfection, in the end, something must be sacrificed, with so trying a task, in the process, and this may be the being at once, nay perhaps even the being without explanation at all, intelligible.[3]

1   L I, p. 54
2   L I, p. 66.
3   L I, pp. 265–6.

The evidence of his last poems, however, suggests that his style was in any case changing: compare 'Tom's Garland' (**pp. 154–6**), written in 1887, the year he decided to add prose arguments, with 'To R. B.' (1889, **pp. 159–60**), and it is clear that intelligibility was becoming less problematic for him.

In other words, Hopkins intended that his poetry should be accessible, if not wholly so on a first reading, then at least in parts, and the whole poem later. Comparatively little historical or cultural knowledge is required for reading Hopkins, though some knowledge of figures and ideas in Christianity is important. Though he himself was highly educated, his poems (compared with, say, Tennyson's or Swinburne's) make few classical allusions, and their references to contemporary events and people are rare. Instead, Hopkins demands from the reader a creative and imaginative approach to the richness and detail of the poems and a willingness to read for the pleasure of the sounds and the phrases that immediately strike home even where the overall meaning of a line is baffling. Working with Hopkins's poetry is a powerful reminder of the fact that reading is an active process, an interaction, not a passive transfer of meaning from text to reader. There is a great deal for the reader to do: interpretation is a deeply satisfying business with poems in which so many phrases and even words are densely packed with meanings, often expressing strong emotions in rich sonic effects. The headnotes and annotations accompanying the texts that follow do not in any sense claim to supply definitive readings, only to act as starting places for individual interpretations.

Unless indicated otherwise, texts of the poems are from the Phillips edition (see Abbreviations).

Key Poems

Heaven-Haven

The first draft of this brief poem was written in July 1864, while Hopkins was an undergraduate in Oxford. He gave a copy to Robert Bridges's cousin Digby Dolben, a young man to whom Hopkins was greatly attracted. The text here is taken from the Williams edition.

Heaven-Haven [1]

A nun takes the veil

I have desired to go
　　Where springs not fail,
To fields where flies no sharp and sided hail [2]
　　And a few lilies blow. [3]

And I have asked to be
　　Where no storms come,
Where the green swell is in the havens dumb,
　　And out of the swing of the sea. [4]

1　The title refers to the last line of the early seventeenth-century Anglican religious poet George Herbert's 'The Size': 'These seas are tears, and Heaven the haven' (*The Poems of Gerard Manley Hopkins*, 4th edn, ed. W. H. Gardner and N. H. MacKenzie (Oxford: Oxford University Press, 1967), p. 248).

2　Phillips compares this line with Tennyson's description of Avilion in 'Morte d'Arthur' (1842): 'Where falls not hail, or rain or any snow / Nor ever wind blows loudly; but it lies / Deep-meadowed, happy, fair with summer-lawns / And bowery hollows crowned with summer seas' (Phillips, p. 311).

3　Hopkins uses lilies as an image for purity in 'The Wreck of the Deutschland', st. 20 and 21, and of beauty in 'Duns Scotus's Oxford'.

4　The image of the haven or harbour is conventional as a metaphor for the contemplative life, but has particular potency in the context of Hopkins's interest in shipwrecks: see 'The Loss of the Eurydice' (in Phillips, pp. 135–8) and of course 'The Wreck of the Deutschland' (Key Poems, **pp. 113–28**).

Where Art Thou Friend

This sonnet has been the subject of conflicting interpretations by Hopkins critics. Robert Bernard Martin identifies the poem as being about Robert Bridges's cousin, Digby Dolben. Julia Saville feels that 'to assume the friend is Dolben, while justifiable, misses the more important point that the love expressed here is considered sublime because the object of yearning is not *visibly* present to the speaker'.[1] But Catherine Phillips argues that the poem has convincingly been shown 'to have quite different origins and implications' and cites Rudy Bremer's argument that the 'friend' may refer to the reader rather than to Dolben.[2,3] The majority of recent critics seem to agree, though, that the poem at least reflects Hopkins's relationship with Dolben. Dated late April 1865, the sonnet was written during a time when Hopkins was anxious about the spiritual consequences of his attraction to the younger man. Norman White suggests that Hopkins had difficulty casting out the thought of Dolben despite encouragement from one of his spiritual advisers: 'it seems likely that Hopkins's confessor, Canon Liddon, forbade him to have contact with Dolben, except by letter; the "forbidden subject" and "dangerous things" occur in [Hopkins's] confessional notes several times within this period.'[4]

'Where art thou friend'

Where art thou friend, whom I shall never see,
Conceiving whom I must conceive amiss?
Or sunder'd from my sight in the age that is
Or far-off promise of a time to be;
Thou who canst best accept the certainty
That thou hadst borne proportion in my bliss,
That likest in me either that or this, —
Oh! even for the weakness of the plea
That I have taken to plead with, — if the sound
Of God's dear pleadings have as yet not moved thee, —
And for those virtues I in thee have found,
Who say that had I known I had approved thee, —
For these, make all the virtues to abound, —
No, but for Christ who hath foreknown and loved thee.

1   Julia Saville, *A Queer Chivalry: The Homoerotic Asceticism of Gerard Manley Hopkins* (Charlottesville, Va.: University Press of Virginia, 2000), p. 45.
2   Phillips, p. xix, p. 319.
3   Rudy Bremer, 'Where art thou friend . . .', *Hopkins Quarterly*, 7(1) (spring 1980), pp. 9–14.
4   White, p. 115.

The Wreck of the Deutschland

When Hopkins decided to become a Jesuit he burnt the poems he had written up to that point and 'resolved to write no more, as not belonging to my profession, unless it were by the wish of my superiors'.[1,2] 'The Wreck of the Deutschland' is a magnificent and extraordinary return to English poetry, composed seven years afterwards. In a letter to Dixon, Hopkins explained:

> when in the winter of '75 the Deutschland was wrecked in the mouth of the Thames and five Franciscan nuns, exiles from Germany by the Falck Laws, aboard of her were drowned I was affected by the account and happening to say so to my rector he said that he wished someone would write a poem on the subject. On this hint I set to work and, though my hand was out at first, produced one. I had long had haunting my ear the echo of a new rhythm which I now realised on paper.[3]

This new rhythm – which Hopkins acknowledged was not his own invention, but had rarely been used except in nursery rhymes and folk poetry – was 'sprung rhythm', a system that involved a set number not of syllables but of stresses in each line.[4] It divided up a line into a number of units, each with one, two, three or four syllables but only one stressed one. Sprung rhythm thus allowed Hopkins to have as many syllables as he needed per line, provided he did not exceed a certain number of stresses. In 'The Wreck of the Deutschland', the number of stresses varies from each line of the stanza to the next. In stanzas 1–10 the count is: 2, 3, 4, 3, 5, 5, 4, 6, and in stanzas 11–35 very slightly different: 3, 3, 4, 3, 5, 5, 4, 6. For example, stanza 2's stress pattern (to my ear) works out thus:

> I did say yes
> O at lightning and lashed rod;
> Thou heardst me truer than tongue confess
> Thy terror, O Christ, O God;
> Thou knowest the walls, altar and hour and night:
> The swoon of a heart that the sweep and the hurl of thee trod
> Hard down with a horror of height:
> And the midriff astrain with leaning of, laced with fire of stress.

Sprung rhythm meant that Hopkins could put stressed syllables together without having to have an unstressed one in between: 'why, if it is forcible in prose to

---

1   L II, p. 14.
2   Obviously this did not mean that all the copies were destroyed.
3   L II, p. 14.
4   About his own contribution to sprung rhythm, Hopkins wrote: 'I do not of course claim to have invented *sprung rhythms* but only *sprung rhythm*; I mean that single lines and single instances of it are not uncommon in English [. . .] but what I do in the *Deutschland* etc is to enfranchise them as a regular and permanent principle of scansion' (L I, p. 45).

say "lashed: rod" [with stresses on both syllables], am I obliged to weaken this in verse, which ought to be stronger, not weaker, into "láshed birch-ród", or something?'.[5] Equally, it meant that he could string together a considerable and variable number of unstressed syllables without having to put stresses in between, as in line 8 of stanza 31: 'Startle the poor sheep back! Is the shipwrack then a harvest, does tempest carry the grain for thee?' Hopkins was immensely interested in rhythm, which for him was not simply part of poetic composition but a fundamental property of all aesthetic experience (towards the end of his life he planned a book on 'Rhythm in general. Indeed it is on almost everything elementary and is much of it physics and metaphysics'[6]), but it is not necessary for most readers of his poetry to pay anything like as much attention to it as he did. Sprung rhythm was intended to be flexible and to allow for dramatic reading aloud: as with so many of Hopkins's poems, to get the most out of 'The Wreck of the Deutschland' it should be read, or heard read, aloud, during which process the basics of the rhythm will become clear.[7]

'The Wreck of the Deutschland' was the most important of the poems that Hopkins tried to have published. He sent it first to the Jesuit journal *The Month*, which was edited by a friend of his, Henry Coleridge. Before seeing the poem, Coleridge gave the impression that he would accept it: he told Hopkins that 'there was in America a new sort of poetry which did not rhyme or scan or construe; if mine rhymes and scanned and construed and did not make nonsense or bad morality he did not see why it shd. not do'.[8] But on seeing the poem, Coleridge asked Hopkins to take out the accents marking the stressed syllables. Hopkins refused to excise them, afraid that without them readers would not scan the lines correctly.[9] Whether or not it was entirely for this reason, *The Month* did not publish the poem, and Hopkins did not venture it with any other journal. Norman White suggests that this failure to publish had a profound effect not only on Hopkins's views on publication but also on his choice of poetic projects: 'any answer to the question why Hopkins never again attempted a poem even half as ambitious as "The Wreck of the Deutschland" has to start with this rejection'.[10]

Robert Bridges, who after his first reading of 'The Wreck of the Deutschland' told Hopkins that he would not 'for any money' read it again, printed a warning for readers of the first edition of Hopkins's *Poems*:

---

5 L I, p. 46.
6 L I, p. 254.
7 See Contemporary Documents, **pp. 34–6**, for an excerpt from Hopkins's detailed account of sprung rhythm.
8 L III, p. 138. The reference to unrhymed, unscanned and unconstruing poetry is probably to Whitman.
9 More than a decade after this débâcle, Hopkins was still defending notation (L I, p. 265):

> My meaning surely ought to appear of itself; but in a language like English, and in an age like the present, written words are really matter open and indifferent to the receiving of different and alternative verse-forms, some of which the reader cannot possibly be sure are meant unless they are marked for him. Besides metrical marks are for the performer and such marks are proper in every art.

It went further than notation for scansion: he looked forward to the day when syntax would be notated also: 'it would be an immense advance [. . .] to distinguish the subject, verb, object, and in general to express the construction to the eye' (L I, p. 265).
10 White, p. 259.

the labour spent on this great metrical experiment must have served to establish the poet's prosody and perhaps his diction: therefore the poem stands logically as well as chronologically in the front of his book, like a great dragon folded in the gate to forbid all entrance, and confident in his strength from past success. This editor advises the reader to circumvent him and attack him late in the rear; for he was himself shamefully worsted in a brave frontal assault, the more easily perhaps because both subject and treatment were distasteful to him. A good method of approach is to read stanza 16 aloud to a chance company.[11]

Reading 'The Wreck of the Deutschland' for the first time, and even after that, can indeed be daunting. But it is one of the nineteenth-century's great and extraordinary masterpieces. See Modern Criticism, **pp. 77–90**, for a sampling of the very large number of critical studies of the poem.

To annotate 'The Wreck of the Deutschland' fully would be a book-length project, and at least two major books of this kind exist.[12] On the other hand, an ideal reading of the poem – particularly a first reading – might be one based on a text with no annotations at all, so that the reader would not be distracted from his or her responses. I have compromised by annotating where the meanings of particular words, phrases or even stanzas seem to me to need a little explanation, and to note some of the lexical usages that connect this poem to others in this sourcebook.

The Wreck of the Deutschland

Dec. 6, 7 1875

to the happy memory of five Franciscan nuns, exiles by the Falck Laws,[13]
drowned between midnight and morning of December 7.[14]

---

11 Robert Bridges, 'Notes,' in *Poems of Gerard Manley Hopkins*, ed. Robert Bridges (London: Oxford University Press, 1918), p. 106; Hopkins refers to Bridges's initial response to the poem in a letter of 1877 (L I, pp. 44–7).

12 John E. Keating, SJ, *'The Wreck of the Deutschland': An Essay and Commentary* (Kent, Ohio: Kent State University Press, 1963) and Peter Milward, SJ, *Commentary on G. M. Hopkins's 'The Wreck of the Deutschland'* (Tokyo: Hokuseido, 1968).

13 Adalbert Falk (sometimes spelt Falck) was the Prussian Minister of Culture under the German Chancellor Otto von Bismarck. Falk had a central part in the attempt to extirpate the influence of the Roman Catholic Church, which – particularly since the announcement of the doctrine of papal infallibility in 1870 – was seen by many powerful Protestants in the newly formed German Empire as a threat to political and social stability. By 1875 the Roman Catholic Church had been dealt severe blows, including the banning of religious (rather than civil) marriages and the expulsion of most priests, monks and nuns from Germany. *Kulturkampf*, the struggle between the Church and Bismarck's government, continued for another decade. Of the victims of a Spanish persecution of Roman Catholics, and the sentiment would likely have held for the victims of German intolerance also, Hopkins wrote: 'to be persecuted in a tolerant age is a high distinction' (L III, p. 106).

14 See Contemporary Documents, **pp. 36–7** for *The Times*'s report of the shipwreck.

Part the First

Thou mastering me
God! giver of breath and bread;
World's strand,[15] sway of the sea;
Lord of living and dead;
Thou hast bound bones and veins in me, fastened me flesh,[16]
And after it álmost únmade, what with dread,
Thy doing: and dost thou touch me afresh?
Over again I feel thy finger[17] and find theé.[18]

2

I did say yes[19]
O at lightning and lashed rod;
Thou heardst me truer than tongue confess
Thy terror, O Christ, O God;
Thou knowest the walls, altar and hour and night:
The swoon of a heart that the sweep and the hurl of thee trod
Hard down with a horror of height:
And the midriff astrain with leaning of, laced with fire of stress.[20]

3

The frown of his face
Before me, the hurtle of hell
Behind, where, where was a, where was a place?[21]
I whirled out wings that spell
And fled with a fling of the heart to the heart of the Host.[22]
My heart,[23] but you were dovewinged, I can tell,

---

15 strand: shore.
16 Compare 'I wake and feel the fell of dark', l. 11: 'Bones built in me, flesh filled, blood brimmed the curse.' See also Job 10:11: 'Thou hast clothed me with skin and flesh, and hast fenced me with bones and sinews' (AV).
17 In a sermon in 1879 Hopkins noted that 'those things which are said [in the Bible] to be done by the Lord's arm are God's works of power, those by his finger are the subtle workings of his wisdom' (S, p. 18).
18 This stanza affirms the speaker's knowledge that he was created by God and that God is in contact with him.
19 i.e. to conversion to Roman Catholicism.
20 Hopkins recalls his religious conversion and describes the process as violent, physical and something like a shipwreck: 'the midriff astrain with leaning of, laced with fire of stress.'
21 Still thinking about the torment of his own state of mind immediately before his decision to convert, the gasping and stammering in l. 3 of this stanza anticipate the extreme breakdown of language in st. 28.
22 The Host is the bread used in Eucharist or Holy Communion, which in Roman Catholic teaching becomes the body of Christ. The heart of the Host, then, is God the Son: Christ.
23 Hopkins addresses his heart in ll. 7–8 of 'Hurrahing in Harvest', l. 3 of 'I Wake and Feel' and l. 7 of 'Spelt from Sibyl's Leaves', as well as in ll. 1–4 of st. 18 and l. 3 of st. 31 of 'The Wreck of the Deutschland'.

Carrier-witted,[24] I am bold to boast,
To flash from the flame to the flame then, tower from the grace to the
    grace.[25]

4

I am sóft síft
In an hourglass — at the wall
Fast, but mined with a motion, a drift,
    And it crowds and it combs to the fall;[26]
I steady as a water in a well, to a poise, to a pane,
But roped with, always, all the way down from the tall
    Fells or flanks of the voel, a vein
Of the gospel proffer, a pressure, a principle, Christ's gift.[27]

5

I kiss my hand
To the stars, lovely-asunder
Starlight, wafting him[28] out of it; and
    Glow, glory in thunder;
Kiss my hand to the dappled-with-damson west:[29]
Since, though he is under the world's splendour and wonder,
    His mystery must be instressed, stressed;[30]
For I greet him the days I meet him, and bless when I understand.[31]

6

Not out of his bliss
Springs the stress felt
Nor first from heaven (and few know this)
    Swings the stroke dealt —
Stroke and a stress that stars and storms deliver,[32]

24 i.e. having a carrier-pigeon's homing instinct.
25 This stanza describes the process of conversion in a gentler but still tumultuous way, imaging
    Hopkins's self as a bird flying to its home.
26 This four-line metaphor likens Hopkins's selfhood to the sand in an hourglass. The sand next to the
    glass appears to be still, but it is undermined by the movement of the sand in the middle falling
    through into the lower chamber: the grains of sand crowd together and the sand is shaped
    (combed, in Hopkins's parlance) by this movement.
27 Hopkins adds a water-based metaphor to the sand-based one: his selfhood is like the apparently
    still water in a well, which is nevertheless constantly fed and agitated by the stream running from
    the hill ('voel' is a rare word meaning a hill). In Hopkins's case that stream is his awareness of
    Christ's gift of redemption to humanity.
28 Him: God.
29 i.e. the sunset.
30 Catherine Phillips explains: 'to complete the communication with Christ requires that the instress
    [impression of Christ's presence] be consciously accepted ("stressed")' (p. 337).
31 Nature's grandeur (particularly the three kinds of light mentioned in this stanza – stars, thunder,
    and sunsets) is a sign of God's presence in the world; the speaker is grateful for it because it gives
    him a sense of God's active love. Although God is the foundation of the world, the speaker is aware
    only intermittently of his presence.
32 Nature's grandeur, specifically the stars we have already heard about in st. 5 and the storm that is to
    come in Part the Second, are signs of God's power not only in nature but over human minds.

That guilt is hushed by, hearts are flushed by and melt —
But it rides time like riding a river
(And here the faithful waver, the faithless fable and miss.)

7

It dates from day
Of his going in Galilee;[33]
Warm-laid grave of a womb-life grey;
Manger, maiden's knee;
The dense and the driven Passion, and frightful sweat;[34]
Thence the discharge of it, there its swelling to be,
Though felt before, though in high flood yet —[35]
What none would have known of it, only the heart, being hard at bay,[36]

8

Is out with it! Oh,
We lash[37] with the best or worst
Word last! How a lush-kept plush-capped sloe
Will, mouthed to flesh-burst,
Gush![38] — flush the man, the being with it, sour or sweet,
Brim, in a flash, full![39] — Hither then, last or first,
To hero of Calvary,[40] Christ,'s feet —
Never ask if meaning it, wanting it, warned of it — men go.

9

Be adored among men,
God, three-numberèd form;
Wring thy rebel,[41] dogged in den,[42]

---

33 i.e. the most affecting part of Christ's story is that of the Incarnation, his life as a man in Galilee (the region in Palestine where he spent most of his life).
34 ll. 3–5 of this stanza allude to Christ's birth to the Blessed Virgin Mary and his Passion, or suffering during crucifixion.
35 The affecting qualities of Christ's story are still just as strong in the present as they were in the past.
36 In hunting, an animal at bay is one that has run as far as it can and turns to face the hunters and defend itself. The soul of the person pursued by God must at last acknowledge his power.
37 Compare 'lashed rod' in st. 2 l. 2.
38 A sloe is a berry whose skin has a slight velvety bloom: if you press a sloe in your mouth it will burst open, releasing juice. This image is often compared to one in Keats's 'Ode on Melancholy' (1819): 'him whose strenuous tongue / Can burst Joy's grape against his palate fine' (ll. 27–8).
39 Human beings are like fruit which bursts in the mouth, releasing flavour, because at the moment of their destruction or their conversion they are filled with the true essence of themselves.
40 Calvary is where Christ's crucifixion is said to have taken place.
41 'Wring' is part of Hopkins's vocabulary of hurt: cp. 'No Worst, There is None', l. 2: 'More pangs will, schooled at forepangs, wilder wring'. See also l. 7 of this stanza. It is characteristic of Hopkins that the word is also part of his vocabulary of intense and pleasurable sensation: e.g. 'Spring', ll. 3–5: '[. . .] thrush / Through the echoing timber does so rinse and wring / The ear, it strikes like lightnings to hear him sing'.
42 The influence on Hopkins of Anglo-Saxon poetry, with its insistent alliterations and medial caesurae, is clearly audible in this line.

Man's malice, with wrecking and storm.
Beyond saying sweet, past telling of tongue,[43]
Thou art lightning and love, I found it, a winter and warm;
Father and fondler of heart thou hast wrung;
Hast thy dark descending and most art merciful then.[44]

10

With an anvil-ding[45]
And with fire in him forge thy will
Or rather, rather then, stealing as Spring
Through him, melt him but master him still:[46]
Whether át ónce, as once at a crash Paul,[47]
Or as Austin, a lingering-out sweet skill,[48]
Make mercy in all of us, out of us all
Mastery, but be adored, but be adored King.

Part the second

11

'Some find me a sword; some
The flange and the rail; flame,
Fang, or flood' goes Death on drum,[49]
And storms bugle his fame.
But wé dréam we are rooted in earth—Dust!
Flesh falls within sight of us, we, though our flower the same,
Wave with the meadow, forget that there must
The sour scythe cringe, and the blear share come.[50]

---

43 cp. 'As Kingfishers Catch Fire', ll. 3–4: '[. . .] each tucked string tells, each hung bell's / Bow swung finds tongue'.

44 Shipwreck imagery returns to imagine God torturing the unfaithful and the wicked for the good of their souls. God's power is both violent and tender.

45 A blow on an anvil. cp. the use of 'anvil' as an instrument of pain that moulds the personality in 'No Worst, There is None', l. 6: 'on an áge-old ánvil wince and sing'.

46 Two different kinds of conversion experience are being described here: one violent and painful, one gentle and almost imperceptible.

47 Saul's conversion to Christianity occurred on the road to Damascus, where 'suddenly there shined round about him a light from heaven' and he heard Christ's voice (Acts 9:3, AV). After the conversion he preached Christianity and under the name Paul became one of the first and most important theologians and missionaries of the new religion.

48 St Augustine of Hippo (another key theologian and a Church Father) was converted to Christianity over a period of several years in the mid-380s.

49 Death, personified, lists causes of death, including warfare and (N. H. Mackenzie suggests) railway accidents ('the flange and the rail'; *A Reader's Guide to Gerard Manley Hopkins* (London: Thames & Hudson, 1981), p. 38). cp. Revelation (Apocalypse, DR) 6:8: 'And I looked, and behold a pale horse: and his name that sat on him was Death, and Hell followed with him. And power was given unto them over the fourth part of the earth, to kill with sword, and with hunger, and with death, and with the beasts of the earth' (AV).

50 Though we see people die around us, we ignore the fact of death. cp. The many biblical metaphors associating flesh (or human life) with grass and flowers, e.g. 1 Peter 1:24: 'For all flesh is as grass, and all the glory of man as the flower of grass. The grass withereth, and the flower thereof falleth away' (AV). Blear: cp. 'God's Grandeur', l. 6: 'all is seared with trade; bleared, smeared with toil;'. Share: ploughshare.

12

On Saturday sailed from Bremen,[51]
American-outward-bound,[52]
Take settler and seamen, tell men with women,[53]
Two hundred souls in the round —
O Father, not under thy feathers nor ever as guessing[54]
The goal was a shoal,[55] of a fourth the doom to be drowned;[56]
Yet díd the dark side of the bay of thy blessing
Not vault them,[57] the million of rounds of thy mercy not reeve even
    them in?[58]

13

Into the snows she sweeps,
Hurling the haven behind,
The Deutschland, on Sunday; and so the sky keeps,
For the infinite air is unkind,
And the sea flint-flake, black-backed in the regular blow,[59]
Sitting Eastnortheast, in cursed quarter, the wind;
Wiry and white-fiery and whírlwind-swivellèd snow
Spins to the widow-making unchilding unfathering deeps.[60]

14

She drove in the dark to leeward,[61]
She struck — not a reef or a rock
But the combs of a smother of sand:[62] night drew her
Dead to the Kentish Knock;[63]
And she beat the bank down with her bows and the ride of her keel;
The breakers rolled on her beam with ruinous shock;[64]

---

51 Bremerhaven was a German inland port giving access to the North Sea.
52 i.e. bound for America.
53 tell: reckon, count.
54 Catherine Phillips notes the echo of Psalm 91:4: God 'shall cover thee with his feathers, and under
    his wings shalt thou trust' (AV) (p. 338).
55 Shoal: sandbank. The *Deutschland* foundered on a sandbank of the coast of England.
56 A quarter of the people on board the ship were fated to drown.
57 vault: cover over.
58 reeve: tie, or twist; hence, to pull or tie together the souls of the drowned crew and passengers for
    God to pull them in (to his presence). 'Reeve' is mainly a nautical term: note Hopkins's adoption
    of terminology associated with ships and the sea for religious points.
59 The waves on the sea have the quality of flints: glassy black tipped with white.
60 The havoc wreaked on families who lose members in the wreck retrospectively gives 'unkind' (l. 4)
    the sense of 'destructive of kinship'. In a letter to Bridges in 1877 Hopkins wrote that one of his
    superiors in the Society of Jesus was 'on the unfathering deeps bound to Jamaica' (L I, p. 44).
61 In English (though not American) usage, 'leeward' (meaning the direction towards which the wind
    is blowing) is pronounced 'loord' and so rhymes with 'endured' (l. 8) and (more or less) with 'drew
    her / D' (ll. 3–4).
62 Phillips glosses 'combs' as 'crests or ridges of the sandbank' (p. 338).
63 Kentish Knock: notoriously dangerous sandbank off the Thames estuary.
64 beam: the side of the ship.

And canvas and compass, the whorl and the wheel
Idle for ever to waft her or wind her with,[65] these she endured.

15

Hope had grown grey hairs,
Hope had mourning on,
Trenched with tears,[66] carved with cares,
Hope was twelve hours gone;
And frightful a nightfall folded rueful a day
Nor rescue, only rocket and lightship, shone,
And lives at last were washing away:
To the shrouds they took,[67] — they shook in the hurling and horrible airs.

16

One stirred from the rigging to save
The wild woman-kind below,
With a rope's end round the man, handy and brave —
He was pitched to his death at a blow,
For all his dreadnought breast and braids of thew:[68]
They could tell him for hours, dandled the to and fro
Through the cobbled foam-fleece. What could he do
With the burl of the fountains of air, buck and the flood of the wave?[69]

17

They fought with God's cold —
And they could not and fell to the deck
(Crushed them) or water (and drowned them) or rolled
With the sea-romp over the wreck.
Night roared, with the heart-break hearing a heart-broke rabble,
The woman's wailing, the crying of child without check —
Till a lioness arose breasting the babble,
A prophetess towered in the tumult, a virginal tongue told.

---

65 The ship went aground on the sandbank and was then stuck there, while the heavy seas (which she could have withstood if she had been able to move in response to the waves) smashed her to pieces. The shock of the grounding and the waves rendered the ship's sails, propellor, steering and navigational equipment broken and useless.
66 Tears have cut lines down the face of the personification of hope.
67 The passengers and crew climbed the rigging.
68 dreadnought: not yet the name for a class of battleship, this word was only a few decades old as an adjective. Braids of thew: thick muscles.
69 The story of this man is told in *The Times*'s report of the wreck:

> One brave sailor, who was safe in the rigging, went down to try and save a child or woman who was drowning on deck. He was secured by a rope to the rigging, but a wave dashed him against the bulwarks [the "walls" around the edge of the deck of the ship], and when daylight dawned his headless body, detained by the rope, was seen swaying to and fro with the waves (see Contemporary Documents, pp. 36–7).

18

Ah, touched in your bower of bone[70]
Are you! turned for an exquisite smart,
Have you! make words break from me here all alone,[71]
Do you! — mother of being in me, heart.
O unteachably after evil, but uttering truth,
Why, tears! is it? tears; such a melting, a madrigal start![72]
Never-eldering revel and river of youth,[73]
What can it be, this glee? the good you have there of your own?

19

Sister, a sister calling
A master, her master and mine! —[74]
And the inboard seas run swirling and hawling;[75]
The rash smart sloggering brine[76]
Blinds her; but shé that weather sees óne thing, one;[77]
Has óne fetch ín her:[78] she rears herself to divine
Ears, and the call of the tall nun
To the men in the tops and the tackle rode over the storm's brawling.[79]

20

She was first of a five and came
Of a coifèd sisterhood.[80]
(O Deutschland, double a desperate name![81]
O world wide of its good!

---

70 bower: generally, a dwelling place: hence, rib-cage (the dwelling place of the heart).

71 For the first time in Part the Second, the speaker connects the story of the shipwreck with his own emotional response to it.

72 madrigal: a song for several parts, using counterpoint (i.e. setting one singer's line against another's); often a love song. Here it seems to indicate an easy expression of emotion: the tears that the story of the wreck causes the speaker to shed are happy as well as sad.

73 Never-eldering: never growing older.

74 A reference to the story of the nun on the wreck who called out (varying from one account to another) 'O Christ, come quickly!' or 'My God, my God, make haste, make haste' (Phillips, p. 338).

75 inboard: inside the ship. Hawling: a Hopkins coinage: meaning unclear, but suggesting powerful movement.

76 sloggering: another Hopkins coinage. The sea gives heavy, crushing blows, as well as stinging ones ('rash smart').

77 she that weather: she in that weather. cp. structure of 'I whirled out wings that spell' (st. 3, l. 4).

78 fetch: primarily, an effort, but 'fetch' is also sometimes used to mean a stratagem or device; it also has nautical meanings. Note how Hopkins uses not just directly nautical terms but also words that echo them.

79 tops and the tackle: platforms on the masts, and rigging.

80 Hopkins believed that the tall nun who cried out was the leader of the five nuns on the ship. A coif is a cap like the kind that nuns wore under their headgear.

81 A desperate name because of the terrible fate of the ship and because of Germany's rejection of Roman Catholicism.

But Gertrude, lily, and Luther, are two of a town,[82]
Christ's lily and beast of the waste wood:
   From life's dawn it is drawn down,
Abel is Cain's brother and breasts they have sucked the same.)[83]

21

Loathed for a love men knew in them,
Banned by the land of their birth,[84]
Rhine refused them, Thames would ruin them;
   Surf, snow, river and earth
Gnashed: but thou art above, thou Orion of light;
Thy unchancelling poising palms were weighing the worth,[85]
   Thou martyr-master: in thý sight
Storm flakes were scroll-leaved flowers, lily showers — sweet heaven was
   astrew in them.[86]

22

Five! the finding and sake[87]
And cipher of suffering Christ.
   Mark, the mark is of man's make
And the word of it Sacrificed.
But he scores it in scarlet himself on his own bespoken,[88]
   Before-time-taken, dearest prizèd and priced —

---

82 St Gertrude was a thirteenth-century Benedictine nun and mystic. Martin Luther (1483–1546) was
    a theologian who questioned the Roman Catholic Church's teachings and practices and contrib-
    uted enormously to the initiating of the Reformation and hence to the splitting of the Protestant
    movement away from the Roman Catholic Church, a split that Hopkins greatly regretted and
    which he prays God to mend at the end of this poem. Both Gertrude and Luther lived in the
    German town of Eisleben.
83 In Genesis 4:8 Cain slays his brother Abel because of jealousy over God's favouring Abel. Eve was
    the mother of both brothers. The sense is that goodness and evil have been closely linked through-
    out the whole of human history.
84 See p. 115, n. 8, on the Falck Laws and German anti-Catholicism under Bismarck.
85 unchancelling: a chancel is a part of a church that is screened off, usually the eastern part in which
    the celebration of communion takes place. Phillips suggests 'God is bringing the nuns into public
    prominence through their deaths' (p. 339). Or perhaps God is himself coming out from the chancel
    into public life as the nuns bear witness to his presence in the world.
86 The snow and waves were like heavenly flower petals strewn around the shipwreck (because of the
    beauty of the sacrifice the nuns were making and the great faith of the nun who called on Christ to
    come quickly).
87 finding: 'emblem' (Phillips, p. 339). Sake: Hopkins wrote to Bridges in his notes on 'Henry Purcell'
    that when he used this word he meant

    the being a thing has outside itself, as a voice by its echo, a face by its reflection, a body by
    its shadow, a man by his name, fame, or memory, *and also* that in the thing by virtue of
    which especially it has this being abroad [i.e. in the world], and that is something distinct-
    ive, marked, specifically or individually speaking, as for a voice and echo clearness, for a
    reflected image light, brightness [. . .]

    (L I, p. 83). So five (the number of nuns on the ship) is the symbol of Christ because of the five
    wounds he suffered on the cross.
88 Christ marks out through suffering those whom he has chosen and loves best.

Stigma, signal, cinquefoil token[89]
For lettering of the lamb's fleece, ruddying of the rose-flake.[90]

23

Joy fall to thee, father Francis,
Drawn to the Life that died;[91]
With the gnarls of the nails in thee, niche of the lance, his
Lovescape crucified[92]
And seal of his seraph-arrival![93] and these thy daughters[94]
And five-livèd and leavèd favour and pride,
Are sisterly sealed in wild waters,
To bathe in his fall-gold mercies, to breathe in his all-fire glances.

24

Away in the loveable west,
On a pastoral forehead of Wales,[95]
I was under a roof here, I was at rest,
And they the prey of the gales;
She to the black-about air, to the breaker, the thickly
Falling flakes, to the throng that catches and quails
Was calling 'O Christ, Christ, come quickly':
The cross to her she calls Christ to her, christens her wild-worst Best.[96]

25

The majesty! what did she mean?
Breathe, arch and original Breath.[97]
Is it lóve in her of the béing as her lóver had béen?[98]
Breathe, body of lovely Death.[99]
They were else-minded then, altogether, the men

---

89 Cinquefoil is a plant whose leaves are made up of five leaflets: again a reference to the five wounds
    of the Crucifixion, particularly important in this context because the nuns were Franciscans, i.e.
    from an order founded by St Francis of Assisi, one of various mystics who are said to have had
    such devotion to Christ and his Passion that they acquired 'stigmata', or wounds on their own
    bodies in the five places where Christ was wounded. 'Five' thus links St Francis and the nuns with
    Christ's physical sufferings.
90 Two images of blood staining pure surfaces. The lamb alludes to the Lamb of God, i.e. Christ, who
    sacrificially takes away the sins of the world.
91 i.e. Christ.
92 A reference to the stigmata of St Francis. Christ's five wounds were made by nails in his hands and
    feet and by a lance in his side.
93 Preceding the appearance of the stigmata St Francis had a vision of a seraph, or angel.
94 i.e. the nuns.
95 i.e. at St Beuno's in north Wales, where Hopkins was studying theology.
96 Another instance of Hopkins using an oxymoron literally: the drowning is both the nun's worst
    experience and her best one, because it will bring her to Christ's presence.
97 Almost an invocation of the Muse, the speaker asks the Holy Spirit to inspire him so that he can
    understand the meaning of the nun's cry.
98 Her lover: Christ.
99 i.e. Christ dying on the cross.

Wóke thee with a *We are perishing* in the wéather of Gennésaréth.[100]
Or ís it that she cried for the crown then,[101]
The keener to come at the comfort for feeling the combating keen?[102]

26

For how to the heart's cheering
The down-dugged ground-hugged grey
Hovers off, the jay-blue heavens appearing
Of pied and peeled May![103]
Blue-beating and hoary-glow height; or night, still higher,
With belled fire and the moth-soft Milky Way,
What by your measure is the heaven of desire,
The treasure never eyesight got, nor was ever guessed what for the
hearing?[104]

27

Nó, but it was nót these.[105]
The jading and jar of the cart,
Time's tásking, it is fathers that asking for ease
Of the sodden-with-its-sorrowing heart,
Not danger, electrical horror;[106] then further it finds
The appealing of the Passion is tenderer in prayer apart:
Other, I gather, in measure her mind's
Burden, in wind's burly and beat of endragonèd seas.[107]

28

But how shall I . . . make me room there:
Reach me a . . . Fancy, come faster—
Strike you the sight of it? look at it loom there,
Thing that she . . . There then! the Master,
Ipse,[108] the only one, Christ, King, Head:
He was to cure the extremity where he had cast her;
Do, deal, lord it with living and dead;

---

100 Three gospels tell the story of Christ and his apostles in a boat: the weather became bad and the
   apostles cried out that they were perishing. Christ rebuked them, calling them 'ye of little faith':
   Matthew 8:23–7, Mark 4:35–41, Luke 8:22–5.
101 i.e. the nun asked for a martyr's crown (in other words, asked for death).
102 More eager to get to the comfort (of death and coming into Christ's presence) because her death
   struggle was sharp.
103 In spring winter's low clouds give way to sky as blue as a jay's plumage.
104 The sense is something like: we are happy when we see blue sky or starlight ('the moth-soft Milky
   Way') instead of clouds, but what is the most desirable sight of all?
105 The speaker is returning to the question he asked in st. 25 l. 1, 'what did she mean?' and rejects the
   answers he has come up with so far.
106 Not sudden shocking danger but life's bumping progress ('the jading and jar of the cart') causes
   ('fathers') people to ask for death ('ease') when the heart is worn out from suffering.
107 It is easier to meditate on the Passion when in peace and solitude; the nun was not in any position
   to engage in meditation while the ship was being wrecked. She had other things on her mind.
108 Himself (Latin).

Let him ride, her pride, in his triumph, despatch and have done with his
doom there.[109]

29

Ah! there was a heart right!
There was single eye![110]
Read the unshapeable shock night
And knew the who and the why;[111]
Wording it how but by him that present and past,
Heaven and earth are word of, worded by?—
The Simon Peter of a soul![112] to the blast
Tárpéïan-fast,[113] but a blown beacon of light.[114]

30

Jesu, heart's light,
Jesu, maid's son,
What was the feast followed the night
Thou hadst glory of this nun? — [115]
Féast of the óne wóman withóut stáin.[116]
For so conceivèd, so to conceive thee is done;
But here was heart-throe, birth of a brain,[117]
Word, that heard and kept thee and uttered thee óutríght.[118]

31

Well, shé has thée for the pain, for the
Patience; but pity of the rest of them![119]
Heart, go and bleed at a bitterer vein for the
Comfortless unconfessed of them —[120]
No not uncomforted: lovely-felicitous Providence
Fínger of a ténder of, O of a féathery délicacy, the bréast of the

---

109 See above, **pp. 86–7**, for Thaïs E. Morgan's account of this stanza as a 'rape fantasy'.
110 The nun's focus was on God only.
111 Her interpretation of the events of the shipwreck allowed her to identify God's purpose in the
   disaster.
112 The nun was as steadfast in her faith as Simon Peter, the apostle to whom Christ said 'Thou art
   Peter, and upon this rock I will build my church' (Matthew 16:18).
113 The Tarpeian rock was the cliff from which Rome executed traitors and murderers; it was named
   after Tarpeia, a vestal virgin crushed to death by invading Sabines with whom she had committed
   treachery. The nun is as strong as the cliff and (perhaps) as virginal as Tarpeia.
114 cp. the rockets and lightships giving forth useless light in st. 15 l. 6.
115 i.e. the celebration in heaven after the nun's death as a martyr.
116 The day after the *Deutschland* was wrecked was the Feast of the Immaculate Conception of the
   Blessed Virgin Mary, when the Roman Catholic Church celebrates Mary's having been born
   without original sin, uniquely among humans.
117 Following the wedding imagery and the mention of conception, Hopkins turns to imagery of
   labour and birth.
118 The nun's hearing, keeping and uttering the name of Christ is compared to the Blessed Virgin
   Mary's conceiving, gestating and giving birth to a baby.
119 i.e. the rest of the victims of the shipwreck.
120 Unconfessed: those who died without making confession of their sins.

Maiden could obey so, be a bell to, ring óf it, and
Startle the poor sheep back! is the shipwrack then a harvest, does
    tempest carry the grain for thee?[121]

32

I admire thee, master of the tides,[122]
Of the Yore-flood,[123] of the year's fall;[124]
The recurb and the recovery of the gulf's sides,
    The girth of it and the wharf of it and the wall;[125]
Stanching, quenching ocean of a motionable mind;[126]
Ground of being, and granite of it:[127] pást áll
    Grásp Gód, thróned behínd
Death with a sovereignty that heeds but hides, bodes but abides;

33

With a mercy that outrides[128]
    The all of water, an ark
For the listener; for the lingerer with a love glides
    Lower than death and the dark;
A vein for the visiting of the past-prayer, pent in prison,
The-last-breath penitent spirits — the uttermost mark
    Our passion-plungèd giant risen,[129]
The Christ of the Father compassionate, fetched in the storm of his
    strides.

34

Now burn, new born to the world,
    Double-naturèd name,

---

121 The speaker rejects his fear that the unconfessed victims of the wreck may have gone to Hell: Providence, God's beneficent care for the world, may have ordained that the nun's cry acted as a call to faith for those who heard her. In other words, perhaps everyone who heard her was reminded to confess their sins and died in a state of grace. The shipwreck might then be not a disaster but a means of carrying many souls to God. Hopkins wrote in a note on death:

    it is seen again and again, I have seen it myself and speak of what I know, that people get the last sacraments just in time, that some happy chance or other falls out in their favour. And when we do not see the providence it may still be there and working in some secret way. [. . .] One of God's providences is by warnings – the deaths of others, sermons, dangers, sicknesses, a sudden thought: beware, beware of neglecting a warning (S, p. 252)

122 i.e. God.
123 Probably Noah's flood.
124 Phillips suggests annual rainfall source (p. 314).
125 This imagery of tides returns to the description of God as 'World's strand, sway of the sea', st. 1 l. 3.
126 Several of the words in this stanza ('fall', 'wall', 'motion') recall st. 4, where the speaker imagines himself as like sand in an hourglass or water in a well, but in st. 32 it is God who is like water and rock, containing apparent change but fundamentally unchanging.
127 Another of the poem's images of rock as solid, reliable and trustworthy, unlike the sands on which the ship foundered.
128 To outride in nautical discourse means to ride out or survive a storm. Note that Hopkins carries the rhyme over from the previous stanza (tides/sides/abides/outrides).
129 Passion-plungèd giant: Christ.

The heaven-flung, heart-fleshed, maiden-furled[130]
Miracle-in-Mary-of-flame,
Mid-numberèd he in three of the thunder-throne![131]
Not a dooms-day dazzle in his coming nor dark as he came;
Kind, but royally reclaiming his own;
A released shówer, let flásh to the shíre, not a líghtning of fíre
hard-húrled.[132]

35

Dame, at our door
Drówned, and among óur shóals,
Remember us in the roads, the heaven-haven of the reward:[133]
Our Kíng back, Oh, upon Énglish sóuls!
Let him easter in us, be a dayspring to the dimness of us, be a crimson-
cresseted east,[134]
More brightening her, rare-dear Britain, as his reign rolls,
Pride, rose, prince, hero of us,[135] high-priest,
Our héarts' charity's héarth's fíre, our thóughts' chivalry's thróng's
Lórd.

Moonrise

Like the later poem 'I Wake and Feel the Fell of Dark' (see Key Poems,
pp. 148–9), this is a nocturne, but the rising rhythm and the insistent alliter-
ation in this brief lyric express intensity of joy rather than of anguish. It is dated
19 June 1876. The caesura marks are Hopkins's own.[1]

Moonrise

I awoke in the Midsummer not to call night, | in the white and the walk
of the morning:

---

130 A reference to Christ's divine origin and incarnation as human.
131 i.e. the second person of the Trinity: God the Father, God the Son and God the Holy Spirit.
132 Christ is asked to come back to the world, specifically to England ('the shire'), not in obscurity as
in his First Coming, nor in apocalyptic violence, but as a king. Note that the line picks up some of
the imagery earlier used in connection with Hopkins's experience of conversion: 'flash' (st. 3 l. 8),
'lightning' (st. 2 l. 2), 'hurled', 'hard' (st. 2 ll. 6–7) but this time instead of describing an individual
conversion it is used to imagine the re-conversion of the country, and the world.
133 cp. Hopkins's early poem 'Heaven-Haven' (p. 111). 'Roads': in nautical discourse, sheltered
water near land, where vessels can anchor in safety. The nun has anchored in safety in Heaven as
a reward for her sacrifice.
134 Three images of renewal signifying the spiritual revival Christ is asked to generate in English
people.
135 See Contemporary Documents, pp. 32–3, for Hopkins's sermon on Christ as hero.

---

1   The text here is taken from the Williams edition. The Phillips edition has slight differences of
punctuation and added accents.

The moon, dwindled and thinned to the fringe | of a finger-nail held to
the candle,[2]
Or paring of paradisaïcal fruit, | lovely in waning but lustreless,
Stepped from the stool, drew back from the barrow,[3] | of dark Maenefa
the mountain;[4]
A cusp still clasped him,[5] a fluke yet fanged him,[6] | entangled him, not
quit utterly.
This was the prized, the desirable sight, | unsought, presented so easily,
Parted me leaf and leaf, divided me, | eyelid and eyelid of slumber.

God's Grandeur

This sonnet was written in the early spring of 1877, on the same day as 'The
Starlight Night'; Hopkins sent both poems to his mother as a birthday present.[1]
'God's Grandeur' has been the subject of a good deal of critical interest. For
recent discussions of the poem in terms of its religious, ecological and gender
interests, see Modern Criticism, **pp. 90–2**. Gardner and Mackenzie point out
that Hopkins made a similar point in the opening argument of this poem in a
note written in the early 1880s on the mystery of the Ascension: 'All things
therefore are charged with love, are charged with God and if we know how to
touch them give off sparks and take fire, yield drops and flow, ring and tell of
him'.[2]

God's Grandeur

The world is charged with the grandeur of God.
It will flame out, like shining from shook foil;[3]
It gathers to a greatness, like the ooze of oil

---

2   Compare an entry in Hopkins's 1866 diary: 'Drops of rain hanging on rails etc seen with only the
    lower rim lighted like nails (of fingers). [. . .] Vermilion look of the hand held against a candle
    with the darker parts as the middles of the fingers and especially the knuckles covered with ash'
    (J, p. 72).
3   barrow: an archaic word for a mountain or hill.
4   Maenefa is the mountain behind St Beuno's, the theological college in north Wales where Hopkins
    had been living and studying for two years.
5   cusp: in astronomy, one of the pointed ends of the crescent moon. Him: the mountain.
6   fluke: 'the triangular-shaped piece of iron near the tip of the arms of an anchor' (Phillips, p. 345).
    Fanged: bit (in the sense of an anchor catching hold).

---

1   White, p. 267.
2   *The Poems of Gerard Manley Hopkins*, 4th edn, ed. W. H. Gardner and N. H. MacKenzie (Oxford:
    Oxford University Press, 1967), p. 264; *The Sermons and Devotional Writings of Gerard Manley
    Hopkins*, ed. Christopher Devlin (London: Oxford University Press, 1959), p. 195.
3   GMH commented 'I mean foil in its sense of leaf or tinsel' and 'shaken goldfoil gives off broad
    glares like sheet lightning, and also [. . .] a sort of fork lightning too' (L I, p. 169). Compare with
    'lightning' in 'Wreck', st. 2 and 9, and 'lightnings' in 'Spring'.

Crushed. Why do men then now not reck his rod?
Generations have trod, have trod, have trod;
   And all is seared with trade; bleared, smeared with toil;
   And wears man's smudge and shares man's smell: the soil
Is bare now, nor can foot feel, being shod.

And, for all this, nature is never spent;
   There lives the dearest freshness deep down things;
And though the last lights off the black West went
   Oh, morning, at the brown brink eastward, springs – [4]
Because the Holy Ghost over the bent
   World broods with warm breast and with ah! bright wings.[5]

The Starlight Night

Hopkins sent a copy of this sonnet, composed around February 1877, to his mother along with 'God's Grandeur' as a birthday present. Norman White speculates about the event occasioning the poem: 'part of the force behind "The Starlight Night" could have been his disappointment [. . .] at having missed the total eclipse of the moon on 28 February because of the community's lack of interest in the night sky.'[1]

The Starlight Night

Look at the stars! look, look up at the skies!
   O look at all the fire-folk sitting in the air!
   The bright boroughs, the circle-citadels there!
Down in dim woods the diamond delves! the elves'-eyes!
The grey lawns cold where gold, where quickgold lies![2]
   Wind-beat whitebeam! airy abeles[3] set on a flare!
   Flake-doves sent floating forth at a farmyard scare!—
Ah well! it is all a purchase, all is a prize.

Buy then! bid then! — What? — Prayer, patience, alms, vows.
Look, look: a May-mess, like on orchard boughs!

---

4   Compare 'Spelt from Sibyl's Leaves', ll. 2–5, which imagine the last evening of the world, with no morning to come.
5   Compare John Milton, *Paradise Lost*, Book 1 lines 19–22: 'Thou [God]from the first / Wast present, and with mighty wings outspred / Dove-like satst brooding on the vast Abyss / And mad'st it pregnant'.

---

1   White, p. 267.
2   Both 'dim woods' and 'grey lawns cold' are metaphors for dark areas of night sky containing few stars. 'Delves': pits, excavations, perhaps mines.
3   abeles: white poplars.

Look! March-bloom, like on mealed-with-yellow sallows![4]
These are indeed the barn;[5] withindoors house
The shocks.[6] This piece-bright paling[7] shuts the spouse[8]
Christ home, Christ and his mother and all his hallows.[9]

As Kingfishers Catch Fire

Though it is now one of the best known of his sonnets, Hopkins seems not to have been satisfied with this poem and did not send it to Robert Bridges, as was his habit. Norman White comments: 'The poem is a determined plea that physical beauty be acknowledged to have moral value, that attraction to aspects of the physical world may be sanctioned by a recognition of their moral status; there is surely also a defence of the poet's practice'.[1] Eric Griffiths compares it with 'Spelt from Sibyl's Leaves' (see, **pp. 152–4**), and argues that though 'more harmonious' than the sounds of the later poem, 'the chain of rhymes from "kingfishers" through "ring" and "string" to "thing" also stands in its milder way for a variety which is bursting at the seams of an orderly scheme of creation'.[2] Compare the poem with Hopkins's meditation on selfhood in 'Comments on the Spiritual Exercises of St. Ignatius Loyola' (Contemporary Documents, **pp. 31–2**).

'As kingfishers catch fire'

As kingfishers catch fire, dragonflies draw flame;
    As tumbled over rim in roundy wells
    Stones ring; like each tucked string tells, each hung bell's
Bow swung finds tongue to fling out broad its name;
Each mortal thing does one thing and the same:
    Deals out that being indoors each one dwells;
    Selves[3] — goes its self; *myself* it speaks and spells,
Crying *What I do is me: for that I came.*

---

4   sallows: willow trees.
5   Catherine Phillips (p. 348) suggests a comparison with Matthew 13:30: 'in the time of harvest I will say to the reapers, Gather ye together first the tares, and bind them in bundles to burn them: but gather the wheat into my barn.'
6   shocks: sheaves (of wheat), a metaphor for the souls of those in heaven.
7   The night sky is imagined as being like a wooden fence or wall separating Earth from Heaven, with the stars as holes through which the light of Heaven shines. A brief lyric of 1866 gives an earlier version of this metaphor of the night sky as a fence: 'The stars were packed so close that night / They seemed to press and stare / And gather in like hurdles bright / The liberties of air' (Phillips, p. 79).
8   spouse: Hopkins is adopting the biblical metaphor of Christ as the bridegroom of the Church.
9   hallows: saints. The *OED* notes that this usage is rare after 1500.

---

1   White, p. 276.
2   Eric Griffiths, *The Printed Voice of Victorian Poetry* (Oxford: Clarendon Press, 1989), pp. 320–1.
3   The *OED* records that Hopkins invented the verb 'to selve'.

I say more: the just man justices;[4]
  Keeps grace: that keeps all his goings[5] graces;
  Acts in God's eye what in God's eye he is—
    Christ. For Christ plays in ten thousand places,
  Lovely in limbs, and lovely in eyes not his
    To the Father through the features of men's faces.[6]

Spring

This sonnet from 1877, like others written in the same year including 'Pied Beauty' and 'The Windhover', uses the octave to celebrate the energy and beauty of nature and in the sestet refers those qualities to God.[1]

Spring

Nothing is so beautiful as spring—
  When weeds, in wheels, shoot long and lovely and lush;
  Thrush's eggs look little low heavens, and thrush[2]
Through the echoing timber does so rinse and wring
The ear, it strikes like lightnings to hear him sing;
  The glassy peartree leaves and blooms, they brush
  The descending blue; that blue is all in a rush
With richness; the racing lambs too have fair their fling.

What is all this juice and all this joy?
  A strain of the earth's sweet being in the beginning
In Eden garden. — Have, get, before it cloy,[3]
  Before it cloud, Christ, lord, and sour with sinning,[4]
Innocent mind and Mayday in girl and boy,
  Most, O maid's child, thy choice and worthy the winning.[5]

---

4 justices: acts justly.
5 That keeps all his activities full of God's grace (but with a suggestion also of physical gracefulness).
6 God recognizes Christ's loveliness in each person.

---

1 The text here is taken from the Williams edition. The Phillips edition has a slight difference in layout.
2 Phillips notes that thrushes' eggs are blue (whence the association with Heaven) (Phillips, p. 350).
3 White comments: 'In the simplicity of this answer [to the question, "What is all this juice and all this joy?"] lie its strength and its weakness. To some people the poem is moving and powerful; to others the interpretation of the spring phenomenon appears incomplete, naïve, or extraneous' (White, p. 280).
4 The sense is that spring in nature is like the part of a human being's life when they are young, pure and unsinful, when they are most dear to Christ. Christ is being addressed directly and asked to 'get' the young people while they are in this fresh, unspoiled state.
5 'Maid's child': Christ, the son of the Virgin Mary.

In the Valley of the Elwy

The River Elwy runs through north Wales, passing near St Beuno's, the college at which Hopkins studied theology from 1874 to 1877. But the first eight lines refer not to Wales but to acquaintances in Shooter's Hill, south of London: Wales is first mentioned in l. 9. Hopkins explained to Bridges that the poem is based on a contrast between the direct and complementary relationship between the kind people in Shooter's Hill and the mismatch between the landscape and the temperament of the people of Wales, with God being called on in the final three lines to help the Welsh come up to the standards of their surroundings (L I, pp. 76–7).[1]

In the Valley of the Elwy

I remember a house where all were good
To me, God knows, deserving no such thing:
Comforting smell breathed at very entering,
Fetched fresh, as I suppose, off some sweet wood.
That cordial air made those kind people a hood
All over, as a bevy of eggs the mothering wing
Will, or mild nights the new morsels of spring:
Why, it seemed of course; seemed of right it should.

Lovely the woods, waters, meadows, combes, vales,
All the air things wear that build this world of Wales;
Only the inmate does not correspond:
God, lover of souls, swaying considerate scales,
Complete thy creature dear O where it fails,
Being mighty a master, being a father and fond.[2]

The Windhover

In 1879 Hopkins told Bridges that this poem was 'the best thing I ever wrote' (L I, p. 85). It was composed at the end of May 1877, when Hopkins had been a student at St Beuno's theological college for nearly three years and had recently been writing poetry fertilely. This poem expands the form of the conventional English sonnet by use of sprung rhythm and what Hopkins called 'outrides', added extra-metrical feet, so that lines 2 and 3, for instance, contain sixteen

---

1   The text here is taken from the Williams edition. The Phillips edition has slight differences of layout.
2   Compare 'Wreck of the Deutschland' st. 9 l. 7: 'Father and fondler of heart thou hast wrung'.

syllables instead of the more usual ten. It describes the speaker watching the flight and hovering of a kestrel and experiencing an epiphanic, ecstatic moment during which he perceives God's beauty in the bird's mastery of the air. In the last three lines Hopkins compares the way that the apparently ordinary natural phenomenon of the bird's flight can suddenly reveal Christ's presence in the world with two other homely ways in which unglamorous things also show beauty.[1]

The Windhover[2]

To Christ our Lord

I caught this morning morning's minion, king-
   dom of daylight's dauphin,[3] dapple-dawn-drawn Falcon, in his riding
  Of the rolling level underneath him steady air, and striding
High there, how he rung upon the rein of a wimpling wing[4]
In his ecstasy! then off, off forth on swing,
  As a skate's heel sweeps smooth on a bow-bend: the hurl[5] and gliding
  Rebuffed the big wind. My heart in hiding
Stirred for a bird, — the achieve[6] of, the mastery of the thing!

Brute beauty and valour and act, oh, air, pride, plume, here
  Buckle![7] AND the fire[8] that breaks from thee then, a billion
Times told lovelier, more dangerous, O my chevalier![9]

No wonder of it: shéer plód makes plough down sillion[10]

---

1 The text here is taken from the Williams edition. The Phillips edition has slight differences of punctuation and added accents.
2 Kestrel (a small falcon).
3 'Dauphin' was the term for the eldest son of the King of France until the fall of the Bourbon monarchy in the revolution of 1830. The reference to the eldest son of a king seems to associate the falcon with Christ, the Son of God the Father.
4 Catherine Phillips glosses this as 'wings quivering in a hover' (p. 352). 'Wimple' has a range of meanings, including to veil, to fall in folds and to move unsteadily. Compare 'wimpled water-dimpled' in 'The Leaden Echo and the Golden Echo' (l. 10).
5 hurl: a violent throwing or falling motion. Compare 'The swoon of a heart that the sweep and the hurl of thee trod', in 'The Wreck of the Deutschland' (st. 2 l. 6).
6 Achievement.
7 Catherine Phillips glosses 'Buckle!' as 'come together' (p. 352). Psalm 91:4 links imagery of God as a bird with imagery of God as armour: 'He shall cover thee with his feathers, and under his wings shalt thou trust: his truth shall be thy shield and buckler' (AV): perhaps 'buckle', which has attracted a great deal of critical attention over the decades, echoes this conjunction of avian and military associations.
8 This fire might be compared with the electrical 'charge' that the world has from the grandeur of God: 'God's Grandeur', l. 1.
9 Hopkins addresses Christ as a knight, using a term which though English as well as French (and Anglicized in pronunciation to rhyme with 'here' and 'dear') echoes the allusion to the French monarchy in 'dauphin'.
10 sillion: an obscure form of a word meaning a strip of land between two furrows. The blade of a plough repeatedly cuts through soil (this agricultural labour is 'sheer plod') and thus becomes shiny.

Shine, and blue-bleak embers, ah my dear,
Fall, gall themselves, and gash gold-vermilion.[11]

Pied Beauty

Like 'Peace' (p. 141), this is an example of a form Hopkins named the 'Curtal-Sonnet': i.e., it is 'constructed in proportions resembling those of the sonnet proper, namely 6 [lines] + 4 [lines] instead of 8 + 6, with however a half line tailpiece'.[1] Along with 'The Windhover' and 'Hurrahing in Harvest', it was written in Wales during the summer of 1877.

Two major aspects of the poem have attracted a great deal of critical attention. One is the complex thought and formal invention involved in its celebration of diversity within a cosmos unified by being the creation of one God; the other is a queer reading of that celebration, in which ll. 7 and 8 are interpreted as coming as close as Hopkins ever does to an acceptance of the 'otherness' of his sexuality. Julia F. Saville comments: 'flying in the face of Victorian respect for reliability, solidity, loyalty, utility, and conformity, he celebrates the unpredictable, the erratic and whimsical, all those creatures and objects that elude easy integration into a specific social agenda'.[2] See above, 'Modern Criticism', pp. 92–6 for extracts from J. Hillis Miller's, Michael Lynch's and Isobel Armstrong's readings of the poem.[3]

Pied Beauty

Glory be to God for dappled things—
  For skies of couple-colour as a brinded[4] cow;
    For rose-moles all in stipple upon trout that swim;[5]
Fresh-firecoal chestnut-falls; finches' wings;
  Landscape plotted and pieced — fold, fallow, and plough;
    And áll trádes, their gear and tackle and trim.[6]

All things counter, original, spare, strange;
  Whatever is fickle, freckled (who knows how?)
    With swift, slow; sweet, sour; adazzle, dim;
He fathers-forth[7] whose beauty is past change:
          Praise him.

---

11 Smouldering ashes in a fire can split open ('gall themselves') and show bright fire inside.

1 Hopkins, 'Author's Preface', in Phillips, p. 109.
2 Julia F. Saville, *A Queer Chivalry: The Homoerotic Asceticism of Gerard Manley Hopkins* (Charlottesville, Va.: University Press of Virginia, 2000), p. 125.
3 The text here is taken from the Williams edition. The Phillips edition has slight differences of layout and added accents.
4 brinded: 'streaked, spotted; brindled' (*OED*).
5 Only live trout have the pinkish-red markings alluded to.
6 Trim is probably used in *OED* sense 6: 'the nature, character, or manner of a person or thing; his or its "way" '.
7 i.e. God generates these beautiful contrasts in the natural world.

Hurrahing in Harvest

Hopkins sent this poem to Bridges with the comment: 'The Hurrahing Sonnet was the outcome of half an hour of extreme enthusiasm as I walked home alone one day from fishing in the Elwy'.[1] It was written in early September 1877, shortly before his ordination and during the last few weeks of his three years at St Beuno's theological college.

Hurrahing in Harvest

Summer ends now; now, barbarous in beauty, the stooks[2] rise
Around; up above, what wind-walks![3] what lovely behaviour
Of silk-sack clouds! has wilder, wilful-wavier
Meal-drift[4] moulded ever and melted across skies?

I wálk, I líft up, Í lift úp heart, éyes,
Down all that glory in the heavens to glean our Saviour;
And, éyes, heárt, what looks, what lips yet gáve you a
Rapturous love's greeting of realer, of rounder replies?[5]

And the azurous hung hills are his world-wielding shoulder
Majestic — as a stallion stalwart, very-violet-sweet! —
These things, these things were here and but the beholder
Wánting; whích two whén they ónce méet,
The heart rears wings[6] bold and bolder
And hurls for him, O half hurls earth for him off under his feet.

Duns Scotus's Oxford

This poem was written in March 1879 while Hopkins was acting as curate in St Aloysius's church, Oxford. Although he felt great affection for the university

---

1   L I, p. 56.
2   stooks: sheaves of harvested corn.
3   Catherine Phillips glosses this as 'fluffy clouds blown across the sky as if making their way along a path' (p. 355).
4   Clouds that are insubstantial like the powdery ground-up 'meal' of grains such as oats or barley.
5   The sense is that the speaker's love of the natural beauty which shows the presence of Christ is returned: Christ and the natural world love him too, as much or more than any human being has. This lover-like relationship with Christ is echoed frequently in Hopkins's poetry and prose, both in joyful and despondent moods: for instance, in a letter to Bridges in 1879 Hopkins wrote: 'feeling, love in particular, is the great moving power and spring of verse and the only person that I am in love with seldom, especially now, stirs my heart sensibly and when he does I cannot always "make capital" of it, it would be a sacrilege to do so' (L I, p. 66).
6   Isobel Armstrong refers to this as the 'Pegasus heart', a heart like the winged horse of Greek legend. See Modern Criticism, p. 83.

(at which he himself had studied from 1863 to 1867, and where he had become a Roman Catholic), he did not wholly enjoy living in the town,[1] but he was able to spend a little time revisiting the countryside that had been familiar to him when he was an undergraduate in Oxford. In the same month as he wrote this poem, he also composed 'Binsey Poplars', about changes that had occurred in one of these rural locations (see **pp. 138–9**).

John Duns Scotus was a Franciscan and a great theologian who engaged in advanced studies at Oxford from 1288 to 1301 before being appointed to a chair of theology at the University of Paris in the very early 1300s. His theology became influential in the Roman Catholic Church from the sixteenth through the eighteenth centuries and was the main alternative to Thomist theology (i.e. theology based on the writings of St Thomas Aquinas). But by the nineteenth century his work was less well known.

Hopkins first read Duns Scotus in 1872 and was immediately very struck by him. One of the major aspects of Scotus's thought that appealed to Hopkins was Scotus's emphasis on the individuality of each created thing: Scotus's term for this individuality, *haecceitas*, is usually translated as 'thisness'. Well before Hopkins read Scotus, he had been writing about the experience of perceiving the unique individuality of particular things (see Modern Criticism, **pp. 74–7**, for comment by J. Hillis Miller about Hopkins's concepts of 'inscape' and 'instress'). Scotus gave Hopkins a theological basis for his thinking about these topics. Hopkins wrote to Bridges in 1875 that he cared for Duns Scotus 'more even than Aristotle and more [. . .] than a dozen Hegels'.[2]

The octave of this sonnet addresses Oxford directly ('thou') and complains about the damage to the city's beauty caused by the erection of new and ugly buildings. The first three lines of the sestet use the city that they both lived in as a way of bringing Hopkins and Scotus together, and the final tercet refers to Hopkins's belief that Scotus was the preeminent theologian of his time and particularly to Scotus's championing of the doctrine of the Immaculate Conception (the idea that Christ's mother, Mary, was born without original sin).[3]

Duns Scotus's Oxford

Towery city and branchy between towers;
Cuckoo-echoing, bell-swarmèd, lark-charmèd, rook-racked, river-
    rounded;
The dapple-eared lily below thee; that country and town did
Once encounter in, here coped and poisèd powers;

Thou hast a base and brickish skirt there, sours
That neighbour-nature thy grey beauty is grounded
Best in; graceless growth, thou hast confounded
Rural rural keeping — folk, flocks, and flowers.

1 White, pp. 305–6.
2 L I, p. 31.
3 The text here is taken from the Williams edition. The Phillips edition has added accents.

Yet ah! this air I gather and I release
He lived on; these weeds and waters, these walls are what
He haunted who of all men most sways my spirits to peace;

Of realty[4] the rarest-veinèd unraveller; a not
Rivalled insight, be rival Italy or Greece;
Who fired France for Mary without spot.

Binsey Poplars

Shortly before the writing of 'Duns Scotus's Oxford', in December 1878, Hopkins was sent by the Society of Jesus back to Oxford, not as a student but as a curate in St Aloysius's Church. Though he wrote to Mowbray Baillie, whom he had met when they were both Oxford undergraduates, that 'Not to love my University would be to undo the very buttons of my being and as for the Oxford townspeople I found them in my 10 months' stay among them very deserving of affection – though somewhat stiff, stand-off, and depressed,'[1] nonetheless Hopkins was miserable during this second Oxford period. In March 1879 he revisited Godstow, not far from Oxford, and found that 'the aspens that lined the river are everyone felled.'[2] The poem he wrote on the occasion is one of the most widely anthologized of his lyrics.[3]

Binsey Poplars

felled 1879

My aspens[4] dear, whose airy cages quelled,
Quelled or quenched in leaves the leaping sun,
All felled, felled, are all felled;
Of a fresh and following folded rank
Not spared, not one
That dandled a sandalled
Shadow that swam or sank
On meadow and river and wind-wandering weed-winding bank.

O if we but knew what we do
When we delve or hew —
Hack and rack the growing green!

---

4   Reality.

1   L III, p. 244.
2   L II, p. 26.
3   The text here is taken from the Williams edition. The Phillips has slight differences of layout and
    accents.
4   Aspens are trees in the poplar family.

Since country is so tender
To touch, her being só slender,
That, like this sleek and seeing ball[5]
But a prick will make no eye at all,
Where we, even where we mean
To mend her we end her,
When we hew or delve:
After-comers cannot guess the beauty been.
Ten or twelve, only ten or twelve
Strokes of havoc únselve[6]
The sweet especial scene,
Rural scene, a rural scene,
Sweet especial rural scene.

Henry Purcell

Henry Purcell (1659–1695) was a great English composer of the Baroque period. Hopkins had been a keen student and would-be composer of music all his life and he admired Purcell's compositions though Purcell himself, as a Protestant, was a highly problematic figure for Hopkins. Indeed he put Purcell alongside Milton (who though a near contemporary of Purcell was far more strongly linked to the Protestant cause) in a letter to Dixon: Milton's poetry 'seems something necessary and eternal (so to me does Purcell's music)'.[1]

In 1883 Hopkins explained to Bridges:

> The sonnet on Purcell means this: [lines] 1–4. I hope Purcell is not damned for being a Protestant, because I love his genius. 5–8. And that not so much for gifts he shares, even though it shd. be in higher measure, with other musicians as for his own individuality. 9–14. So that while he is aiming only at impressing me his hearer with the meaning in hand I am looking out meanwhile for his specific, his individual markings and mottlings, 'the sakes of him'. It is as when a bird thinking only of soaring spreads its wings: a beholder may happen then to have his attention drawn by the act to the plumage displayed. – In particular, the first lines mean: May Purcell, O may he have died a good death and that soul which I love so much and which breathes or stirs so unmistakeably in his works have parted from the body and passed away, centuries since though I frame the wish, in peace with God! So that the heavy condemnation under which he

---

5   i.e. an eyeball.
6   Compare 'selves – goes itself' in 'As kingfishers catch fire', l. 7.

1   L II, p. 13.

outwardly or nominally lay for being out of the true Church
may in consequence of his good intentions have been reversed.[2]

Henry Purcell

The poet wishes well to the divine genius of Purcell and praises him that, whereas
other musicians have given utterance to the moods of man's mind, he has, beyond
that, uttered in notes the very make and species of man as created both in him and
in all men generally.

Have fáir fállen, O fáir, fáir have fállen, so déar
To me, so arch-especial a spirit as heaves in Henry Purcell,
An age is now since passed, since parted; with the reversal
Of the outward sentence low lays him, listed to a heresy, here.

Not mood in him nor meaning, proud fire or sacred fear,
Or love, or pity, or all that sweet notes not his might nursle:[3]
It is the forgèd feature[4] finds me; it is the rehearsal[5]
Of own, of abrupt self there so thrusts on, so throngs the ear.

Let him oh! with his air of angels then lift me, lay me! only I'll
Have an eye to the sakes[6] of him, quaint moonmarks,[7] to his pelted
    plumage under
Wings: so some great stormfowl, whenever he has walked his while

The thunder-purple seabeach, plumèd purple-of-thunder,
If a wuthering of his palmy snow-pinions scatter a colossal
smile
Off him, but meaning motion fans fresh our wits with wonder.[8]

---

2   L I, pp. 170–1.
3   Phillips glosses 'nursle': 'to nurse, foster, cherish' (p. 359).
4   'Inescapable impress of personality' (Phillips, p. 359).
5   i.e. repetition.
6   Hopkins explained to Bridges that 'sake' in this instance meant 'distinctive quality in genius' (L I,
    p. 83).
7   'By *moonmarks* I mean crescent shaped markings on the quill-feathers' (L I, p. 83)
8   Hopkins commented:

    'The sestet [. . .] is not so clearly worked out as I could wish. The thought is that as the
    seabird opening his wings with a whiff of wind in your face means the whirr of the
    motion, but also unaware gives you a whiff of knowledge about his plumage, the marking
    of which stamps his species, that he does not mean, so Purcell, seemingly intent only on
    the thought or feeling he is to express or call out, incidentally lets you remark the indi-
    vidualising marks of his own genius.   (L I, p. 83)

Peace

This poem, like 'Pied Beauty', is a curtal sonnet, i.e., a poem written in the same proportions as a regular English sonnet but with fewer lines in each section. Written during the period in 1879 when Hopkins was a curate in Oxford, the poem uses reversals of syntax in lines 2 and 4 ('under be my boughs': be under my boughs, and 'own my heart': my own heart). White comments 'the consolatory ending is less powerful than the complaining start'.[1,2]

Peace

When will you ever, Peace, wild wooddove, shy wings shut,
Your round me roaming end, and under be my boughs?
When, when, Peace, will you, Peace? I'll not play hypocrite
To own my heart: I yield you do come sometimes; but
That piecemeal peace is poor peace. What pure peace allows
Alarms of wars, the daunting wars, the death of it?

O surely, reaving Peace, my Lord should leave in lieu[3]
Some good! And so he does leave Patience exquisite,
That plumes to Peace thereafter. And when Peace here does house
He comes with work to do, he does not come to coo,
      He comes to brood and sit.

Felix Randal

Felix Randal (real name Felix Spencer: perhaps Hopkins changed the name for purposes of rhyme) was a shoer of horses, a parishioner of Hopkins's in Liverpool, who died at thirty one in April 1880. The sonnet was written a week later.[1] Critics interested in the overlap of Hopkins's Christianity and his male-centred sexuality have commented on the admiration with which Hopkins portrays this working man's powerful physique. Julia F. Saville points out that the final tercet 'leaves us with an image of Felix not as a spiritual child receiving grace in his corporeal humiliation but as the invulnerable, energetic Victorian

---

1   White, p. 314.
2   The text is taken from the Williams edition. The Phillips edition has very slight differences in
    punctuation and layout.
3   Hopkins explained that 'reave' means 'rob, plunder, carry off' (L I, p. 196).

---

1   The text here is taken from the Williams edition. The Phillips edition has a slight difference in
    punctuation and added accents.

Vulcan, working only or and amid the physically mighty'.[2] Joseph Bristow argues that the emphasis on impressive strength connects Felix with other figures in Hopkins's poetry, including 'Tom's Garland' and the sailor in 'The Wreck of the Deutschland':

> these supposedly ox-like working men [. . .] could provide an imaginative license to a poet who looked to an "other" world liberated from respectable middle-class constraints, providing emblems upon which a remarkably emancipated and conspicuously modern kind of poetry might be modeled. Infused in them, of course, was the potency of God.[3]

Felix Randal

Félix Rándal the fárrier, O is he déad then? my dúty all énded,
Who have watched his mould of man, big-boned and hardy-handsome
Pining, pining, till time when reason rambled in it and some[4]
Fatal four disorders, fleshed there, all contended?

Sickness broke him. Impatient, he cursed at first, but mended
Being anointed[5] and all; though a heavenlier heart began some
Mónths éarlier, since Í had our swéet repriéve and ránsom
Téndered to him.[6] Áh well, God rést him áll road éver he offénded![7]

This séeing the síck endéars them tó us, us tóo it endéars.
My tongue had taught thee comfort, touch had quenched thy tears,
Thy tears that touched my heart, child, Felix, poor Felix Randal;

How far from then forethought of, all thy more boisterous years,[8]
When thou at the random grim forge, powerful amidst peers,
Didst fettle[9] for the great grey drayhorse his bright and battering
  sandal![10]

2 Julia F. Saville, *A Queer Chivalry: The Homoerotic Asceticism of Gerard Manley Hopkins* (Charlottesville, Va.: University Press of Virginia, 2000), p. 164.
3 Joseph Bristow, ' "Churlsgrace": Gerard Manley Hopkins and the Working-Class Male Body', *ELH* 59 (1992), pp. 693–711 (p. 709).
4 Robert Bridges attacked the handsome/and some rhyme in his 'Editor's Preface' to the first edition of Hopkins's poetry: see above, **p. 52.**
5 i.e. anointed with oil blessed by a bishop: Extreme Unction is one of the three Last Sacraments in Roman Catholic practice. Hopkins wrote that though Extreme Unction can perform extraordinary feats of healing, it is also 'meant to strengthen you for your death agony, for the last struggle with your spiritual enemy [. . .] Moreover it quits you of either all or some of the remains of sin [. . .] it may save your soul' (S, p. 249).
6 i.e. administered Holy Communion to him.
7 i.e. God forgive him for all the sins he ever committed. 'All road' was a Lancashire dialect phrase.
8 i.e. how little you looked ahead in your boisterous years to the time of sickness and death.
9 Archaic or dialect word meaning 'to make ready': in this instance, to forge.
10 i.e. the iron shoes on the horse's feet.

Spring and Fall

This is probably the most widely anthologized of Hopkins's poems, though he was perhaps not writing at his best or most characteristic here. It was written in 1880 and does not describe a real incident.[1,2]

Spring and Fall

to a young child

Margaret, are you grieving
Over Goldengrove unleaving?
Leaves, like the things of man, you
With your fresh thoughts care for, can you?
Ah! as the heart grows older
It will come to such sights colder
By and by, nor spare a sigh
Though worlds of wanwood leafmeal lie;
And yet you will weep and know why.
Now no matter, child, the name:
Sorrow's springs are the same.
Nor mouth had, no nor mind, expressed
What heart heard of, ghost guessed:
It is the blight man was born for,
It is Margaret you mourn for.[3]

The Leaden Echo and the Golden Echo

While working as a curate at Bedford Leigh in Lancashire in 1879, Hopkins began a verse tragedy telling the story of St Winefred's martyrdom. He was not confident about his ability to finish the play, though he wrote that 'I seem to find myself, after some experiment, equal to the more stirring and critical parts of the action, which are in themselves the more important, but about the filling in and minor parts I am not sure how far my powers will go. I have for one thing so little varied experience.'[1]

Winefred, according to legend, was a seventh-century Welsh nobleman's daughter who wished to devote her life to Christ but who was wooed by Caradoc, a local lord. When Winefred refused his suit he killed her, but her

---

1 L I, p. 109.
2 The text here is adapted from the Williams edition (I have left out his accents). The Phillips edition has slight differences of punctuation and added accents.
3 i.e. the child's sorrow over the leaves falling comes from the same spring as an adult's sorrow at the thought of his or her own mortality.

1 L I, p. 92.

relative Beuno (later St Beuno) raised her from the dead. At the spot where her blood had flowed, a stream of water sprang from the ground; the location became a place of pilgrimage and was known as Holywell. The water was said to have miraculous healing properties.

By 1885 Hopkins's melancholy state of mind meant that he could make no further progress with his play about St Winefred.[2] During a holiday in Wales the following year he worked on the play again,[3] but it was not finished when he died three years later. 'The Leaden Echo and the Golden Echo' is the best-known of the surviving fragments of the play; Hopkins wrote to Bridges that it was 'dramatic and meant to be popular'[4] and told Dixon that he had never written 'anything more musical'.[5]

Robert Bridges evidently told Hopkins that he thought 'The Leaden Echo and the Golden Echo' bore comparison with the poetry of the contemporary American writer Walt Whitman. Hopkins agreed that Whitman's rhythms, which he thought were on the point of 'decomposition into common prose', were indeed like the sprung rhythm of his own poem. But he insisted that 'The long lines [of "The Leaden Echo and the Golden Echo"] are not rhythm run to seed: everything is weighed and timed in them.'[6]

The Leaden Echo and the Golden Echo
(Maidens' song from *St. Winefred's Well*)

The Leaden Echo —

How to keep — is there ány any, is there none such, nowhere known
    some, bow or brooch or braid or brace, lace, latch or catch or key to
    keep[7]
Back beauty, keep it, beauty, beauty, beauty, . . . from vanishing away?[8]

---

2 L I, p. 219.
3 L I, p. 227.
4 L I, p. 106.
5 Phillips, p. 368.
6 L I, p. 157.
7 Phillips points out that Hopkins was not satisfied with the first line. '[T]he thought is of beauty as of something that can be physically kept and lost and by physical things only, like keys' (Phillips, p. 368).
8 Phillips quotes Hopkins: '*Back* is not pretty, but it gives that feeling of physical constraint which I want' (Phillips p. 368). In 1930 the English poet and critic T. Sturge Moore (1870–1944) suggested that the opening lines could have been better like this:

> 'How to keep beauty? is there any way?
> Is there nowhere any means to have it stay?
> Will no bow or brooch or braid,
>   Brace or lace
>   Latch or catch
> Or key to lock the door lend aid
> Before beauty vanishes away?'

F. R. Leavis commented ferociously '[Sturge Moore]has discarded, not merely a certain amount of music, but with the emotional crescendo and diminuendo, the plangent rise and fall, all the action and substance of the verse' (*New Bearings in English Poetry: A Study of the Contemporary Situation*, (London: Chatto & Windus, 1932, repr. with 'Retrospect 1950', 1950; Harmondsworth: Penguin (Peregrine), 1963), p. 141).

Ó is there no frowning of these wrinkles, rankèd wrinkles deep,
Down? no waving off of these most mournful messengers, still
   messengers, sad and stealing messengers of grey?—
No there's none, there's none, O no there's none,
Nor can you long be, what you now are, called fair,
Do what you may do, what, do what you may,
And wisdom is early to despair:
Be beginning; since, no, nothing can be done
To keep at bay
Age and age's evils, hoar hair,
Ruck and wrinkle, drooping, dying, death's worst, winding sheets,
   tombs and worms and tumbling to decay;
So be beginning, be beginning to despair.
O there's none; no no no there's none:
Be beginning to despair, to despair,
Despair, despair, despair, despair.

The Golden Echo

Spare!⁹
There is one, yes I have one (Hush there!);
Only not within seeing of the sun.
Not within the singeing of the strong sun,
Tall sun's tingeing, or treacherous the tainting of the
   earth's air,
Somewhere elsewhere there is ah well where! one,
One. Yes I can tell such a key, I do know such a place,
Where whatever's prizèd and passes of us, everything that's
   fresh and fast flying of us, seems to us sweet of us and swiftly
   away with, done away with, undone,
Undone, done with, soon done with, and yet dearly and
   dangerously sweet
Of us, the wimpledwater-dimpled, not-by-morning-matchèd face,
The flower of beauty, fleece of beauty, too too apt to, ah! to fleet,
Never fleets more, fastened with the tenderest truth
To its own best being and its loveliness of youth: it is an
   everlastingness of, O it is an all youth!
Cóme then, your ways and airs and looks, locks, maidengear,
   gallantry and gaiety and grace,¹⁰
Winning ways, airs innocent, maidenmanners, sweet looks, loose locks,
   long locks, lovelocks, gaygear, going gallant, girlgrace —
Resign them, sign them, seal them, send them, motion them
   with breath,
And with sighs soaring, soaring sighs, deliver
Them; beauty-in-the-ghost, deliver it, early now, long before death

9 Spare!: Stop!
10 Hopkins invented 'maidengear' for this poem. It means something like 'the things that maidens
   possess'.

Give beauty back, beauty, beauty, beauty, back to God beauty's self
    and beauty's giver.
See; not a hair is, not an eyelash, not the least lash lost; every hair
Is, hair of the head, numbéred.[11]
Nay, what we had lighthanded left in surly the mere mould[12]
Will have waked and have waxed and have walked with the wind what
    while we slept,[13]
This side, that side hurling a heavy-headed hundredfold
What while we, while we slumbered.
O then, weary then whý should we tread? O why are we so haggard at
    the heart, so care-coiled, care-killed, so fagged, so fashed, so cogged,
    so cumbered,[14]
When the thing we freely fórfeit is kept with fonder a care,
Fonder a care kept than we could have kept it, kept
Far with fonder a care (and we, we should have lost it) finer,
    fonder
A care kept. — Where kept? do but tell us where kept, where. —[15]
Yonder. — What high as that![16] We follow, now we follow. — Yonder, yes
    yonder, yonder,
Yonder.

To Seem the Stranger

Hopkins's conversion to Roman Catholicism caused both an immediate and a long-term estrangement from his family, to whom he had previously been close. He wrote to his father in October 1866, once he had made the decision to convert: 'You ask me if I have had no thought of the estrangement. I have had months to think of everything'.[1] His father's reply mourned the 'hard & cold' tone of Hopkins's letter and returned to the question of the rift in the family Hopkins's decision was creating:

> the manner in which you seem to repel & throw us off cuts us to the heart. All we ask of you is for your own sake to take so

---

11 Compare Matthew 10.30: 'But the very hairs of your head are all numbered'. In a meditation on death, Hopkins wrote: '*the hairs of your head*, Christ says, *are numbered*; if when the hair is parted God counts and knows how many hairs fall to the right side and how many to the left how much more does he take account of the parting of soul and body!' (S, p. 252).

12 Characteristic Hopkins inversion: the sense is something like 'what we carelessly left without seeing through to completion'. Phillips notes that Hopkins wrote that this line means 'Nay more: the seed that we so carelessly and freely flung into the dull furrow, and then forgot it, will have come to ear [matured and be ready for harvest] meantime' (Phillips, p. 369).

13 Waxed: grown.

14 Fagged: exhausted. Fashed: a Scottish and northern English dialect word meaning troubled. Cogged: Phillips suggests 'perhaps "vexed", "blocked" ' (p. 369).

15 The dashes indicate that the voices are here in dialogue: the 'Leaden Echo' asks 'Where kept? do but tell us where kept, where' and is answered by the 'Golden Echo'.

16 'What high as that!': What, as high up as that (presumably referring to Heaven).

---

1 L III, p. 94.

momentous a step with caution & hesitation; have we not a right to do this? [. . .] you answer by saying that as we might be Romanists if we pleased the estrangement is not of your doing. O Gerard my darling boy are you indeed gone from me?[2]

Though the initial breach was later healed, Hopkins's life as a priest meant that he could visit his family only rarely. In February 1884 he was sent to live in Dublin, to work as Professor of Greek at the new Roman Catholic University. Ireland at that time was under British rule. The 1870s and 1880s saw increasingly bad relations between Ireland and England; the Home Rule movement was agitating for Irish autonomy and the British Prime Minister, William Ewart Gladstone, made concessions on important and controversial issues including land tenure, culminating in 1886 with his failed attempt to pass a Home Rule Bill. English popular sentiment was mainly against Home Rule, partly because of fears about the effects of the unbridled influence of the Roman Catholic clergy on Irish politics. For Hopkins, an English convert, living in Ireland during this turbulent time was a powerful emotional experience that brought his English and Roman Catholic loyalties into sharp focus. 'The grief of mind I go through over politics, over what I read and hear and see in Ireland about Ireland and about England, is such that I can neither express it nor bear to speak of it', he wrote to his mother in 1885.[3]

In the same year Hopkins wrote a number of poems which later critics have grouped together under the name 'Sonnets of Desolation' or more commonly the 'Terrible Sonnets', including 'I Wake and Feel', 'No Worst, There is None', 'Carrion Comfort', 'Patience, Hard Thing' and 'My Own Heart Let Me Have More Pity On'. He told Bridges: 'four of these came like inspirations unbidden and against my will.[4] And in the life I lead now, which is one of a continually jaded and harassed mind, if in any leisure I try to do anything I make no way – nor with my work, alas! but so it must be'.[5] Hopkins was unhappy, lonely, ill and exhausted in Dublin: the poems written at this time generally reject the metrical innovations of the sonnets written in Wales (such as 'The Windhover') and use a more conventional sonnet form, though they maintain lexical innovations and syntactical inversions. See Modern Criticism, **pp. 96–106**, for recent critical discussion of this group of poems, and **pp. 102–4** for Eric Griffiths's reading of this poem in particular. Norman White calls this 'the loneliest of poems, written for himself and seen by no one else while he lived'.[6]

'To seem the stranger'

To seem the stranger lies my lot, my life
Among strangers. Father and mother dear,

2   L III, p. 96, p. 97.
3   L III, p. 170
4   Scholars do not agree on which four Hopkins meant.
5   L I, p. 221.
6   White, p. 260.

Brothers and sisters are in Christ not near
And he my peace/my parting, sword and strife.

England, whose honour O all my heart woos,[7] wife
To my creating thought, would neither hear
Me, were I pleading, plead nor do I: I wéar-
Y of idle a being but by where wars are rife.

I am in Ireland now; now I am at a thírd
Remove.[8] Not but in all removes I can
Kind love both give and get. Only what word

Wisest my heart breeds dark heaven's baffling ban
Bars or hell's spell thwarts. This to hoard unheard,
Heard unheeded, leaves me a lonely began.

I Wake and Feel

Norman White calls this poem 'a chaotic and unresolved sonnet, a profoundly realistic representation of psychological struggle'.[1] Like 'Moonrise' (**pp. 128–9**), the poem begins with the speaker waking in the night but where the earlier poem gives a vision of natural beauty that almost undoes the speaker ('parted me leaf and leaf'), this sleepless night is full of pain.

'I wake and feel'

I wake and feel the fell of dark, not day.
What hours, O what black hours we have spent
This night! what sights you, heart, saw; ways you went!
And more must, in yet longer light's delay.

With witness I speak this. But where I say
Hours I mean years, mean life. And my lament

---

7   Compare with Hopkins's marching song for English soldiers: 'What Shall I Do for the Land that Bred Me', which begins: 'What shall I do for the land that bred me, / Her homes and fields that folded and fed me? — / Be under her banner and live for her honour: / Under her banner I'll live for her honour' (Phillips, pp. 181–2). Hopkins tended to think of art and patriotism as supporting one another: in 1886 he wrote to Bridges: 'A great work by an Englishman is like a great battle won by England' (L I, p. 231). And of Wordsworth's great poem 'Ode: Intimations of Immortality' (publ. 1807), he wrote to Dixon: 'For my part I shd. think St. George [patron saint of England] and St. Thomas of Canterbury [St Thomas Becket] wore roses in heaven for England's sake on the day that ode, not without their intercession [i.e. heavenly help], was penned' (L II, p. 148).

8   Catherine Phillips suggests that the first remove was the rift with his family over his conversion and the second the separation of the English people from the Roman Catholic faith (p. 373).

---

1   White, p. 401.

Is cries countless, cries like dead letters[2] sent
To dearest him that lives alas! away.

I am gall,[3] I am heartburn. God's most deep decree
Bitter would have me taste: my taste was me;
Bones built in me, flesh filled, blood brimmed the curse.[4]

Selfyeast of spirit a dull dough sours. I see
The lost[5] are like this, and their scourge[6] to be
As I am mine, their sweating selves; but worse.

No worst, There Is None

Another of the 'Terrible Sonnets', this poem is more experimental in its lexis than 'To Seem the Stranger' or 'I wake and feel'.[1] In May 1885 Hopkins, worn out from work at the university and miserable in Ireland, wrote to Bridges: 'I think that my fits of sadness, though they do not affect my judgment, resemble madness'.[2] Lines 9–11 of this sonnet echo *King Lear*, a play very much about madness provoked through unbearable suffering (see Modern Criticism, **pp. 99–100**, for W. H. Gardner's analysis of the Shakespearean echoes in this and the other Terrible Sonnets). Opening with the idea that suffering has no limit, that pain can always grow worse, the poem asks the Holy Spirit and the Blessed Virgin Mary for help, but there is no answer: the only voice other than the speaker's is that of 'Fury', urging itself on to inflict further torments. In the sestet the imagery turns to landscape, but not the external, beautiful landscapes of the St Beuno poems (such as 'Hurrahing in Harvest'): rather this is an internal, mental or emotional landscape of dangerous precipices. The only consolation the speaker can find by the end of the poem is that death and sleep bring pain to an end. In 'I Wake and Feel', Hopkins extends his vision of pain beyond death to include the punishment of damned souls; this poem gives no sense that death is not final. Norman White calls this idea 'unChristian':[3] perhaps this is the poem that best illustrates J. Hillis Miller's argument that Hopkins had, among all his Victorian contemporaries, 'the most shattering experience of the disappearance of God'.[4]

---

2 Undelivered letters.
3 A bitter substance (literally, produced by the liver).
4 Compare 'The Wreck of the Deutschland', st. 1 l. 5: 'Thou hast bound bones and veins in me, fastened me flesh'.
5 i.e. the damned in Hell.
6 Literally a whip; figuratively, torture or divine chastisement.

---

1 This text is taken from the Williams edition. The Phillips edition has slight differences in punctuation and layout, and added accents.
2 L I, p. 216.
3 White, p. 395.
4 See above, Modern Criticism, **p. 105**.

'No worst'

No worst, there is none. Pitched past pitch of grief,
More pangs will, schooled at forepangs, wilder wring.[5]
Comforter,[6] where, where is your comforting?
Mary,[7] mother of us, where is your relief?
My cries heave, herds-long; huddle in a main, a chief
Woe, world-sorrow; on an age-old anvil wince and sing —
Then lull, then leave off. Fury had shrieked 'No ling-
ering! Let me be fell:[8] force[9] I must be brief'.

O the mind, mind has mountains; cliffs of fall
Frightful, sheer, no-man-fathomed. Hold them cheap
May who ne'er hung there. Nor does long our small
Durance deal with that steep or deep. Here! creep,
Wretch, under a comfort serves in a whirlwind:[10] all
Life death does end and each day dies with sleep.

(Carrion Comfort)

Some critics and editors refer to this poem, to which Hopkins did not give a title, as '(Carrion Comfort)' (the parentheses indicating that the title is not original), others as 'Not, I'll Not, Carrion Comfort, Despair'.

The speaker in this sonnet sets his face resolutely against suicide (though that word is never used). In Roman Catholic doctrine, despair is considered a mortal sin, a conscious transgression of divine law, because it implies that one has made a decision that God cannot or will not help one save one's soul. Despair is 'carrion comfort' in the sense that it is dead, taboo and unappealing. Rather like the first stanzas of 'The Wreck of the Deutschland', the poem is full of metaphors of punishment and violence describing Hopkins's experience of God.

(Carrion Comfort)

Not, I'll not, carrion comfort, Despair, not feast on thee;
Not untwist — slack they may be — these last strands of man

---

5 The sense is that each moment of anguish builds on earlier ones ('forepangs') and instead of becoming hardened, the sufferer experiences each new pain as worse than previous ones.
6 In a sermon preached in Liverpool, Hopkins explained the 'Paraclete' or 'Comforter' in Roman Catholic theology: 'A Paraclete is one who comforts, who cheers, who encourages, who persuades, who exhorts, who stirs up, who urges forward, who calls on' (S, p. 70). He identifies both Christ and the Holy Ghost as performing this role.
7 i.e. the Blessed Virgin Mary.
8 fell: fierce, savage; cruel, ruthless; dreadful, terrible (OED).
9 Necessarily, perforce.
10 i.e. 'under a comfort that serves in a whirlwind'.

In me ór, most weary, cry *I can no more.* I can;
Can something, hope, wish day come, not choose not to be.

But ah, but O thou terrible, why wouldst thou rude on me
Thy wring-earth right foot rock? lay a lionlimb against me? scan
With darksome devouring eyes my bruisèd bones? and fan,[1]
O in turns of tempest, me heaped there; me frantic to avoid thee
        and flee?

Why? That my chaff might fly; my grain lie, sheer and clear.
Nay in all that toil, that coil, since (seems) I kissed the rod,[2]
Hand rather,[3] my heart lo! lapped strength, stole joy, would laugh,
        cheer.[4]

Cheer whóm though? The héro whose héaven-handling[5] flúng me, fóot
        tród
Me? or mé that fóught him? O whích one? is it eách one? That níght,
        that year
Of now done darkness I wretch lay wrestling with (my God!) my God.

My Own Heart

The last of the 'Terrible Sonnets' included in this sourcebook, this poem is less
violent and in a very subdued way perhaps more optimistic than the others,
acknowledging that though relief from suffering seems to be completely
vanished, joy may reappear at a time the speaker cannot predict.

'My own heart'

My own heart let me more have pity on; let
Me live to my sad self hereafter kind,
Charitable; not live this tormented mind
With this tormented mind tormenting yet.

---

1   Hopkins turns from carnivore imagery to images of threshing: 'fanning' wheat blows the chaff
    away, leaving only the grain.
2   Catherine Phillips suggests that 'kissed the rod' (a standard phrase meaning 'agreed to be obedient')
    might here mean 'accepted depression [. . .] as a test set by God' (p. 375) (but see below).
3   i.e. 'or rather, kissed (not the rod but) the hand', perhaps recalling the ceremony of ordination at
    which Hopkins would have kissed the hand of the bishop, or a general image of obedience associ-
    ated with his conversion. But Eric Griffiths suggests that it is his own hand the speaker is kissing,
    perhaps in a gesture of graceful compliance or gratitude; he compares this image with 'I kiss my
    hand to the stars' ('Wreck of the Deutschland', st. 5, l. 1) (Griffiths, *The Printed Voice of Victorian
    Poetry* (Oxford: Clarendon Press, 1989), p. 332).
4   For the first time in the Terrible Sonnets Hopkins acknowledges memories of happier times.
5   i.e. handling from heaven: again, compare with the first stanzas (esp. st. 2) of 'The Wreck of the
    Deutschland', where God buffets Hopkins during the period of his coming to conversion.

I cast for comfort I can no more get
By groping round my comfortless than blind
Eyes in their dark can day or thirst can find
Thirst's all-in-all in all a world of wet.[1]

Soul, self; come, poor Jackself, I do advise
You, jaded, lét be; call off thoughts awhile
Elsewhere; leave comfort root-room; let joy size[2]

At God knows when to God knows what; whose smile
'S not wrung, see you; unforseentimes rather — as skies
Betweenpie[3] mountains — lights a lovely mile.[4]

Spelt from Sibyl's Leaves

F. R. Leavis thought that 'Spelt from Sibyl's Leaves' was 'one of the finest things that [Hopkins] ever did', and that 'it exhibits and magnificently justifies most of the peculiarities of his technique':

> in comparison with such a poem of Hopkins's as this, any other poetry of the nineteenth century is seen to be using only a very small part of the resources of the English language. His words seem to have substance, and to be made of a great variety of stuffs. Their potencies are correspondingly greater for subtle and delicate communication.[1]

Hopkins called the poem 'the longest sonnet ever made and no doubt the longest [in the] making'[2] (it was begun in 1884 but not finished until 1886). He

---

1   Robert Bridges glossed ll. 5–7 as 'I cast [around] for comfort, (which) I can no more find in my comfortless (world) than a blind man in his dark world' (*Poems of Gerard Manley Hopkins*, ed. by Robert Bridges, 2nd edn (London: Oxford University Press, 1930, repr. 1938), p. 117. Lines 7–8 recall the plight of the Ancient Mariner in Coleridge's poem, whose ship was becalmed with no drinking water: 'Water, water, everywhere, / And all the boards did shrink; / Water, water, everywhere, / Ne any drop to drink.' (ll. 115–18).
2   Increase in size.
3   Catherine Phillips glosses 'betweenpie' as 'probably a verb, suggesting either that the sky seen between mountains makes a pied or variegated pattern with them, or that sunlight falling into a valley changes the colour of those parts of the mountains it touches' (p. 377).
4   The sense is that the smile (which may be God's or joy's) cannot be forced, but (as Laura Riding and Robert Graves put it, 'comes as suddenly and unexpectedly as when, walking among mountains, you come to a point where the sky shines through a cleft between two mountains and throws a shaft of light over a mile of ground thus unexpectedly illumined for you' (*A Survey of Modernist Poetry* (London: Heinemann, 1927), p. 92).

---

1   F. R. Leavis, *New Bearings in English Poetry: A Study of the Contemporary Situation* (London: Chatto & Windus, 1932, repr. with 'Retrospect 1950', 1950; Harmondsworth: Penguin (Peregrine), 1963), p. 148, p. 151.
2   L I, p. 245.

told Bridges that it was written 'for performance and that its performance is not reading with the eye but loud, leisurely, poetical (not rhetorical) recitation, with long rests, long dwells on the rhyme and other marked syllables, and so on. This sonnet shd. be almost sung'.[3]

The poem begins with a description of the changing light at evening and moves into imagining the *final* evening of the world, i.e., the evening of the Day of Judgement when, according to Christian tradition, Christ will return to the earth to judge all human souls and the world will then be destroyed. For Hopkins this destruction is a process of unbinding the 'dapple' or variegated-ness, mixedness, of the world into only two kinds: those to be preserved, and those to be lost. The title refers to the Cumaean Sibyl or female prophet of classical myth, who was said to have written her prophecies on leaves. Many critics have compared the poem to the 'Dies Irae', a thirteenth-century Latin poem by Thomas of Celano, formerly used in the Roman Catholic funeral and requiem mass, which begins by associating the Day of Judgement with both the Sybil and King David:

> The day of wrath, that dreadful day of anger, will dissolve the world into ashes, as David and the Sybil foretold.
> How great the trembling will be when the judge descends from heaven to scrutinize everything.

Eric Griffiths comments on the 'extreme density of internal rhyme' in the poem, noting that 'it is as if the moral consciousness of the poem were itself whelmed by the descent of a sonic night which blots out the discriminations that consciousness tries to make. The remarkable, created tussle within the poem, its impeded movement, thought making its way through language as through a muddy and a clogging earth, produces a self-retorting eloquence'.[4]

Spelt from Sibyl's Leaves

Earnest, earthless, equal, attuneable, | vaulty, voluminous, . . . stupendous
Evening strains to be tíme's vást, | womb-of-all, home-of-all, hearse-of-all night.
Her fond yellow hornlight[5] wound to the west, | her wild hollow hoarlight[6] hung to the height
Waste; her earliest stars, earlstars,[7] | stars principal, overbend us,
Fíre-féaturing héaven. For éarth | her béing has unbóund; her dápple is at énd, as-

---

3   L I, p. 246.
4   Eric Griffiths, *The Printed Voice of Victorian Poetry* (Oxford: Clarendon Press, 1989), p. 319.
5   i.e. moonlight.
6   i.e. starlight.
7   Compare 'The Starlight Night', ll. 1–2: 'Look at the stars! look, look up at the skies! / O look at all the fire-folk sitting in the air!'

Tray or aswarm, all throughther,[8] in throngs; | self ín self stéepèd and
    páshed — qúite
Disremembering,[9] dismembering | all now. Heart, you round me right
With: Óur évening is óver us; óur night | whélms, whélms, ánd will
    énd us.
Only the beakleaved boughs dragonish | damask the tool-smooth bleak
    light;[10] black,
Ever so black on it. Óur tale, O óur oracle! | Lét life, wáned, ah lét life
    wínd
Off hér once skéined stained véined varíety | upon, áll on twó spools;
    párt, pen, páck
Now her áll in twó flocks, twó folds — bláck, white; | ríght, wrong;
    réckon but, réck but, mínd
But thése two; wáre of a wórld where bút these | twó tell,[11] éach off the
    óther; of a ráck
Where, selfwrung, selfstrung, sheathe- and shelterless, | thóughts agáinst
    thoughts ín groans grínd.[12]

Tom's Garland

Hopkins sent this difficult poem to Dixon in December 1887 along with 'Harry
Ploughman',[1] and remarked: 'they are of a "robustious" sort and perhaps "Tom's
Garland" approaches bluster and will remind you of Mr. Podsnap with his back
to the fire.[2] They are meant for, and cannot properly be taken in without,
emphatic recitation; which nevertheless is not an easy performance'.[3] Dixon
apparently found the sonnet difficult to understand even with 'emphatic recita-
tion' and wrote to Bridges to see if he could explain it. Hopkins commented:

---

8 Catherine Phillips glosses 'throughther' as a dialect word meaning 'confused, disorderly' (p. 380).
9 An Irish dialect word meaning 'forgetting'.
10 F. R. Leavis explains: 'the trees are no longer the beautiful, refreshing things of daylight; they have
    turned fantastically strange, hard and cruel, "beak-leaved" suggesting the cold, hard light, steely
    like the gleam of polished tools, against which they appear as a kind of damascene-work ("dam-
    ask") on a blade'. *New Bearings in English Poetry* (London: Chatto & Windus, 1932, repr. with
    'Retrospect 1950', 1950; Harmondsworth: Penguin (Peregrine), 1963), p. 150.
11 Eric Griffiths argues that 'ware' is ambiguous: 'he means both that the heart should be aware of
    such a world ["where right and wrong are seen with absolute clarity to be all that matters"] and also
    beware of such a world' (*The Printed Voice of Victorian Poetry* (Oxford: Clarendon Press, 1989),
    p. 320).
12 I. A. Richards commented: 'It is characteristic of this poet that there is no repose for him in the
    night of traditional morality. As the terrible last line shows, the renunciation of all the myriad
    temptations of life brought no gain. It was all loss' ('Gerard Hopkins', *The Dial*, September 1926,
    quoted in Gerald Roberts, ed., *Gerard Manley Hopkins: The Critical Heritage* (London: Routledge
    & Kegan Paul, 1987), p. 144).

---

1 In Phillips, p. 177.
2 In Charles Dickens's *Our Mutual Friend* (1864–5), Podsnap is small-minded, self-satisfied,
    pompous and absurd. Hopkins is acknowledging that he may be like Podsnap in being opinionated.
3 L II, p. 153.

I laughed outright and often, but very sardonically, to think you and the Canon [Dixon] could not construe my last sonnet; that he had to write to you for a crib [a translation]. It is plain I must go no farther on this road [of experimentation with obscure poetics]: if you and he cannot understand me who will?'.[4]

Obligingly Hopkins explained to Bridges the poem's thought ('O, once explained, how clear it all is!'[5]). The poem is concerned with contemporary British class politics. The central figure, 'Tom', is a composite, standing for the labouring classes. The poem argues that despite the discomforts and hard work that make up their lives, labourers are lighthearted. Hopkins added in his explanation to Bridges: 'the witnessing of which lightheartedness makes me indignant with the fools of Radical Levellers',[6] i.e. advocates of the abolition of private property rights: probably Hopkins means socialists.

But presently [the speaker in the poem remembers] that this [lightheartedness] is all very well for those who are in, however low in, the Commonwealth [i.e. of British society] and share in any way the Common weal [i.e. good]; but that the curse of our times is that many do not share it, that they are outcasts from it and have neither security nor splendour [. . .]. And this state of things, I say, is the origin of Loafers, Tramps, Cornerboys, Roughs, Socialists and other pests of society.[7]

Hopkins's politics are in some ways difficult to categorize neatly. In 'Tom's Garland' he uses the socially conservative image of the nation as a single body, with 'lordly head' (the monarch) and 'mighty foot' (the labourers), implying that the interests of one class are the interests of all and that internal strife (such as agitation for the rights of the poor) is nonsensical and counterproductive. He describes the unemployed and dispossessed – those who do not share the legitimate social position even of the poor labourers – in animal terms, as 'Hangdog' and 'Manwolf', an infestation. But he recognizes that the causes of their dehumanization are socially produced: despair and rage at being shut out from the benefits of belonging.

Evidence for unemployment rates in the nineteenth century is far from complete, but it is clear that unemployment was a common experience particularly among manual workers, and that in the 1880s and 1890s in particular it was seen as a growing threat to a stable society and economy. In 1871 there had been a major breach in Hopkins's friendship with Bridges, a rift that lasted for more than two years and that was occasioned by Bridges's rejection of Hopkins's political stance towards the dispossessed. Hopkins had written to

4   L I, p. 272.
5   L I, p. 273.
6   L I, p. 273.
7   L I, pp. 273–4.

Bridges about his concern for the unemployed and his consequent sympathy for those who offered radical solutions:

> Horrible to say, in a manner I am a Communist. Their ideal bating some things[8] is nobler than that professed by any secular statesman I know of (I must own I live in bat-light[9] and shoot at a venture[10]). Besides it is just. [. . .] it is a dreadful thing for the greatest and most necessary part of a very rich nation to live a hard life without dignity, knowledge, comforts, delight, or hopes in the midst of plenty – which plenty they make. They [working-class radicals] profess that they do not care what they wreck and burn, the old civilisation and order must be destroyed. This is a dreadful look out but what has the old civilisation done for them?[11,12]

This much later poem addresses the same questions.

Hopkins called 'Tom's Garland' a sonnet with two codas (each of the two-and-a-half line sections at the end of the poem is one coda)[13,14].

Tom's Garland

upon the Unemployed

Tom — garlanded with squat and surly steel
Tom; then Tom's fallowbootfellow piles pick
By him and rips out rockfire homeforth — sturdy Dick;
Tom Heart-at-ease, Tom Navvy: he is all for his meal
Sure,'s bed now.[15] Low be it: lustily he his low lot (feel
That ne'er need hunger, Tom; Tom seldom sick,
Seldomer heartsore; that treads through, prickproof, thick
Thousands of thorns, thoughts) swings though. Commonweal
Little I reck ho! lacklevel in, if all had bread:
What! Country is honour enough in all us[16] — lordly head,

---

8 i.e. with the exception of some things.
9 i.e. obscurity.
10 i.e. am guessing.
11 Critics sometimes refer to this as Hopkins's 'red letter'.
12 L I, pp 27–8.
13 Phillips, p. 383.
14 The text here is taken from the Williams edition. The Phillips edition has slight differences of punctuation and added accents.
15 Hopkins wrote to Bridges:

> the scene of the poem is laid at evening, when they are giving over work and one after another pile their picks, with which they earn their living, and swing off home, knocking sparks out of mother earth not now by labour and of course but by the mere footing, being strongshod and making no hardship of hardness, taking all easy.   (L I, p. 273)

16 Compare 'England, whose honour O all my heart woos' ('To seem the stranger', l. 5).

With heaven's lights high hung round, or, mother-ground
That mammocks, mighty foot. But no way sped,
Nor mind nor mainstrength; gold go garlanded
With, perilous, O nó; nor yet plod safe shod sound;
    Undenizened,[17] beyond bound
Of earth's glory, earth's ease, all; no one, nowhere,
In wide the world's weal; rare gold, bold steel, bare
    In both; care, but share care —
This, by Despair, bred Hangdog dull; by Rage,
Manwolf, worse; and their packs infest the age.

That Nature is a Heraclitean Fire

This sonnet with three codas was written in July 1888. Heraclitus was a Greek cosmologist working around 500 BC. He argued that the multiplicity and vari-ousness of the world should really be understood as having an underlying unifying order or structure. This doctrine has parallels with Hopkins's religio-aesthetic interest in the way the dappledness and piedness of nature revealed the presence of God.

The title alludes to the central argument of the poem: nature is in a constant state of flux, and the fire that Heraclitus thought was the most important element in the physical world is also within the human soul. When the fire is put out in death, the soul is submerged in darkness and might be forgotten or obliterated. But Christ's return from the dead (resurrection) promises that death will not be obliteration but instead a coming to true selfhood: after death the soul will emerge from the dross of physical life and its concerns and be recognizable as being made of the same material as Christ.

In September 1888 Hopkins wrote to Bridges reminding him that he had sent him this sonnet, 'in which a great deal of early Greek philosophical thought was distilled; but the liquor of the distillation did not taste very Greek, did it?'[1].[2]

That Nature is a Heraclitean Fire and of the comfort of the Resurrection

Cloud puffball, torn tufts, tossed pillows | flaunt forth, then chevy[3] on
    an air-

---

17 i.e. lacking citizenship.

1 L I, p. 291.
2 The text here is taken from the Williams edition. The Phillips edition has slight differences of
    punctuation and an added accent.
3 chevy: to race or scamper (OED).

built thoroughfare: heaven-roysterers, in gay-gangs | they throng; they
  glitter in marches.[4]
Down roughcast, down dazzling whitewash, | wherever an elm arches,
Shivelights[5] and shadowtackle in long | lashes lace, lance, and pair.
Delightfully the bright wind boisterous | ropes, wrestles, beats earth bare
Of yestertempest's creases; | in pool and rut peel parches
Squandering ooze to squeezed | dough, crust, dust;[6] stanches, starches
Squadroned masks and manmarks | treadmire toil there
Footfretted in it. Million-fuelèd, | nature's bonfire burns on.
But quench her bonniest, dearest | to her, her clearest-selvèd[7] spark
Man, how fast his firedint,[8] | his mark on mind, is gone!
Both are in an unfathomable, all is in an enormous dark
Drowned. O pity and indig | nation! Manshape, that shone
Sheer off, disseveral,[9] a star, | death blots black out; nor mark
        Is any of him at all so stark
But vastness blurs and time | beats level. Enough! the Resurrection,
A heart's-clarion! Away grief's gasping, | joyless days, dejection.
        Across my foundering deck[10] shone
A beacon, an eternal beam. | Flesh fade, and mortal trash
Fall to the residuary worm; | world's wildfire, leave but ash:
        In a flash,[11] at a trumpet crash,
I am all at once what Christ is, | since he was what I am, and
This Jack,[12] joke, poor potsherd,[13] | patch, matchwood, immortal
  diamond,
        Is immortal diamond.

Justus quidem tu es, Domine

The poem is sometimes known by the English translation of its part of its title,
'Thou art indeed just'. (The poem proper starts after the completion of the

---

4 The behaviour of clouds shows the vitality and carefreeness of nature. Compare 'Hurrahing in
   Harvest', ll. 2–4.
5 'Splinters of light' (Phillips, p. 385).
6 The wind causes water to evaporate, so that soggy ground becomes a little drier. Heraclitus argued
   that the elements are in flux.
7 i.e. most clearly selved, most distinctive.
8 A compound word invented by Hopkins, meaning something like 'a blow of fire' and signifying
   selfhood.
9 Another Hopkins coinage. To dissever includes the meaning 'to divide'; so 'disseveral' suggests
   'divided off from', i.e. unique.
10 The shipwreck imagery picks up the idea in l. 13 of the individuality of (a) man being 'drowned' in
   the cosmic dark after death.
11 Compare 'The Wreck of the Deutschland', st. 3, l. 8: 'To flash from the flame to the flame then,
   tower from the grace to the grace.'
12 Compare 'My own heart let me have more pity on', l. 9, where the speaker addresses himself as
   'Jackself'.
13 potsherd: a fragment of broken pottery. Compare Genesis 3:19: 'dust thou art, and unto dust shalt
   thou return' (AV).

quotation from Jeremiah.) It was written in March 1889, several years after the 'Terrible Sonnets', and just a few months before Hopkins's death. In 1888, Hopkins had written that he felt

> loathing and hopelessness [. . .] which made me fear madness [. . .] I could therefore do no more than repeat *Justus es, Domine, et rectum judicium tuum*[1] and the like [. . .] What is my wretched life? Five wasted years almost have passed in Ireland. I am ashamed of the little I have done, of my waste of time, although my helplessness and weakness is such that I could scarcely do otherwise. [. . .] All my undertakings miscarry: I am like a straining eunuch. I wish then for death: yet if I died now I should die imperfect, no master of myself, and that is the worst failure of all'.[2,3]

Justus guidem tu es, Domine, si disputem tecum: verumtamen justa loquar ad te: Quare via impiorum prosperatur? &c.[4]

> Thou art indeed just, Lord, if I contend
> With thee; but, sir,[5] so what I plead is just.
> Why do sinners' ways prosper? and why must
> Disappointment all I endeavour end?
>   Wert thou my enemy, O thou my friend,
> How wouldst thou worse, I wonder, than thou dost
> Defeat, thwart me? Oh, the sots[6] and thralls of lust
> Do in spare hours more thrive than I that spend,[7]

1   From Psalm 118 in the Vulgate, 119 in AV, verse 137, translated in AV as 'Righteous art thou, O Lord, and upright are thy judgments'. DR (Ps. 118): 'Thou art just, O Lord: and thy judgment is right'.
2   S, p. 262.
3   The text here is taken from the Williams edition. The Phillips edition has slight differences of punctuation and layout.
4   The Latin comes from the Vulgate, the Bible translated by St Jerome around AD 400 and formally adopted as the exclusive Bible of the Roman Catholic Church in the mid-sixteenth century. The AV translates the verse from which the poem takes its title as: 'Righteous art thou, O Lord, when I plead with thee: yet let me talk with thee of thy judgments: Wherefore doth the way of the wicked prosper?' The verses go on:

> wherefore are all they happy that deal very treacherously?
>   Thou hast planted them, yea, they have taken root: they grow, yea, they bring forth fruit: thou art near in their mouth, and far from their reins.
>   But thou, O Lord, knowest me: thou hast seen me, and tried mine heart toward thee: pull them out like sheep for the slaughter, and prepare them for the day of slaughter.

(Hopkins replaces this blood-thirsty plea with the gentler 'send my roots rain'.) DR gives: 'Thou indeed O Lord art just, if I dispute with thee, but yet I will speak just things to thee: Why doth the way of the impious prosper [. . .]?'
5   Hopkins addresses God as 'sir' in l. 20 of an unfinished poem, 'Thee, God, I come from': 'I have life left with me still / And thy purpose to fulfil; Yea a debt to pay thee yet: / Help me, sir, and so I will.' (Phillips, p. 169).
6   Drunks.
7   cp. l. 9 of 'God's Grandeur': 'And, for all this, nature is never spent;'.

Sir, life upon thy cause. See, banks and brakes[8]
Now, leavèd how thick! lacèd they are again
With fretty[9] chervil, look, and fresh wind shakes
Them; birds build — but not I build; no, but strain,
Time's eunuch,[10] and not breed one work that wakes.
Mine, O thou lord of life, send my roots rain.[11]

To R. B.

Norman White argues that this sonnet, written shortly before Hopkins became ill with the typhus that killed him, was written in terms that would be more congenial to its dedicatee, Robert Bridges, than the religious tenor of 'Thou Art Indeed Just, Lord'.[1] The central metaphor of the octave is sexual and generative and has been the subject of much interest from feminist critics investigating its gendering of the creative process: see Modern Criticism, **pp. 64–5**, for Gilbert and Gubar's reading of the poem. Many critics have commented on the irony that Hopkins's last completed poem should demonstrate exactly the creativity it fears that he lacked.[2]

To R. B.

The fine delight that fathers[3] thought; the strong
Spur, live and lancing like the blowpipe flame,[4]
Breathes once and, quenchèd faster than it came,
Leaves yet the mind a mother of immortal song.
Nine months she then, nay years, nine years she long
Within her wears, bears, cares and combs[5] the same:

---

8 Clumps of bushes.
9 An archaic word in Hopkins's time, 'fretty' is a heraldic term meaning interlaced. The serrated leaves of the chervil plant interlace one another.
10 See L I, p. 222: 'if I could but produce work I should not mind its being buried, silenced, and going no further; but it kills me to be time's eunuch and never to beget' (September 1885).
11 Compare a sentence from the previous letter to Bridges: 'there is a point with me in matters of any size when I must absolutely have encouragement as much as crops rain; afterwards I am independent' (l I, pp. 218–19).

---

1 White, pp. 451–2.
2 The text here, with the exception of one word (see p. 160, note 5), is taken from the Williams edition. The Phillips edition has slight differences in layout.
3 Compare 'Pied Beauty', l. 9: 'He fathers-forth whose beauty is past change'.
4 Catherine Phillips notes that in a sermon Hopkins talked about seeing 'a glassblower breathe on a flame; at once it darts out into a jet taper as a lance head and as piercing too' (Phillips, p. 388; S, p. 242).
5 Combs: shapes, brings to completion. Compare 'The Wreck of the Deutschland', st. 4, l. 4: 'And it crowds and it combs to the fall'. In the first edition Bridges changed 'combs' to 'moulds'; this alteration was preserved in the second edition. F. R. Leavis commented: 'good metaphor need not be a matter of consistently worked out analogy or point-for-point parallel; and the shift represented by "combs" imposes itself as "right" on the unprejudiced sensibility, and is very characteristic of Hopkins' (New Bearings in English Poetry (London: Chatto & Windus, 1932, repr. with 'Retrospect 1950', 1950; Harmondsworth: Penguin (Peregrine), 1963, p. 156).

The widow of an insight lost she lives, with aim
Now known and hand at work now never wrong.
  Sweet fire the sire of muse, my soul needs this;
I want the one rapture of an inspiration.
O then if in my lagging lines you miss
The roll, the rise, the carol, the creation,
My winter world, that scarcely breathes that bliss
Now, yields you, with some sighs, our explanation.

4

Further Reading

Further Reading

Recommended Editions

Four editions of Hopkins's poetry have been published, each adding to the material presented in the last. The first (1918; edited by Robert Bridges) is rare; the second (1930; edited by Charles Williams) is likely to be found in research libraries; the third (1948, revised 1956, edited by W. H. Gardner) and fourth (1967, edited by W. H. Gardner and N. H Mackenzie) are no longer in print but are reasonably widely available in university libraries. Based on the fourth edition, Catherine Phillips's Oxford Authors volume *Gerard Manley Hopkins* (Oxford University Press, 1986), has been reprinted in the Oxford World's Classics series as *Gerard Manley Hopkins: The Major Works*, and is authoritative and extremely thorough. Recently several presses have published selections of the poetry; some, such as Vintage's *Mortal Beauty, God's Grace: Major Poems and Spiritual Writings of Gerard Manley Hopkins* (2003) also include extracts from Hopkins's prose. Penguin's excellent selection, edited by W. H. Gardner, *Gerard Manley Hopkins: Poems and Prose* (1974), is inexpensive and reliable.

For the authoritative scholarly editions of Hopkins's correspondence and prose writings, see the list in Abbreviations (**p. xv**). Gerald Roberts's *Gerard Manley Hopkins: Selected Prose* (Oxford University Press, 1980) is now out of print but very useful where available through libraries. It gives an excellent selection from all five volumes of Hopkins's prose (L I, L II, L III, S and J) and has helpful, interesting notes.

Those interested in investigating Hopkins's compositional practice should consult the two volumes of facsimiles of the poetry edited by N. H. Mackenzie: *The Early Poetic Manuscripts and Note-books of Gerard Manley Hopkins in Facsimile* (New York: Garland, 1989) and *The Later Poetic Manuscripts of Gerard Manley Hopkins in Facsimile* (New York: Garland, 1991).

Recommended Critical Works

General Works

Norman H. Mackenzie, *A Reader's Guide to Gerard Manley Hopkins* (London: Thames & Hudson, 1981).

Donald McChesney, *A Hopkins Commentary* (London: University of London Press, 1968).

Graham Storey, *A Preface to Hopkins* (London: Longman 1981, 2nd edn 1992).

All three of the above are excellent starting places.

Margaret Bottrall, ed. *Gerard Manley Hopkins, Poems: A Casebook* (London: Macmillan, 1975).
Gives a valuable selection of the critical material available up to its date of publication, but since Hopkins criticism has changed considerably in the three decades since the casebook came out, the volume must be used in conjunction with more recent studies.

Gerald Roberts, ed. *Gerard Manley Hopkins: The Critical Heritage* (London: Routledge & Kegan Paul, 1987).
Brings the selection rather more up to date, but the same consideration applies as to the casebook.

Norman White, *Hopkins: A Literary Biography* (Oxford: Clarendon Press, 1992).
An excellent and very detailed biography.

Specialist Works

The materials presented in the Modern Criticism section of this sourcebook are extracts, mostly from book-length studies of Hopkins in particular or Victorian or other poetry more generally. In all cases, the full-length studies are likely to form part of any secondary reading list in Hopkins studies, but since the bibliographical information about them is given with the extracts, there is no need to repeat it here. This list contains only studies not excerpted in this sourcebook.

John Pick, *Gerard Manley Hopkins: Priest and Poet* (London: Oxford University Press, 1942, 2nd edn 1966).

Alfred Thomas, *Hopkins the Jesuit: The Years of Training* (London: Oxford University Press, 1969).
A critical strand not significantly represented in this sourcebook is theological studies of Hopkins. These two books did very valuable groundwork for this aspect of Hopkins criticism.

Walter J. Ong, *Hopkins, the Self and God* (Toronto: University of Toronto Press, 1986).

W. A. M. Peters, *Gerard Manley Hopkins: A Critical Essay Towards an Understanding of his Poetry* (Oxford: Blackwell, 1970).

These two works listed above are among the many good examples of studies by scholars whose lives as Jesuit priests gave them unique insight into Hopkins's theological training and its impact on his work.

Immortal Diamond: Studies in Gerard Manley Hopkins, edited by Norman Weyland (London: Sheed & Ward, 1949).

A collection of essays written by Jesuits: one notable contribution is Walter J. Ong's essay on sprung rhythm and English poetry.

Another aspect of Hopkins criticism not addressed in this sourcebook's extracts – though far fewer studies have yet been written in this area than in theological criticism – focuses on Hopkins and science. The surge of critical interest in the relations of nineteenth-century science and literature generally has included some excellent work on Hopkins.

Daniel Brown, *Hopkins's Idealism: Philosophy, Physics, Poetry* (Oxford: Clarendon Press, 1997).

Difficult but very stimulating.

Tom Zaniello, *Hopkins in the Age of Darwin* (Iowa City, Iowa: University of Iowa Press, 1988).

Focuses on Hopkins in the context of the life and earth sciences.

Particularly useful recent collections of critical essays include the following:

Francis L. Fennell, ed. *Rereading Hopkins: Selected New Essays* (Victoria, BC: University of Victoria Press, 1996).

Gary Bouchard's essay on Hopkins's later sonnets is especially useful.

Anthony Mortimer, ed., *The Authentic Cadence: Centennial Essays on Gerard Manley Hopkins* (Fribourg: Fribourg University Press, 1992).

Alison G. Sulloway, ed., *Critical Essays on Gerard Manley Hopkins* (Boston, Mass.: Hall, 1990).

Eugene Hollahan, ed., *Gerard Manley Hopkins and Critical Discourse* (New York: AMS, 1993).

Includes an extremely helpful critical survey by Jerome Bump, 'The Hopkins Centenary: the Current State of Criticism'.

Electronic Resources

Two electronic resources have been particularly useful in preparing this sourcebook and should prove valuable to readers of Hopkins. One is the online version of the Catholic Encyclopaedia, originally published between 1907 and 1914, which provides very detailed information on an enormous range of theological, devotional and other topics relevant to Hopkins studies. It is available at <http://www.newadvent.org/cathen>. Also helpful is the concordance to Hopkins's poetry at <http://www.dundee.ac.uk/english/wics/gmh/framconc.htm>. The online concordance produced by the web concordance project based at the English

Department in the University of Dundee allows speedy online searching of the poems for any given word; this is a wonderfully useful tool for a study of Hopkins's diction, imagery, linguistic invention, and so forth. The concordance is currently based on the first (1918) edition of the *Poems*, so quotations need to be checked against the more recent editions.

A Concordance to the English Poetry of Gerard Manley Hopkins, compiled by Robert J. Dilligan and Todd K. Bender (Madison, Wisc.: University of Wisconsin Press, 1970).
A hard copy concordance for the poems.

William Foltz and Todd K. Bender, *A Concordance to the Sermons of Gerard Manley Hopkins* (New York: Garland, 1989).

Index

Printed in Australia
AUHW012347051219
320886AU00008B/41